MECHANICS··
MERCANTILE
LIBRARY.

New Atlantis

New Atlantis

Musicians Battle for the Survival of New Orleans

JOHN SWENSON

OXFORD
UNIVERSITY PRESS

OXFORD
UNIVERSITY PRESS

Oxford University Press, Inc., publishes works that further
Oxford University's objective of excellence
in research, scholarship, and education.

Oxford   New York
Auckland   Cape Town   Dar es Salaam   Hong Kong   Karachi
Kuala Lumpur   Madrid   Melbourne   Mexico City   Nairobi
New Delhi   Shanghai   Taipei   Toronto

With offices in
Argentina   Austria   Brazil   Chile   Czech Republic   France   Greece
Guatemala   Hungary   Italy   Japan   Poland   Portugal   Singapore
South Korea   Switzerland   Thailand   Turkey   Ukraine   Vietnam

Published by Oxford University Press, Inc.
198 Madison Avenue, New York, New York 10016

www.oup.com

Library of Congress Cataloging-in-Publication Data

9 8 7 6 5 4 3 2 1

Printed in the United States of America
on acid-free paper

By the year 2100, the city of New Orleans may be extinct, submerged in water. A future akin to the fabled sunken city of Atlantis? Yes, according to Dr. Chip Groat, Director of the United States Geological Survey (USGS) in Washington, D.C., "With the projected rate of subsidence (the natural sinking of land), wetland loss, and sea level rise," he said, "New Orleans will likely be on the verge of extinction by this time next century."

—From the University Of New Orleans *Science Daily*,
January 21, 2000 (New Orleans)

CONTENTS

New Atlantis

CHAPTER 1

Voice of the Wetlands

Mother Nature smiled on New Orleans during the first week of 2005. The trees still held an autumnal glow as the temperature hovered around the midseventies with only a smattering of rain. It was warm enough that the icy waters from the north surging down the Mississippi created spectacular fog banks at night, fog so thick it turned the city's New Year's Eve fireworks display into a pastel haze. Captains on the river tugboats said it was the worst fog in ten years.

Having grown up in Brooklyn, New York, I was really enjoying such magnificent January weather. The streets of New Orleans were filled with revelers as the New Year celebrations spilled over into the beginning of the carnival season, which would climax on Fat Tuesday—Mardi Gras.

But not everyone was out on those streets enjoying themselves. Down the block from my house on Piety Street in the downtown New Orleans neighborhood of Bywater, engineer and producer Mark Bingham was hunkered down at his place of business, Piety Street studios, fine-tuning preparations for a recording session that would set the tone for 2005. The only barometers Bingham and assistant engineer Wesley Fontenot were paying attention to were the ones measuring what was going on inside the building's thick walls.

Several of the most notable bandleaders in New Orleans had come to the cavernous white stucco building at 728 Piety Street for what amounted to a summit meeting of Louisiana music superheroes. Tab Benoit, Dr. John, Cyril Neville, Monk Boudreaux, Anders Osborne, George Porter Jr., Johnny Vidacovich, Johnny Sansone, and Waylon Thibodeaux were joining forces to combat an insidious enemy that was destroying Louisiana's wetlands and threatening the future of New Orleans. The group planned to educate the public about the dangers posed by erosion of the region's wetlands with a recording that at once extolled the area's natural beauty and warned of its vulnerability to the encroaching Gulf of Mexico. They called themselves the Voice of the Wetlands All-Stars.

The project came about after Benoit, a Cajun blues guitarist and vocalist, decided to use his musical talents to campaign for the preservation of the

Louisiana wetlands. Rueben Williams, Benoit's manager, assembled the band, but when the group arrived at Piety Street, no one was sure what would happen. The day the sessions started, Williams picked up Monk Boudreaux at his home on Valence Street and drove him to the studio. Monk, dressed casually and wearing his ever-present canvas rain cap with the brim turned down, looked without comment at the enormous studio, studied the brown and white tin ceilings of its thirty-foot-high vaulted roof, then took a seat on the torn leather couch in the control room of Studio A and waited. Though Boudreaux is not big or tall, his taciturn demeanor and African Indian creole features lend him a quiet power befitting his status as a former chief of the Wild Magnolias and the current big chief of the Golden Eagles Mardi Gras Indians. However, Monk's most dramatic quality offstage is his presence. He can say more with the determined look on his face than most people can with a two-hour speech.

Bingham, whose wit, love of philosophical exchange, and unvarnished gift for gab runs to the opposite extreme, knew that Boudreaux would be a key element of this recording. Bingham's first New Orleans project was a 1982 remote recording of a Mardi Gras Indian practice at the H&R Bar. This historic session caught Monk in action at a time when these Sunday-night sessions were still part

Figure 1. 728 Piety Street. Behind these modest doors New Orleans musicians are reviving the city's legendary sound. Photo by John Swenson. Used by permission of John Swenson.

of what was essentially a secret society, so Bingham was well aware of how Monk Boudreaux worked. He didn't have to discuss strategy or give directions. When the music was right, Monk would begin his spontaneous declamations and cause a kind of spiritual transformation in the room.

Bingham opened Piety Street the weekend before 9/11. The huge building at the corner of Piety and Dauphine bears the inscription "Leonhard 1927" on its façade. Leonhard owned the whole block, including a dry cleaner and the Bargain Center grocery store up Dauphine Street. He leased what is now the studio space to the federal government; until 1980 the building served as the Bywater post office. After that it became the Louisiana Center for Retarded Citizens, an organization whose mail is still delivered at the building. Bingham quickly built a reputation at Piety, where he recorded Dr. John, Vida Blue, the Black Eyed Peas, Nick Lowe, Less than Jake, 12 Stones, Superjoint Ritual, Dr. Michael White, Jon Cleary, Ryan Adams, and John Gros.

Williams and Bingham chatted as the band members started arriving. Benoit drove in from the bayou near Houma, where he had grown up. With his short brown hair, well-kempt beard-and-moustache combo, and easy smile, the strong-shouldered Benoit exuded Cajun-country charm as he greeted his colleagues. "Tab, have you got any songs written?" Williams joked, knowing full well that Benoit liked to work spontaneously.

"No, I don't, but I'll have something soon," Benoit replied, picking up a yellow writing pad and carrying his guitar out to the backyard, where he immediately began working on a song. Anders Osborne wandered out to smoke a cigarette and began trading ideas with Benoit on a song about how well Louisiana musicians work together: "We Make a Good Gumbo." Osborne, a quiet, contemplative Swede who'd become one of the most accomplished songwriters and producers in New Orleans since emigrating to the city in the 1980s, traded guitar licks and lyrics with Benoit in an easy exchange that augured well for the recording.

Cyril Neville arrived with bustling, energetic purpose. A great vocalist and the youngest of the city's vaunted band of musical siblings, The Neville Brothers, Cyril was eager to pursue the project's aesthetic and political goals. He wanted the band to record a bucolic anthem he'd written with Rusty Kershaw years before about the glories of the local habitat, "Louisiana Sunshine."

Mac "Dr. John" Rebennack was the last to arrive for the session, making a regal entrance with his felt fedora, elegant suit, alligator shoes, and hand-carved voodoo walking stick. Though the sixty-four-year-old musician moved at a slow, creaky pace, there was still a jaunty lilt to the cadence of his progress. Every gesture had meaning, from the warm smile he offered to studio manager, Shawn Hall, to the subtle hand signal acknowledging his departed friend and songwriting partner, Doc Pomus, whose thickly bearded visage beams out from a photo on the entrance wall to Studio A. Mac had been at Piety recently to record his tribute to New Orleans R&B, *Dis, Dat, or D'Udda,* so he was right at home. He ambled over to his spot in the far corner of the room, nestled between the grand piano and the Hammond B-3 organ, and the music commenced.

The proceedings in Studio A took on aspects of sacred ritual as the session progressed, aided by the atmospherics of Piety Street's unique lighting. By day the room is filled, cathedral-like, with natural light that filters through the high windows in a mellow, golden hue. At night a few subdued lights and candles mixed with moonlight give the place a burnished, shadowy glow. The whole session was cut live with everything in the same room except the guitar amps, which were isolated. Mac's keys faced Johnny Vidacovich's drum kit at an angle, George Porter's bass was plugged directly into the board, and all of the vocal microphones were live. The band quickly arrived at a desired tempo and cut "We Make a Good Gumbo" to an easy Cajun two-step beat.

An electric feeling ran through the room, and the players started conversing in small groups, talking about ideas for other songs. Porter began absentmindedly playing a bass-line pattern, and the proverbial light bulb of inspiration went off over Cyril Neville's head. He walked over to Porter and said "Man, let's do something with that." Benoit joined the two of them and began suggesting lyrics back and forth with Cyril. The band decided to cut the song right on the spot. Porter counted off the time, and Bingham flicked the switches on the board and started recording. Porter gently suggested the changes and order of solos over the vocal microphone as the band played the beautiful "Bayou Breeze," which became the first track on the album.

Neville also conferred with the Rev. Goat Carson and Dr. John on the lyrics to one of the most confrontational songs on the record, "We Ain't Gonna Lose No More (without a Fight)." The song was an explicit attack on the Bush administration, a sentiment that Dr. John would elaborate on in subsequent songs. In the piece Dr. John sang about money being wasted on wetlands in Iraq while the Louisiana wetlands were being exploited by the oil industry. "We want our damn money back," sang Mac.

Other contributions by Dr. John were more sanguine. He sang a song written by his friend Bobby Charles, "Clean Water," which could have been about spiritual cleansing as much as environmental concerns. He also played a beautiful version of Earl King's ballad, "Weary Silent Night," which included the prescient line "What is Louisiana without a bayou?"

When Monk finally took the microphone, the spirits inhabited the room. The slow, eerie cadence of "Lightning and Thunder" crept through eight minutes of ominous beats as Monk declaimed in short, urgent bursts, summoning the elements and evoking scraps of Mardi Gras Indian dreamscape as Cyril Neville played congas and Johnny Vidacovich laid down a stately drum beat. When

Dr. John played a funky one-chorus solo, Monk vowed, "I won't bow down/ when I go downtown."

Monk had one more trick up his sleeve. "He sang the unaccompanied first lines of "Me Donkey Want Water" and Vidacovich began to smack out a brisk dance beat pushed along by Neville's percussion and building to a surging war dance with the whole band chugging along on the groove. Monk improvised as the music moved faster, turning into tighter circles, and the people in the room began chanting an answer to each of Monk's statements.

When it was all over, everyone marveled at what had taken place, as if the music had had a mind of its own. The musicians had created an album's worth of music powerful enough to convince the world that the disappearing wetlands of Louisiana were a harbinger of certain destruction that was targeting a significant portion of the United States, including one of its oldest and most important cities, New Orleans. By making the record, Benoit felt he was giving voice to the sacred ground he was brought up on.

Like many of his south Louisiana neighbors Benoit grew up in an "oil family":—His father and grandfather worked on oil wells in the Gulf of Mexico. "My grandfather was out there when the rigs were just wooden towers," said Benoit. Benoit himself worked as a pilot, ferrying workers from the rigs to the mainland. "I've been flying airplanes since I was a kid," he said. "I was fourteen years old the first time I had my hands on a stick, and I've had my pilot's license since I was seventeen. I grew up around oil rigs. I would go out and fly to oil rigs with my dad, fly out to different locations in seaplanes, and I always enjoyed that. I noticed that the happiest guy on the oil rig was always the guy who was flying the airplane back to town that night. I thought, 'That looks like the kind of job I would want to have, working in the oil field.' Music wasn't my first choice. I wanted to be a pilot for a living. I got a good job working out of Lakeview airport, out of Houma airport, flying back and forth."

Benoit had a bird's-eye view of the creeping destruction of his homeland as the gulf rapidly inundated the Mississippi's alluvial marshes with deadly salt water. When he saw the land that was so familiar to him disappearing, he decided he had to do something about the problem himself and in 2003 formed the Voice of the Wetlands. Benoit then realized he had musician friends who were also allies in the wetlands cause. He had been writing songs with Cyril Neville and began talking about his plans for the Voice of the Wetlands (VOW) organization. Neville quickly joined forces with Benoit, and the nucleus of the VOW All-Stars was in place.

"It all started with me writing songs with Tab for his records," said Neville. "We started talking about this, and we realized we had a lot in common about a lot of different things, one in particular being how the loss of wetlands was threatening New Orleans. When he started talking about the Voice of the Wetlands organization, I was very interested in it from the beginning."

Benoit found another willing VOW partner in Dr. John, who had spoken out about the dangers of coastal erosion even before Tab founded his group. "Mac's dad was talking about this in the forties," Benoit explained. "That's how he got hooked up with us. We were friends for a long time, but I saw his eyes light up when I started talking about forming this organization."

In fact, Dr. John was eager to talk about his partnership with Benoit. "My father was interested in savin' da wetlands around the late forties," he said in his distinctive style of explication:

> They've been disappearin' for an awful long time. A lot of people don't understand dis. When you live around dis country and you're watching the lands disappear, from way back, this ain't recent. Not just my father, a lot of guys who lived out in the country in south Louisiana saw all of that. They'd say to my father, "Hey, dis is what's happening." You could see it wit' your own eyeballs even back then. He would tell me about it, but I was too young to know what he was talking about back then. He used to go fishin', huntin', anything. Dat's how people lived back then. Everybody down here lived off the land, whether it was fishin' or huntin'. A lot of people lived off the fishin' and everything you could get out [of] the water. You shot whatever you could to eat something. It wasn't just my life, it was the way everybody lived as far as I know. Louisiana people always ate seasonal. You ate the foods that grew seasonal. Today people expects to eat anything any time of the year. They don't respect eatin' and livin' seasonal.

Although Dr. John had made some statements about the disappearing wetlands, he jumped at the larger opportunity to address the issue by participating in Benoit's project. "I was just grateful that Tab was doin' somethin'," he said. "I said, 'Well, man, I wanna do dis thing because of the memory of my father.' I felt I was doing something to respect the memory of my father. I was just grateful that Tab and Cyril and everybody was involved in dis."

Benoit came up with the idea to form an All-Star record to raise funds for the cause. A small festival in Houma in early October 2004 provided the seed money for the benefit record. The first time this group played together was that day in January 2005, when they showed up at Piety Street studios to make the first Voice of the Wetlands album. Benoit and Cyril Neville had worked on some material together, but everyone else walked in cold.

All-star groups are notorious for producing bad music in the service of good causes even though their hearts are in the right place. Giant egos are often unable to get out of each other's way. Nonetheless, a spirit of cooperation ruled this gathering, a camaraderie that Dr. John recognized from his early days collaborating with many of the biggest names in New Orleans R&B history.

"Ain't anybody tryin' to be a front man," he explained. "It's just everybody bein' part of a band. Everybody's a piece of somethin'. Chunks of it got written right in the studio. George Porter arranged chunks of it right there, too. Dat's what you call community skull arrangements. Dat's where the music of New Orleans all came from, everybody working in unison to do somethin'. Dat's where the whole thing came from."

Other members of the VOW All-Stars recalled that things came together quickly. "We had clusters of different musicians off in corners throwing ideas around," said Neville. "There was a lot of mutual respect. It was a great experience, really. We had fun, and everybody meant what they were saying. A lot of the conversations we were having ended up in songs."

Fortunately, George Porter Jr., who knew everyone in the project and had played with several members as guests in his Trio gigs with Vidacovich, was on hand to take on the role of musical director. As such, he dictated the general flow and arrangement strategy for the session. "The cohesion of the musicians and the music happened as the record was being made," Porter recalled. "There was a lot of cooperation in the studio. Someone needed to step to the front of the room and get these nine bandleaders on the same page with all these different songs. Everything I knew about the music was delivered that day when we got to the studio. I wrote the music for a couple of songs, [and] Tab and Cyril wrote the lyrics for some."

Piety Street owner Mark Bingham and his chief engineer, Wes Fontenot, ran the board and kept things moving smoothly on the technical end, while other musicians and friends of the band—Papa Mali, Shannon McNally, the Reverend Goat Carson, Chris Boone, and Shawn Hall—joined in on the background vocals. In a few days this patchwork of brilliant Louisiana musical fabrics was sewn into a fabulous garment, an album that would stand as a tribute to the region's cornucopia of American roots music. Little did the participants realize that their collaboration was not merely a reflection of past glories but a vision of the future.

"Voice of the Wetlands was trying to stylistically encompass the entire Louisiana music culture into a band," said Osborne:

> Mix all these different characters together, and come up with something completely new. Every time we play together we're always blown away by the fact that all these styles fit together so naturally. We cowrote some stuff on the spot and rehearsed on the spot. We got it together, and then we started the process. I've always liked spontaneous recording, and I try to use it myself when I produce. What was particularly

amazing about that project was to have that many solo artists working together like that. Each one of us is a solo career artist, and we all got together. There were no session players. That's pretty unique. The tempo was great; it was a really creative environment. Everybody was relaxed. I think all of us were on a pretty friendly basis prior to this even though we had never recorded as a unit.

Osborne had worked on several projects with Monk Boudreaux and often performed live with him. They formed an unlikely combination—a Swedish-born rock guitarist and an African American/Native American Creole Mardi Gras Indian big chief—but their bond of brotherhood virtually defined the sacred mystery of New Orleans music.

"It's a really big spiritual connection first of all," said Osborne. "The music is so trancelike and hypnotic. It feels like what I can imagine being African music being performed here. When I play with him, I feel like I'm entering a place that is very New Orleans, but it goes beyond that. There's a cultural and musical experience I get playing with him that takes me really, really far, really deep without having to think about anything. It makes me think less when I play and feel more."

"It was all a natural evolution," Osborne said of their friendship. He first met Monk at an impromptu gig at the Funky Butt on North Rampart Street:

It clicked, and it was a superbly exciting night. We both felt the same. Monk and me were looking at each other across the stage, going "Damn, you're a bad motherfucker." We became friends, and it's still like that to this day. I love Monk in a way I can't express in words. It's like he's my older brother [because] he shows me the way in so many ways. I just respect him so much, and I get the same feeling from him, and therefore everything seems easy. We just get together: I get inspired, I write something, he throws some lyrics on, or vice versa. I don't have any questions about who I am as a musician when I play with him.

Benoit scheduled his second Voice of the Wetlands festival in Houma for October 1 and 2, 2005. The occasion would celebrate the release of the album, which was to be called *Louisiana Sunshine,* and feature the first live performance of the Voice of the Wetlands All-Stars.

Sometimes it doesn't pay to be right. Benoit and the other VOW participants had warned against the very calamity that actually came to pass on August 29, when Hurricane Katrina slammed into the Gulf Coast. Multiple levee failures left most of the city under water for weeks, scattering the entire population.

When the record was finally released a month later, on September 29, the title had been changed to *Voice of the Wetlands*. This crucial document, which warned of the perils to the Gulf Coast, was overlooked in the confusion after the storm and never accorded the attention such an important piece of cultural history deserved. *Voice of the Wetlands* was ironically overshadowed by the very calamity it was attempting to warn people about. "It was hard to be focused on-promoting a record at that time—because it was so chaotic," Osborne noted. "It definitely got lost."

"By the time people paid attention to it, there were about nine million Katrina records out there," said Neville. "Everything that we went into the studio talking about happened," added Porter. "It was like 'We were saying this all along.' Unfortunately, the record came out after the fact. It was recorded before, but it was never released until after the fact, which made it sound like just another hurricane record. I think that's the reason it wasn't heard by more of the right people. I don't believe this record was really intended for the everyday record-buying public. I think it was meant to be heard by the powers that be. People who can change something."

Porter admitted that he wasn't really thinking in political terms when he made the record, which is why the content moved him so much when he heard the finished product only after Katrina hit. "When we did this record, it was before the political aspect of it had really had an impact on me," he said:

> To me it was just a recording session. I was more interested in ensuring that it was musically correct. I walked away from the project feeling that that purpose had been served. It wasn't until after Hurricane Katrina that I actually heard the finished product. I put the record on while I was driving along the I-10. I had to pull over to the side of the highway because I started fucking crying like a baby. I cried for a good forty-five minutes on the side of the highway—listening to this record—because it broke my heart.

CHAPTER 2

African Americans and Indians

Many cities are built in defiance of nature, located on fault lines or natural harbors that expose them to the temperament of the waters. Their steel and granite edifices are carved out of the land and suspended high in the air, defying gravity as they push skyward, triumphant statements of civilization's ability to impose strict statistical order on nature's realm.

New Orleans is one city that feels, day in and day out, as if nature is poised to reimpose its claim to the territory at a moment's notice. Trees seem to grow before your eyes, and plants certainly do, exploding in the calm nights to shock you with their progress. Insects engage in a relentless attack, a species war in which waves of flies, mosquitoes, voracious ants, pitiless termites, and all manner of crawling, flying, swarming beetles, spiders, water bugs, and roaches lay siege to the city in a relentless series of suicide attacks. Streets and sidewalks are no match for nature's realm, disappearing in one spot through sinkholes and flying out of the ground elsewhere, pushed by giant roots. The sun works its inexorable, caustic hammer and anvil most of the year, while roof-shearing winds jump up from out of nowhere in any season. We all know about the hurricanes, but a hard rain on a May night in the French Quarter can make you vividly aware that you're standing in a spot that looked and felt exactly the same two hundred years ago. In January the humid breezes meet the water coming downriver from the frozen north in an explosion of fog that can linger for nights on end.

For all its terrible power, nature graces New Orleans with all manner of soothing gestures, from the gentle gulf winds that ease the heat on a hot summer night to the narcotic fragrance of jasmine, gardenias, and magnolias, the lush beauty of oleander, the twisting vines of honeysuckle and wisteria, the bounty of tart, burnt-orange kumquats hanging within arm's reach all over the city, lofty banana trees sprouting tiny bunches of fragrant fruit, the brilliant bougainvilleas, and the riot of crape myrtle in every shade of red from amaranth to fuchsia. The city can feel like a dark, desolate landscape one moment and a garden paradise the next.

Back when this spirit-beloved land was the realm of the nature-worshiping Native Americans, the animate power of that flora, bathed in the realm of the elements, was understood to be an essential part of life, not something merely to be lived with but instead welcomed as an essential partner. The Africans who were brought to America as slaves were able to understand and relate to the Native Americans' approach to the land and its creatures much more than the development-minded European colonists who came here to subdue this wild landscape. The natural affinity between people brought in chains from Africa and the Native Americans (whom a bewildered Columbus mistakenly called "Indians") made for all kinds of alliances. The African slaves, who were brought to work on plantations, were predominantly male, and many of them began producing offspring with Native American women, establishing an African/Native American bloodline that is a strong and underrecognized undercurrent in American genealogy. The French colonists realized the explosive potential of this alliance immediately and nearly lost the colonial stronghold in 1719, when slaves and Native Americans joined forces and defeated them briefly in the "Natchez rebellion." The French regained control of the colony but were so wary of another alliance between African slaves and Native Americans that they stopped the slave trade in the 1730s.

Native American farmers, trappers, and craftsmen knew every inch of the land between the New Orleans ramparts and Bayou St. John, as well as the cypress swamps up- and downriver. Escaped African slaves hid in those swamps and lived together with the Native Americans, creating their own unique version of creole culture.

The French and later the Spanish administrations encouraged slaves and free blacks to trade in public. By the mid-eighteenth century, the Place des Nègres, just outside the city limits, had become a bustling Sunday trading post. The nickname of the area, "Back o' Town," has persisted over the centuries.[1] The market place, which later became known as Congo Square and was eventually encompassed by the Treme neighborhood, ended with dances that reflected the culture the slaves had brought over from Africa. Under French and Spanish rule, slaves were allowed to buy their freedom, making Treme, the neighborhood just past the walls of Rampart Street, one of the first places in the New World where freed slaves bought and lived on their own land.

The parades of various groups to the Place des Nègres for the Sunday market and attendant festivities probably resembled the parades later held by the African American gangs of New Orleans, who dressed in Native American costumes and became popularly known as Mardi Gras Indians. The phrase was invented by someone who saw these gangs parading on the backstreets of the city on Mardi Gras day, but the gang members refer to themselves by the names of the organization they belong to: Black Indians. The gangs were organized into hierarchies for their street excursions—big chiefs and second chiefs, spy boys who scouted for opposition gangs, flag boys who relayed that information to the chief, and the wild man who scared people away from the procession. These Indians had their own rituals, as well as a sacred, coded language, and played their own music as they sang and paraded. Those parades anticipated the ongoing culture of the New Orleans Social Aid and Pleasure Clubs, and their parades were known as "second lines." To this day second lines generally take place every Sunday in African American neighborhoods throughout the city.

The Black Indian gangs paraded on Mardi Gras day and used elaborate Native American images sewn into the ceremonial suits worn during their public appearances, so the outsider phrase "Mardi Gras Indians" works well enough for descriptive purposes. While the connections to Native American culture are obvious, these gangs were also clearly carrying on African-based traditions culled from the various regions their ancestors came from. The ceremonial wearing of feathers, masks, and costumes are traditions that date back to African religious practices. The parades were statements of freedom from interference by civil authorities—the Black Indians surreptitiously practiced their rituals, chose their parade routes in secret, and played the ritual folk music that accompanied those parades themselves on drums and shakers and found percussion instruments.

After the Louisiana Purchase in 1803, the American authorities were far less tolerant of African American culture, and the traditionally interracial city became more and more divided along color lines. Even though the slaves were emancipated in 1865 and Reconstruction brought black officials into government, by the end of the nineteenth century a strict apartheid system had been imposed on New Orleans culture. Around the time, observers began commenting on the number of African Americans masquerading in Native American garb on Mardi Gras day. The Black Indians had good reason to hold their parades on Mardi Gras day because the local authorities were too busy attempting to control the mainstream carnival activities happening downtown to try to interfere with what was happening in the ghetto neighborhoods. At this point the Black Indian gangs were at once a link to the cultural activities of their African past and an acknowledgement of the creole bloodline of Africans and Native Americans.

If we accept the reasonable hypothesis that the Black Indian parades were at least partly reflections of African culture that go back to the early years of French colonial life in the lower Mississippi, it becomes clear that the diaspora following Katrina, in which the entire city of New Orleans was depopulated and restricted from returning for months, was indeed what Cyril Neville called a kind of ethnic cleansing, in which 250-year-old African traditions were forced out of existence.

What is certain is that the Black Indian parades, with their characteristic rhythms, have had a long-range influence on virtually all New Orleans music, from the nineteenth-century classical compositions of Louis Gottschalk and ragtime to the twentieth-century inventions of jazz and R&B to rock, hip-hop, and contemporary New Orleans pop. The rituals and dances of the Mardi Gras Indians lie at the cultural heart of this imperiled place. The fate of that culture is intertwined with all popular music in the city, which is why the people who played New Orleans music before the storm returned to their city and fought so hard to reclaim the culture that nurtured them.

CHAPTER 3

The Constantinople of the New World

When I returned to New Orleans after the federal flood[1] the waters had finally receded after sitting for the better part of a month. The city was still under curfew and was essentially occupied by National Guard units from other states since the Louisiana Guard had been sent to Iraq. Eventually some of the local troops were redeployed back home. One of their bases was a parking lot on Royal Street, nicknamed "Camp Lucky."

Air travel into New Orleans was limited, but I got a seat on a Jet Blue flight that was filled to capacity. It seemed like all of the passengers on the flight were making their first trip in since the storm. I was used to seeing tourists on excursion to New Orleans, merrymakers who got their party rolling early, but this was a somber crowd not of revelers but of residents returning to pick up the uncertain fragments of their lives. There was an eerie quiet on the plane in the final minutes before landing. As we descended from the sky on that bright afternoon, the city offered an almost giddy vision from the air, covered in a sea of swimming-pool blue. Every roof of a house that hadn't been completely washed away seemed to have a blue FEMA tarp over it.

On the ground it was a different story. The ride into the city was my first view of the miles of total devastation, my first taste of the oily, dusty death smell that pervaded New Orleans. I got off at the Elysian Fields exit of I-10 on the way into the Ninth Ward, where the destruction was total—awesome in some unimaginable way, familiar streets lined with gap-toothed skulls of ruined houses, mile after mile. Miraculously, just across St. Claude Avenue in the five blocks closest to the Mississippi River, the houses were not completely inundated. Homes on slabs had been flooded, but those built off the ground had not. Wind had removed a sizable portion of the roof on my Piety Street home and part of the side of the house. As a result rainwater had gotten in, bringing mold and ruin from above, but at least the house didn't need to be gutted. Only some of the walls had to be stripped and rebuilt.

My brother Ed had returned to the house around the same time, driving in with his friend Jimmy Mac, a horseplayer who stayed with us during the Fair Grounds racing season. With only intermittent power in the city, we needed a generator, a propane stove to cook on, drinking water, and other basic supplies, but there was nothing available this side of Baton Rouge. We finally found a store that had some of these necessities in stock. As I reached for the last bottle of water on the shelf, a woman shoved past me to snag it. One thing you could not buy anywhere was a shotgun. In any event, this was never an item that I had considered necessary for survival until the days after Katrina, when there was no protection for your home available from either civilian or paramilitary predators in the city. Residents got a true glimpse of the postapocalypse America so popular in contemporary films.

The storm was followed by an intense heat wave broken up by another hurricane, Rita, that caused additional wind damage to the city. The heat wave didn't break until early November, and it was more than a little strange to be back in New Orleans on the first coolish night after that brutal summer. A mustard-gas death smell that pervaded the neighborhood had backed off, and the relentless heat and humidity had eased to a simmer. Mountains of garbage, parts of houses, and all manner of flotsam and jetsam lay in the street, while dead, stinking refrigerators were strewn along sidewalks all through the city.

New Orleans's seventeen voting districts, known locally as wards, generally run out from the Mississippi River toward Lake Pontchartrain like rough slices of an enormous pie. Various neighborhoods are subdivisions of the wards. Our neighborhood, a stretch of ground along the Mississippi River called Bywater, is part of the Ninth Ward. We're in what's known as the upper Ninth, separated from the lower Ninth by the Industrial Canal, which connects the Mississippi River with the lake. During Katrina, a barge crashed through the levee on the downriver side of the Industrial Canal, causing the entire lower Ninth to flood to the rooftops.

Those of us down in Bywater were the lucky ones, along with the rest of the city on the high ground close to the Mississippi. Our houses were torn by wind and rain, but we were able to move back, to congregate at Markey's Bar down on Royal Street, and to tell our stories over and over. Our neighborhood was surrounded by devastation that stretched for miles toward the lake in one direction and downriver in the other. Much of the New Orleans we knew was dead and gone. The city had lost an essential part of its identity. The social clubs and neighborhood joints of African American enclaves like Treme, Mid-City, Gentilly, and the lower Ninth Ward, which nurtured the culture of street parades, brass bands, and the magnificence of the Mardi Gras Indians were gone, along with the departed residents of those ghost-town neighborhoods. Few believed that the intricate family-based institutions that had been built over the span of numerous generations would reassemble in force.

New Orleans has always attracted itinerant adventurers, runaways, bohemians, outcasts from conservative southern communities, and those who just didn't fit in with their local culture. Street musicians and self-described anarchist clowns had established a presence in our neighborhood before the flood, but they returned in greater numbers afterward, arriving by the busload and squatting in abandoned houses. These were not TV clowns by any means, nor were they advertising to perform at children's parties. They were street corner clowns—mimes, actors, artists, jugglers, amateur musicians, and sideshow performers more than comedians, dressed in colorful, disheveled thrift-store outfits, and they fit the dysfunctional mood of the city perfectly. The capacity of New Orleanians to be whimsical in the face of disaster was never more needed than it was then.

It was early November, and my brother and a group of friends from the Blue Nile nightclub were sitting outside after a day's work on our house, cooking chicken legs on a propane stove, and listening on a battery-powered CD player to Davis Rogan singing "Hurricane," a song about staying in New Orleans during a hurricane. The song is steeped in the carefree, whistle-past-the-graveyard spirit that New Orleanians have long exhibited in the face of imminent disaster, a kind of defiant innocence that makes the ultimate irony of "Hurricane" not the fact that it was written before Katrina but that it would be that much harder to write in the face of all that had happened since:

> Well, you're standin' on the corner with your um-be-rell-a in your hand/
> Standin' on the corner keepin' out the pouring rain/
> Um-be-rell-a won't help ya when they hit you wit' the hurricane/
>
> I'm gonna buy me a pirogue lash it to my balcony/
> It's a little boat, baby, enough room for you and me/
> When the water comes to meet us, we'll float on out to sea /
>
> (chorus) Well, they're all evacuatin' (I ain't goin!)/
> Some folks ain't waitin'(I ain't goin!)/
>
> My house outlasted Betsy, and it stood through Camille/
> When they built my house, they were building houses for real/
> I'm stayin' on the premises so I can be here to deal/
>
> Well, I got me my water (I ain't goin!)/
> Camp stove and a shotgun (I ain't goin'!)/
> You can do what you oughta (I ain't goin!)/
> But I'mana stay here some/
> I'm stayin' in New Orleans with a cold drink in my hand!

After dark we went into the house and played the piano in a room illuminated by candlelight. The funky one-hundred-year-old upright piano was like all old uprights in New Orleans—the humidity and heat do things to the strings and the action of the keys that makes each piano a unique instrument, full of bizarre microtonal variations on standard tuning, every one of them an ill-tempered clavier. One of the clowns from up the block heard the commotion and joined the fray. He said his name was Stubbs, and he brought his own can of beer and his girlfriend along with him. He had a guitar and played some good slide with a butter knife while singing in an incomprehensible mumble, but his descriptions of the songs were fascinating: "This is a song about a friend of mine who lived in a hobo jungle and hopped freight trains. He died under mysterious circumstances." My guess is that, after the storm, people were making music like this all over town—or at least where they didn't have electricity, just like they did in the nineteenth century.

All across New Orleans, musicians were returning and looking to play anyplace that would let them. All kinds of venues opened up to accommodate them despite problems with intermittent electricity service and the curfew. Mayor Ray Nagin had issued an evacuation order for the city, and a dusk-to-dawn curfew enforced by National Guard units made New Orleans even more of a city of isolated neighborhoods than it had been before the flood. Residents were forced to stay close to home, and neighborhood bars became key places to trade information, unwind with a few beers, and hear the reassuring music of New Orleans played by returning musicians. Even in some of the blighted areas the music was back in action almost immediately.

I've made friends with many New Orleans musicians over the years and interviewed them for articles in *United Press International, Reuters,* several national magazines, and the New Orleans publications *OffBeat* and *Gambit.* One of the most interesting conversations was with Shannon McNally, the last person I interviewed in New Orleans before Katrina. McNally, a very good singer and songwriter with a strong feel for the roots music influences now called Americana, had been groomed by Capitol to be an Alanis Morrisette knockoff on her first album. Something told McNally this was too high a price to pay for her freedom. She took off for New Orleans, made a terrific roots rock record, *Geronimo,* and ended up marrying her drummer, Wallace Lester.

McNally was scheduled to be the cover subject of the September 2005 issue of *OffBeat,* a magazine devoted to Louisiana music and culture. I met her at Sound Café, a popular coffeehouse just across the railroad tracks from our neighborhood, on an early August afternoon when a lazy, sun-dappled breeze offered no indication of what nature had in store for the city later that month. McNally's long, straight, black hair was swooped up into a bun against the heat. Both of us were dealing with damage from the 2005 New Orleans tropical storm that nobody talks about, Cindy, which knocked a tree onto my house and split a crape myrtle in McNally's backyard.

With the emotional precision of a good storyteller, McNally articulated what draws certain musicians to New Orleans. She talked of going to Mardi Gras Indian practice sessions, Sunday second lines, meals at the Bywater eatery, Elizabeth's, and interaction with local musicians, poets, and artists. But McNally said there was something else that drew her to New Orleans. "It's very specific to the ground the city's built on," she said as her hazel eyes conspiratorially monitored my response:

> The energy that's trapped here, that lives here, is very unique, and it's very powerful, and I think that's what we all feel. It's transmitted in a million ways. That's why the music is like it is. I believe music comes out of the ground. I don't think it comes out of the sky or your head. It comes out of the ground, and it has something to do with the vibrations of the earth wherever you are.
>
> The earth here, this plot of ground, it's a combination of elements— the fact that [much of it is] below sea level; the heat; its history as a port town and a portal into the whole western hemisphere for Europeans and Africans; and then the millions and millions of people who lived here already. It's like the Constantinople of the New World. Everything is exaggerated here: The beauty is exaggerated, the poverty is exaggerated, the brutality, the music, the food. If you're a person whose senses are acute, there's no way of getting around it. You just feel it.

McNally was feeling what she was calling her "North American ghost music" hard; something very, very exaggerated was on the horizon.

I walked into the *OffBeat* office on Frenchmen Street just after publisher Jan Ramsey and managing editor Joseph Irrera reopened it following the storm. With little money and serious damages to address, the magazine's future hung in the balance. No staff members were left, and there were no means to hire new ones. I immediately volunteered to help them get back on their feet. By the time we got the first post-Katrina issue out, Jan and Joseph had already resurrected the magazine's online edition, *Weekly Beat,* which was providing one of the key social links for New Orleans musicians. Many went missing for a long time before being tracked down in the numerous destinations where they'd scattered to after the storm, and *OffBeat* religiously kept a list of who'd been contacted and who was still missing.

New Orleans musicians landed all over the country—some had been on tour when the storm hit and watched their homes disappear from afar; others evacuated, thinking they'd return home in a matter of days. Many attempted to continue their careers in various places, but the large majority intended to return as soon as they could, any way they could. Those musicians we contacted had amazing stories—sad, funny, and tragic. Every tale was the story of a journey through sorrow, a certain acceptance of loss, and a detailed explanation of what was required to keep going. None of the journeys had ended; five years later that's still true except for those who have since passed away.

Bassist George Porter Jr., one of the godfathers of New Orleans funk, had been enjoying a banner year highlighted by the historic reunion of the Meters at the 2005 New Orleans Jazz and Heritage Festival. Porter had also been working with several side groups, including PBS, with drummer Russell Batiste and guitarist Brian Stoltz; another group with drummer Johnny Vidacovich and guitarist June Yamagishi; and his own group, which had just finished recording an album at his home studio. Porter lost two houses, his studio, and a warehouse where he kept his equipment.

Porter had played until five in the morning the Saturday before the storm hit at the Maple Leaf Bar. "I went to bed about six, woke up about ten, and was sitting outside on the gazebo in front of the house," he recalled. "I love the smell when the marsh is rising. I wasn't planning on going. I was sitting on a swing in the gazebo when my granddaughter came up to me and sat down next to me. And she had that look on her face. She just looked up and said, 'Grandpa, when are we leaving?' And I said, 'Go tell your mama to go pack her bags.' And before she could even get to the door, she just kind of high-signed everybody, and they all went walking out the door with their bags. They were just waiting for me to say 'We're going.' "

Porter's daughter Katrina was so upset by the storm that she wanted to change her name. "I'm constantly telling her don't change her name," said Porter. "I love her name. She was freaked out."

Porter put his family up in a new house a little more than fifty miles from New Orleans. Meanwhile, he set to work fixing up his New Orleans base and began to work from there as best he could. "I can't stay away too long," he confessed. "I go crazy when I stay away from New Orleans too long."

Porter's story was repeated over and over again as musicians tried to return to doing what they were doing before the flood. Houses took a lot of time to rebuild. Restaurants could reopen in limited ways but were ultimately held hostage by the damage to crucial parts of the city's infrastructure, like water, electricity, and gas. While everything in the city was still broken, a musician could start singing, blow into an instrument, or strum a guitar and be back in business. However, this wasn't the business of the mainstream record industry, making videos and selling recordings, which was never the New Orleans music business in the first place. These musicians were instantly back in the business of entertaining people with live music, and they found an audience desperate for their ministrations.

A lot of unreleased music that was archived or in the process of being recorded before the flood was lost forever, but there were some spectacular rescues. One of the more dramatic stories involved Davis Rogan. Rogan, a tall, animated keyboardist and music teacher with a quick smile, had a voracious appetite for Jameson's Irish whiskey, and the relentlessly loquacious storyteller's attack associated with a peculiar brand of New Orleans bon vivant. His charm could lose its luster when girlfriends, employers, or authority figures of any description were concerned, and he had a bad habit of being thrown out of bars from time to time, but he was about as genuine a New Orleans character as you were ever likely to meet. When Katrina hit, Davis had just finished recording *The Once and Future DJ*, a reference to his alter ego, DJ Davis, who promoted brass-band music and local hip-hop as a radio personality on WWOZ. He put the master out for delivery via USPS express mail the day before the storm. Rogan had fronted the experimental Brass Band All That for a decade, and *The Once and Future DJ* was a marked departure, his first album under his own name.

"I dropped it off and went to Liuza's by the Track and had an Oyster Rockefeller soup and watched the people watching TVs, one of which was tuned to a baseball game and the other to the approaching hurricane," he recalled. "Sunday morning it was evident that we were gonna be hit with a category five hurricane, so I went to Baton Rouge, but my disc was stranded in New Orleans. My disc was six feet under water in the outgoing express mail."

Fortunately for Davis, his engineer had kept a safety copy of the album on his hard drive, and Davis was able to release the album anyway. However, his attempts to return to New Orleans were more problematic. "I picked a great day to be there, 9/11," he said. "I'd been turned away twice at gunpoint. Then, when I finally got in, what I saw was too heavy to talk about. I saw the dead body on the fence on Airline Highway. I drove past the Seventh Ward, where I smelled the stink of the drug dealers who had been murdered by the New Orleans Parish police department. It's all way too fucking heavy. It's huge, it's tragic. It's terrifying, it's awful. Some people will use this as a reason to crawl in a hole and die. Some people will say, 'I'm going back to New Orleans to rebuild.' Others will say, 'Dude, I'm gonna stay the fuck away from New Orleans for a while to get my head together,' and that's a valid response."

In fact, it was the response Davis took for a couple of months, couch-surfing in New York City and Europe before returning home. "I'm not going to compare my suffering and loss to anyone else's," he said.

> [T]his affected so many people on so many different levels, all I can
> talk about is me personally. It made me think that, when this happened,
> I was teaching and trying to live on the straight and narrow and slowly

driving nails into my coffin one binge at a time, resenting it. I'm just trying to make the best of it and look at it as a way to start over.

I've never been good at shoveling, but standing onstage and telling
a story is something I'm good at. I believe in myself, and when it all
comes down to this, the hurricane is not much different than being told
you have six months to live. I've taken up smoking. It's all or nothing.
I feel deeply for my city, and the best thing I can do for myself and my
city is to make a statement. So that's what I'm gonna do. I'll keep coming back. I'll be in New Orleans on Mardi Gras day.

Davis did come back—a lot sooner than Mardi Gras. He hand-delivered copies
of his album to the local record store, Louisiana Music Factory, and played at *Off-
Beat*'s Best of the Beat awards show in January. Meanwhile, *The Once and Future
DJ* served as a bridge between pre- and post-Katrina reality in New Orleans.

The record was unadulterated Davis, a rambling rumble through the streets of
New Orleans, populated with characters from in and out of town. The principle
character, of course, was Davis himself. As a white guy living in the predominantly black neighborhood of Treme before the storm, Davis had a bird's-eye
view of the gentrification taking place in New Orleans during the real-estate
boom of the mid-2000s. In general, Davis was against the white incursion into
one of America's first black neighborhoods, but he approved of one aspect of it, a
sentiment that inspired the song "Hookers" ("I got hookers moving to my neigh-
borhood/You can call it gentrification, but I'mana call it good"). Davis claimed
to have been fired from his DJ job at local New Orleans radio station WWOZ
for playing hip-hop, and he closed the album with the revenge anthem "I Quit,"
detailing his gripes with the station in graphic terms. Davis recruited the bounce
rapper Cheeky Blakk to deliver some of the nastiest invective. The bristling anger
and sense of injustice Davis expresses on this song resonates with anyone who's
ever gotten a raw deal at the office. The song goes a long way toward explain-
ing why some people find Davis's caustic honesty and teenage angst refreshing,
whereas others abhor it.

Other musicians watched the developing disaster with members of their
family who lived outside New Orleans. The Radiators' keyboardist, Ed Volker,
evacuated to a relative's house in Baton Rouge, where he tracked the flood via
computer. "We were watching the storm hit New Orleans on the satellite picture," he recalled.

We could see individual streets and houses through the whole city.
When the storm passed, it was obvious from the satellite picture that
the city had weathered the blow. Then we gradually saw the grid system begin to turn dark, nearly all at once in some places, and block by

block in others, and we realized that the city was under water. All kinds of thoughts went through my head: "What's going to happen to the people who are still there? Where am I going to live? How am I going to keep the band together?"

Volker couldn't return to his Bayou St. John home for several months, during which time he joined a cell of New Orleans musicians who lived in Austin, Texas. Members of the Radiators and another displaced New Orleans band, the Iguanas, played a weekly gig at Austin's Continental Club as the Texiles. Cyril Neville and local Austin musicians like guitarist Papa Mali often played with them.

Glen David Andrews had just returned from four months in Perugia, Italy, when the storm hit. He and his cousin Terence Andrews tried to weather the storm in their grandmother's house on North Robertson Street in the Treme neighborhood, where Andrews grew up surrounded by countless musically inclined relatives. The cousins heard about the flooding in the lower Ninth Ward before the levees that flooded the rest of the city failed—and prepared for the worst.

"We put my horns and our passports inside a bass drum, screwed the bass drum back together, covered it with tape, and that way we preserved the horn and preserved the drum and all of our vital information, and we put it all in the roof," Andrews explained. "After we did that, the back part of the house collapsed on us. We had to dig out of the house and get out of the water. It was all fucked up."

The cousins retreated to the projects, where they holed up while listening to the radio, which gave them descriptions of the anarchy going on outside. "We had a lot of gadgets that we buy from Europe, a lot of telephones and computer stuff that was still working," said Andrews.

But we couldn't let people see that because there was a lot of anarchy and dog-eat-dog shit going on. At the same time the police was [sic] robbing people. We knew the buses was [sic] coming because we had radios. So I got on a bus to Houston, and Corey Henry was there to pick me up. It was really cool because the people there had all heard about me, and they wanted to meet me. They gave us places to live and a place to play, so we had a great time in Houston. But after about six months I had to get back because I love New Orleans too much to be away from it for long. I might leave 100 times, but I'll come back 101 times.

Helen Gillet, a Belgium-born cellist who moved to New Orleans before the flood and was involved in the city's classical, jazz, and experimental music scenes, lost her uptown home and also found herself in Texas before she had a chance to return to New Orleans. "After Katrina hit, everyone lost their band," she said, "so I was by myself actually living in a school bus in Texas doing henna tattoos. My friend was working at the Texas Renaissance festival after Katrina. I was looking for any job I could get, and she said come and do henna tattoos. So I went over there, and my first henna tattoo was the largest Tinker Bell you could possibly imagine. I had to learn the ropes."

Along with the countless lives lost in the flood and roughly 80 percent of the city's housing stock, the cultural history that vanished was unimaginable. Unique collections of music, art, and artifacts were gone forever along with the utter tragedy of the human loss. The Neville Brothers, long known as the "first family" of New Orleans music, lost unknown treasures of unrecorded music along with homes, office, and studio. Aaron Neville, the golden-voiced singer best known for the 1966 hit "Tell It Like It Is," was forced to relocate to Nashville for health reasons, and Cyril Neville settled his family in Austin. The great clarinetist Dr. Michael White, a direct descendent of some of the earliest performers of New Orleans jazz, lost an irreplaceable collection of original artifacts personally given to him by those musicians—instruments, mouthpieces, and an enormous library of recordings, books, sheet music, and paper ephemera.

Cyril Neville ran into Michael White shortly after the flood while both musicians were on the road. "I saw Michael White in Memphis right after the storm," said Neville. "We wound up playing together in [a documentary] called *New Orleans Music in Exile*, and we were talking about it then. We knew that the most important thing for us to do is to try to go back and rebuild the culture. When you wipe out a culture, there's no way to replace it."

Neville and White were two of the musicians interviewed in *New Orleans Music in Exile*, which was directed by Robert Mugge and made in the months after the storm. Instead of concentrating on the city itself, Mugge followed New Orleans musicians who were displaced to other cities, particularly those who relocated to Austin, Texas, and Memphis, Tennessee. The documentary details how Austin musicians became a support group for their homeless colleagues by arranging places for them to stay and providing them with work.

Cyril Neville had always been a strong voice against social injustice in New Orleans. His gaunt frame and penetrating gaze lend him the aspect of a philosopher or religious figure. Unlike his older brothers, who came of age in the 1950s and early '60s as part of the golden age of New Orleans R&B, Cyril was a child of the mid- to late 1960s, growing up during the turbulent political era of the antiwar and civil rights movements. Even before Katrina, Cyril was one of the most confrontational New Orleans artists, challenging the political status quo in both his songwriting and his public statements.

After the storm Cyril became a central player in one of the best post-Katrina projects, *Sing Me Back Home,* an all-star collection of musicians called the New

Orleans Social Club, which also included Neville's *Voice of the Wetlands* partners, Dr. John and Monk Boudreaux, as well as his older brother, Charles Neville, his nephew Ivan Neville, and other displaced New Orleanians, including John Boutté, Trombone Shorty, Henry Butler, Willie Tee, and Irma Thomas. The record was made in Austin in the months after the flood.

Cyril was overwhelmed by the kindness offered to him during his exile in Austin, which, in public statements, he contrasted negatively to the treatment he received in his hometown. He had argued that New Orleans was mistreating its African American community through gentrification and police brutality even before the storm, but his argument grew more heated after the flood, when he began to accuse authorities of conducting a kind of ethnic cleansing in New Orleans, remarks that were amplified and distorted in media sound bites. Though he was trying to make a case for his community, Neville's comments were interpreted by some as kicking the city when it was down, generating hostility that took a while to abate.

"Our family, just like all those other families, is scattered everywhere all over the place," said Neville.

> Instead of a ten-minute ride or a five-minute walk, now it's a plane ticket or a ten-hour drive just to be with your loved ones. Just like thousands and thousands of other people from New Orleans, they got scattered everywhere. I didn't just wake up one morning and say, "I'm moving to Austin." I got there the same way a lot of other people wound up in places that they never thought they would be in. This is an ongoing agony for a lot of us. We've still got a lot of folks that don't know what became of some other members of their family. I feel blessed that, even though our family is scattered everywhere, we know that everybody is all right. A lot of people don't have that. There's a lot of just broken families, period. Then you've got to deal with the fact that you've got children and elders going through posttraumatic stress who don't really know what's happening to them. It's a hell of a burden to walk around with. Your city don't care about you, the government don't care about you. Then you get your sea legs, and you're still walking, and you realize "I got to bear this burden."

Neville would not let up on the notion that political forces were trying to thin out the African American community in New Orleans. "There are stories out there that haven't been told about the ethnic cleansing that went on," Neville argued.

> They put a gun in your face and told you to put your ass on that bus. That ain't no rescue. That's an armed roundup. Basically the scatterings

of the people of New Orleans after Katrina was the cleanup of a crime scene, getting rid of all the witnesses they could. They say it was because of Katrina, but Katrina had nothing to do with it. They scattered people from New Orleans to forty-nine states. I ain't heard no stories about people being moved to Hawaii, but I did hear about brothers getting forced to get on a bus, then got off a plane in Alaska wearing nothing but shorts, tank top, and flip-flops with a plastic bag containing all of their possessions.

New Orleans was also missing most of the stars of its once-thriving hip-hop scene. Some of them, like Mystikal and C. Murder, were in jail. However, the city's wildly successful rap label, Cash Money, followed its biggest star, Li'l Wayne, out of town (he had left New Orleans before the storm), depriving the city of one of its most effective music-industry economic engines. The absence of Li'l Wayne and Cash Money was a metaphor for the decimation of the city's African American communities every bit as much as the truncated brass bands, Mardi Gras Indian gangs, and high school marching bands. It's easy to see why they decided to leave—New Orleans hip-hop was not about the past, and it certainly was not about the future. The message, the sound, and the context are relentlessly and only about the here and now. It had a Big Easy genius for celebrating partying, vanquishing your opponents, gratifying every desire, and not making excuses for your actions. Li'l Wayne coined the now ubiquitous term *bling*, a reference to the diamonds and gold chains that are required habiliments of the hip-hop champion and which bear an eerie resemblance to the glittering bits of broken glass and bottle caps that the Mardi Gras Indians once used to fashion their beautifully elaborate costumes.

4

Sad Night in Jackson Square

On September 15, 2005, seventeen days after Katrina's landfall, James Andrews stood in Jackson Square with his younger brother, Troy ("Trombone Shorty") Andrews, surveying a scene from his worst nightmare. The gated park in front of the triple spires of Saint Louis cathedral was bathed in high-powered spotlights, which gave it a surreal, made-for-television appearance. Television crews from all over the world were on hand to broadcast President Bush's statement about the future of New Orleans. The park had been spruced up for the event. It was now an oasis of calm and beauty amid the chaos and destruction that surrounded it.

James and Troy had been brought in to perform at the ceremonies surrounding the president's speech, but they were not in a mood for celebration. Like the Nevilles, all of the members of the Andrews family had left town after the flood, and many of them were still unaccounted for. Their grandmother Dorothy Hill was among the missing, and James and Troy feared the worst. During an interview with the brothers on MSNBC, Troy begged for anyone watching to send them news about their grandmother. He gave out his cell phone number.

Both brothers had played many times in Jackson Square over the years, but the location had always been a short walk from their home across Rampart Street in Treme, where hundreds of their relatives had lived. Now those relatives were scattered across the country. The only two members of the Andrews family left in New Orleans had lost their sense of place in the middle of their hometown. Their cousins Glen David and Terence Andrews stayed through the storm but evacuated to Houston only days before James and Troy returned.

The brothers, born sixteen years apart, looked more like father and son. James, a big man with a thick neck and a perpetual smile, presented a stately presence that befitted his status as the oldest of more than a dozen musical cousins and the organizer of the group they all sometimes played in, the Andrews Family Band. His gold trumpet, a gift from the Johnny Carson–era *Tonight Show* bandleader, Doc Severinsen, suited his regal bearing. Troy, then barely out of his teens, was thin and wiry with a hard, wary visage and a restless athleticism that forecast a maelstrom of virtuoso musicianship. He hefted his trombone with the sense that it was far more than an instrument, more like an Excalibur he used to slay dragons.

"A friend of ours called us and asked us to play," said Troy.

> That was about a week after the storm or so. We were able to go to the house and look at it, but nobody was in town. It was just the National Guard, police from everywhere in the country, some dignitaries, and us. We played in Jackson Square, and that's the first time I actually heard my horn echo in the city. There was no traffic, no people at all. It was an empty city, maybe there were five hundred people, most of them police officers. We couldn't find my grandmother.

Shorty had been on a world tour with Lenny Kravitz when the storm hit. "We had like a two-week break from the tour, and then Katrina happened," Troy recalled.

> After all that Katrina stuff and helping the family get settled, I had go to back on tour with Lenny to finish out the rest of the leg of the tour. At that point we still hadn't talked to people about the family. It was hard being on the road and knowing that we still hadn't found all our family members. I was out for six more months. It was tough. Eventually we found everybody. Thank god we didn't lose anyone.

James recalled the reunion at Jackson Square with conflicting emotions. "I was up in Monroe, Louisiana, and my brother Troy was in Houston, but we came back to play this show," James said. "We were happy to see each other, but it was difficult to be positive. Every time you look around, you see sadness. Everything was destroyed; there were no people in New Orleans at that time. No places open, no food stores. It was sad."

But something good came out of their return to the city. "Someone saw our grandmother up in a shelter in Baton Rouge," said James. "She had been stuck on the highway, then she walked all the way to the bridge to try to get out of the city. She was with the people the police shot at to stop them from crossing the river. 'They drew guns on us,' she said. That's how I know that story is true." James was referring to an incident on the Crescent City Connection, a bridge across the Mississippi River, during which police from the west bank fired shots over a crowd of people trying to leave New Orleans after the storm.

James Andrews was one of the most visible musicians in New Orleans after Katrina. He participated in so many key events that it seemed as if he was try-ing to bring New Orleans back by the sheer strength of his will. Of course, no one gesture could overcome the emotional impact of the events that followed the levee failures, but there were isolated moments when individual musicians managed to summon the spirit of New Orleans music and use its saving grace as a balm to ease the pain.

The most striking thing about watching Andrews sing and play in those months after the storm was how much the traditional songs he performed took on added meaning for him in the aftermath of the city's destruction. Before Katrina, James Andrews had been a strutting crowd pleaser adept at wielding the power of compositions that had entertained visitors to New Orleans for generations. Afterward, that magic overwhelmed him, and tears streamed down his face more than once as he played music that he'd played thousands of times before. Those songs had been light entertainment before the storm, but in its wake they became powerful vehicles of transcendence.

Andrews was one of the musicians who helped quickly put New Orleans music back in business shortly after the first traditional aspect of the city's life returned, the public tavern. Johnny White's bar on Bourbon Street in the French Quarter never closed, not even during the storm itself, as the bartender Marcy Kreiter did brisk business with journalists and emergency workers (and there's no way to lock the door even if they wanted to close). Other bars in the Vieux Carré, as the original grid of the French colonial settlement is called, were open soon after Katrina. When the bars reopened—with or without electricity—the music followed.

Musicians did more than just play when they came back. A group led by Bonerama's Craig Klein formed the Arabi Wrecking Krewe, a group of musicians and friends who worked on gutting ruined homes in between gigs. Klein's own house in Arabi was destroyed in the flood, which is where his story begins:

"When disaster happens, people come together, and some good things come out of it," said the tall, sandy-haired trombonist.

> I married a girl from Arabi in Saint Bernard Parish. This last house I had down there we had built from the ground up. It was a pretty nice house. After the storm I couldn't get back for a month or so, and when I saw it, I thought, "I can't deal with this. It's too much for me." I had a friend named Armand "Sheik" Richardson, and he came over and said, "Let's just take it one step at a time. Let's start getting this stuff outta here and see what it looks like." So we started bringing some of the stuff out, and he took a hammer to the sheet rock, and we said, "He's a one-man wrecking crew." He replied, "We're the Arabi Wrecking Krewe." So me and these other three guys gutted my house. While we were doing it, we were talking about the music and how it may never happen here again in New Orleans and how we could help get the musicians back

because the culture of New Orleans was all scattered across the U.S. So we decided we would start gutting musicians' ruined houses. That would be the actual first step of getting these musicians back to New Orleans.

Klein knew a lot of musicians around New Orleans and started making calls to see who he could help:

> We started gutting houses of musicians, and it started snowballing, people starting calling us, offering to help. It was really a selfish thing for me because I wanted my friends to be back here in New Orleans so I could play music with them. I was doing it for myself because I wanted to get New Orleans back like it was. I was afraid that it wouldn't come back, so my attitude was "whatever it took."

As Klein organized email contacts and started getting donations, he realized that the project was expanding well beyond what he had envisioned:

> People were contacting us, asking us to help them. I was gutting houses by day and playing gigs at night. It was getting kind of exhausting, really. There was something about bringing all the things out of the house to the curb. It was sad, but it also felt good. We were getting it done, getting rid of some of the tragedy, and as we did it to house after house I kept getting that feeling over and over again. In some kind of crazy way deep down it felt good. So we would make announcements over the Internet: "We're gonna be at this house at this time, and we're gonna gut it." I was surprised at how many people came out, but it showed me how much people cared, like I cared, about what really could happen if we lost all those musicians.

The Arabi Wrecking Krewe went on to partner with a musician's relief group called Sweet Home New Orleans to provide a new home for New Orleans R&B singer Al ("Carnival Time") Johnson in the Musicians' Village.

Andy J. Forest, a neighbor down the block from my house on Piety Street, and his wife, Gwen, opened a badly needed community center and coffeehouse called Cofféa. Forest, a tall, angular man, always fashionably attired, with a dark, piercing gaze over his jutting jaw and a perennial fedora capping his vertiginous frame, was a pioneer presence in the neighborhood after the flood. Forest plays harmonica in the Washboard Chaz Trio and is an accomplished songwriter and vocalist who plays guitar and frattoir when fronting his own band. Like many local musicians he is also a visual artist—music and the visual arts have a closer relationship here in New Orleans than anywhere else in America—and he displayed his paintings of classic blues musicians on Cofféa's walls. With Anders Osborne producing him, Forest recorded some of the best recent songs about life in New Orleans before the federal flood. In fact, he wrote one of the best pre-Katrina hurricane songs, "Hurricane George."

Forest stayed clear of the Big Easy clichés to write about real people and events, a talent that seemingly reached its apotheosis on the beautiful tribute to his upper Ninth Ward home, the ironically titled "Deep Down Under in the Bywater."

Forest's post-Katrina release, *Real Stories,* wasn't maudlin or sorrowful. It was an angry, op-ed-style documentary that opened with the Swiftian satire "Let 'Em Die": "C. Ray had a party down in New Orleans," he declaimed as Osborne played an irresistible R&B vamp along with Heggy Vezzano, the guitarist from the Italian blues band that backed Forest on the session: "If you didn't have a car or other means of transportation, you were invited down to the Superdome, where things got out of hand." Forest continued the commentary until he reached the line the song turned on: "The U.S. government decided to let them die." Even though everyone knew the story already, the line was gut wrenching, and in the

Figure 2. Andy J. Forest writes about postflood reality in "Trailerless Man." Photo by John Swenson. Used by permission of John Swenson.

context of the song it hit like the perfect Joseph Conrad sentence, putting a stark meaning on the government's decision to federalize the rescue effort, thereby abandoning the populace of an American city for a week.

The vamp went on and on, and the chorus chanted its grim message over and over: "Let 'em die, let 'em die, let 'em die!" Forest made other disaster-era comments in "Trailerless Man" and "Breach in the Levee," but the rest of the album dealt with day-to-day observations like "Stinkin' Lincoln," the white whale of a car that had sat in front of Forest's Piety Street home for years, or "4:20 A.M.," an account of postgig activities that speaks for itself.

Coco Robicheaux, a blues guitarist, singer, and songwriter, was a fixture on the lower French Quarter and Marigny music scene. Dressed in a suit, cowboy boots, and Native American talismans, with long, graying hair hanging in a thick braid down his back, Robicheaux cut a memorable figure. He possessed a growl of a baritone and accompanied himself on guitar, singing eccentric original material with titles like "The Ten Commandments of the Blues," and also had an encyclopedic knowledge of American folk tradition. Robicheaux was one of a number of New Orleans musicians who claimed to have been the first to play live music in the city after Katrina. He had stayed through the storm, he said, because he had several upcoming gigs scheduled at various bars on Frenchmen Street in the Faubourg Marigny. Those gigs never materialized, but Robicheaux found a haven in Molly's at the Market, a Decatur Street bar run by Jim Monaghan.

"I was at Molly's when the lights came on," he said. "I said to Monaghan, 'What does that mean to you?' He said, 'I'm back in business. My beer cooler's on.' I said, 'It means music to me. I got my shit parked right outside.'" Robicheaux set up and started playing Jimmy Reed's classic blues tune "You Don't Have to Go."

The bar filled with people drawn to the music. "Girls were dancing on the bar," Robicheaux smiled, "removing clothing. Everybody was partying. I just kept playing, never took a break. I have no idea how long I played, longer than usual, and I usually play four or five hours. There was a curfew, but we didn't care. Monaghan said, 'The hell with it, man.'"

Uptown, Hank Staples was eager to get his club, the Maple Leaf, back in action. He decided to put on a show on September 30 and immediately got support from all over. Even though the neighborhood didn't have power, local technical crews donated generators for the occasion. Drummer Kevin O'Day put together a band featuring New Orleans guitarist and singer Walter ("Wolfman") Washington called the MREs, named after the military-style "meals ready to eat," which everyone in town was relying on after the storm. O'Day's spin on the acronym was "Music Ready to Enjoy," and he reckons that a crowd of roughly 550 locals and journalists came to the show.

"We started really early, about 4 o'clock in the afternoon," said O'Day:

My wife, Julie, cooked red beans in a huge pot. There were a lot of mixed emotions, but it was incredible from the first moment until the end of the concert just to be playing. It was like the music was really serving its purpose. All the practice and years of playing really meant something to everyone at that time. We did what we were supposed to do, which was uplift the souls of everybody. It was an intensely spiritual moment for me.

The concert ran past curfew, and eventually the National Guard came in to break it up about 8 P.M., but the message was clear—even in a lawless town, music set its own rules, and in New Orleans it was treated like a religion. Music most certainly was a kind of religion to most of those who had already returned and to the majority of those who would be back within months. In every neighborhood some variation on this theme was taking place during the weeks after the storm. Places that had never hosted music before suddenly became clubs, and other places that hosted limited shows expanded their schedule. Right at the edge of the greatest devastation on the uptown side of the Industrial Canal, which separates the lower and the upper Ninth Ward, the Poland Avenue wine store, Bacchanal, reopened, using its windswept backyard as a garden club. Davis Rogan was one of the musicians who held court there, singing about quitting his job and riding out hurricanes on his front porch. A few blocks away, Cindy Wood reopened Vaughan's on October 13 and before long had lured trumpeter Kermit Ruffins back from Houston to do his regular Thursday-night gig. Wood started booking music on other nights as well, bringing in Washboard Chaz on Wednesdays and the Treme Brass Band on Sundays. "If we want musicians to come back to town, we have to provide gigs for them," reasoned Wood, "so I need to have music more than one night a week."

Other places were providing musicians with all the work they could handle. On October 14, three days after power was restored to Frenchmen Street, New Orleans's flagship jazz club, Snug Harbor, reopened with a local jazz all-star band assembled for the occasion, Ed Peterson and the Ultimate Test, featuring Peterson, Steve Masakowski, Don Vappie, and Ricky Sebastian.

In the depths of Mid-City, a neighborhood that had been almost totally destroyed by the flood, Maria Guth opened her place, the Banks Street Bar, despite heavy water damage and zero electricity. She got musicians to play acoustic shows by candlelight and used coolers for tables. On Magazine Street, Pepper Keenan, guitarist with the hard-core New Orleans metal band Down, reopened his club, Le Bon Temps Roule, with Chris Boone and members of Soul Fiya playing with special guests like Anders Osborne, Willie Green, and Stanton Moore. Before long, the Hot 8 Brass Band was playing there as well. A few blocks away on Lyons Street the Plowboys played at the Kingpin.

By the middle of October, roughly six weeks after Katrina but only a month after the aftershock produced by Hurricane Rita, a skeleton crew of New Orleans musicians had returned but were still waiting for the spark that would rekindle the city's cultural fire. Helen Gillet was struck by how quiet the city was, a peace she took advantage of by playing in Jackson Square with her acoustic band. She played in a few other locations as well.

"I got back to New Orleans for the first time in early October and found my place and started cleaning," she said. "I remember playing at Cafe Brasil by candlelight with people passed out on [club owner] Ade's mattresses that he pulled out for people to take a nap. I did that for a few weeks, then took a break to visit my mother in Chicago for Thanksgiving, then moved back in December. I was ready to come back. I didn't want to be far away from it. It's like a sick friend. You fall in love with a city, and it gets sick. You want to go to the hospital with flowers."

James Andrews played one of the most significant performances after the storm, the reopening of the Ogden Museum's "Ogden after Hours" series. These Thursday early-evening shows began before the storm but picked up momentum during the recovery and soon became emblematic of the way the New Orleans arts and music communities worked together to forge a new vision for the city's culture in the wake of the flood. Libra LaGrone, then special-events director at the Ogden, was among the earliest of the returnees—she was in the crowd at Coco Robicheaux's impromptu concert at Molly's. Her efforts were largely responsible for the Ogden's earning the distinction of being the first mainstream cultural institution to open its doors to the public after Katrina. LaGrone said the museum was initially trying to reopen on October 1, but Hurricane Rita's unwanted visit pushed the date back to October 27.

"James was a logical choice, being from Treme," LaGrone said of her decision to reopen the series with Andrews, "considering the devastation that happened to that historic neighborhood, as well as his importance to the city as a musician and member of an accomplished musical family." The series had been drawing an average of 145 people a night before the flood, and LaGrone was expecting roughly 200 for the reopening. She was shocked when 600 people showed up.

"When James hit his first note, I remember standing outside the museum," she said:

> There were hundreds of people everywhere, and I was home. There was no looking back. Despite all the things I lost in the storm, I realized how fortunate I was to work for an institution that cares about the city and cares about the musicians and artists in the city. The museum became a meeting place to find out where your family and friends were. After

9/11, people posted pictures and signs of all of their friends. Well, after Katrina, people were coming to the museum to hear the music, have a drink, and find out where all of their friends were. It was absolutely beautiful. There were parents with newborns and two-year-olds, and there were grandmothers and grandfathers. There were some contractors and some military people, but I'd say 80 percent of it was local. Every race, age, you name it—they were here. It was a truly remarkable evening.

CHAPTER 5

Return of the Spirits

Halloween is a sacred time in New Orleans, second only to Mardi Gras as an occasion for ritual celebration. Like Mardi Gras, it occurs over a season rather than just on a single day. Halloween-themed costume parties usually begin in earnest at least a weekend before October 31. Promoter Steven Rehage identified Halloween season in New Orleans as a likely time to hold a contemporary music festival, and his Voodoo Fest, a next-generation version of the New Orleans Jazz and Heritage Festival, has become a spectacular success.

It's not just the costumes and the merriment that make Halloween so important to New Orleans culture. Like most things that matter in this antique territory, it's a celebration of ancestral spirits. Halloween is literally the eve of All Hallows' or All Saints' Day. Celebrated on November 1 on the Gregorian calendar, All Saints' Day acknowledges those who've been beatified in heaven, while the following day, November 2, is All Souls' Day, a remembrance of those who died in a state of grace but have yet to reach heaven. Like many Christian rituals, it was adopted from an ancient pagan tradition, the Feast of the Lemures, in which the spirits of the dead were offered sacrifices to appease them. The New Orleans celebrations also dovetail with the start of Mexico's *día de los muertos* rituals, in which altars are built to honor the ancestors, whose spectral presence in the world of the living is acknowledged. Practitioners of the Haitian religion, vodou ("voodoo" is the Anglicization of the word), in New Orleans celebrate All Saints' Day with elaborate ceremony. My next-door neighbor, Sallie Ann Glassman, is a vodou priestess who operates the Isle of Salvation botanica down the street. She's also a talented painter and writer who has published an excellent book on the spiritual practice, *Vodou Visions*. Glassman assembles her group, dressed in white and purple, every November 1 to make a candlelight pilgrimage to a nearby cemetery, where they offer gifts to the souls of the departed.

The first Halloween after the flood was a particularly important moment in the city's recovery, and musicians ruled the day with special performances all over town, including a truncated version of Voodoo Fest, which was held on the

Figure 3. Sally Ann Glassman's Island of Salvation Botanica & Magical Pharmacy at 835 Piety Street. Photo by John Swenson. Used by permission of John Swenson.

grounds of the Audubon Zoo. The musicians who played that day felt the spirits urging them on. "It was an astonishing feeling, as if we were in some alternate dimension," said Cowboy Mouth's Paul Sanchez, one of the musicians whose house was gutted by the Arabi Wrecking Krewe. Cowboy Mouth, a veteran New Orleans rock band, had written a pair of Katrina-related songs since the storm, and one of them, "On the Avenue," received the biggest ovation of the day from a crowd that responded to its vow to return to the city and revisit the glories of Mardi Gras:

> *Because the marching bands will roll/I'll find my city in my soul/Because I plan on growing old/On the avenue.*

Several bands played at Voodoo that afternoon and elsewhere in town that night. Rebirth Brass Band actually played three gigs that day—one at Voodoo, another in the French Quarter, and yet another that night at Tipitina's. "When everybody was scattered about all over the place, we pulled it together weeks after the storm," said Rebirth sousaphone player Phil Frazier. "We all made it back quick. Even my brother [bass drummer Derek Frazier], who's living in Dallas, he was on the phone every day. We all got together and played."

Halloween was a moment when it all seemed possible again. "A big turning point for me was when we performed Halloween night at One-eyed Jack's," said Josh Cohen of Morning 40 Federation:

> The curfew was still on. When the place got packed, I realized that the people will go out and party and not necessarily wallow in their misery or hold their head in their hands. They were there to have fun and celebrate the moment. The high points to me are when everything's perfect between the crowd and the band; you're in New Orleans and somehow this whole combination of stuff creates perfect moments in life.

The weather that fall and winter in New Orleans was beautiful; falling leaves carpeted the ground in gold. At the same time the city was still filled with mounds of garbage, tens of thousands of dead refrigerators, and wasted, abandoned cars everywhere. Hope and despair lived side by side. Bodies were still being found in the rubble of collapsed houses, the "Katrina cough" (a respiratory ailment related to the swirls of toxic dust from mold and chemical spills that the wind swept across the city) kept making its rounds, and money to rebuild was scarce.

Nonetheless, the music kept performing miraculous feats of recovery. Deep in the heart of Mid-City, past scores of desolate blocks of flooded-out houses along lightless streets, the parking lot at Mid-City Lanes "Rock 'n' Bowl" was packed for the November reopening night of this famous music club and bowling alley. The ground-floor bar and stage were completely ruined, but the original upstairs bar (on the level of the bowling alley) was high enough off the ground to be salvaged and restored to action. The tops of the bottles of Miller High Life were rusty, but the beer tasted sweet as New Orleans R&B icon Eddie Bo led an all-star band featuring members of Archie Bell and the Drells through a multiple-hour set of great music. The crowd was a little unusual with so many members from "Camp Lucky" on hand, but when Eddie Bo swung into a twenty-minute version of "Check Your Bucket," it was clear that this was the last place on earth you could hear music played like this.

Baty Landis had reopened Sound Café, and Helen Gillet became one of the regular performers there, playing her cello and singing songs she remembered from her childhood in Belgium. "When I came back to New Orleans, I met up with Daron Douglas. She's an amazing woman and a really good friend, and we just decided to have a coffee shop get-together at the Sound Café," said Gillet:

> I was still practicing, really, and Daron would have my back, filled out the melodies so I could take a break from singing. It was just me and Daron at that point. We were just coming up with a name for the event. We called it Christmas in the Trenches because with that postapocalyptic

environment we were all living in, with all the worrying that we were all experiencing, it just sort of felt like this was such a great respite to go to the Sound Café and hang out for three hours and play these songs that I loved from my childhood that I was never able to sing and play, and this was opening up a whole new world for me. So we were there for about a year under the name Christmas in the Trenches, and then we became Wazozo. The band grew from there—we added guitar, and then my dear friend Luke from college moved down here. He was a clown in the Barnum and Bailey circus, and he decided to come here and play the harp. So we started playing these songs together, and I decided to record them. It's an all-string band. There's no drums. The band's obviously not a typical New Orleans band.

Another key element in the resumption of the city's musical culture came in November, when New Orleans witnessed the first major second-line parade since the storm, part of a jazz funeral for chef Austin Leslie. Second-line parades are central to New Orleans's unique lifestyle. They are an integral part of the traditional jazz funerals organized by the city's Social Aid and Pleasure Clubs, but that's not their only function. A jazz funeral will always include a second line when the mourners and band return from the cemetery after burying the deceased. The "second line" refers to the people who join the procession on its return from the cemetery as the mourners celebrate the liberated spirit's passage to the next world. However, a second-line parade can also be an event in itself, a street party accompanying a wide range of functions from holiday celebrations to political events.

Davis Rogan, an ardent participant in the second-line culture that permeates his Treme neighborhood, summed up the all-purpose nature of the second line by using a grammatical example taken from his teaching experience. "'Second line' can be used as a verb or a noun," he said, waving his hands in the air for emphasis. "So I can be second-lining with the second-liners at the second line."

These awe-inspiring public outpourings of emotion are the very soul of a city whose celebrations are designed to cover the deep, miserable scars of the past. The second-line parade for Austin Leslie passed a playground filled with hundreds of automobile corpses, the detritus of cars destroyed by the floodwaters and left behind by their owners. Brass bands performed the ritual music that the second-liners always dance to as they sashay down the street. People banged on impromptu percussion instruments and sang ecstatically. Everyone was kinetic, dancing to the rhythms in small, ecstatic movements when one of the kids in the crowd leaped atop the sea of dead cars and started dancing, then jumping from one car to another.

Paul Sanchez witnessed this second line and had an epiphany. "It was amazing," he recalled. "It was a statement, but not a violent statement. It was an expression of frustration, of dancing on the abandoned city. The whole day had been beautiful, white people and black people dancing together, celebrating New Orleans in that very unique way, doing a second line. Dancing on the abandoned vehicles. Dancing past the destroyed homes. That's New Orleans, that's the jazz funeral right before your eyes."

The second-line festivities Sanchez attended were marred by a shooting in which three people were wounded. A few months later at another second line, a man was killed by a gunman, and police wounded the shooter. Using the spurious argument that these incidents led to violence, the authorities cracked down on second lines. However, you didn't need a parade to inspire violence in post-Katrina New Orleans. Moreover, police harassment of second-line parades and Mardi Gras Indian celebrations had begun even before Katrina, an issue that Cyril Neville had been bringing up for years prior to the storm. Just two months before Katrina, a gathering of Mardi Gras Indian elders went to a city council meeting to protest police harassment of the Saint Joseph's Day Mardi Gras Indian celebration earlier that year. During an emotional address to the council, Yellow Pocahontas Big Chief Allison Tootie Montana, the elder statesman of black Indians, collapsed and died right in the council chambers.

"Katrina didn't cause that. That was going on before," said Neville:

> Public gatherings were being stopped in the street by the police. Tootie Montana died at a city council meeting protesting how the police were treating the Mardi Gras Indians, one of the oldest aspects of our culture. The oldest masking Mardi Gras Indian at that time was Tootie Montana. It was precipitated by something that happened on Saint Joseph's night, another tradition that had been going on as long as anybody can remember. He died over this. This gentrification of the city was going on for ten, fifteen years before Katrina came along. It's amazing, the times that we're living in to see this all happen here in a major American city.

Second-line parades are a signature of life in New Orleans, a crucial metaphor for the city's spiritual recovery, and a social organization system in which displaced New Orleanians could reconnect with their former neighbors. Originally a practice indigenous to New Orleans's African American community, the street parties have become popular in virtually all of the city's neighborhoods and overlap with the Mardi Gras parades. In fact, it seems like New Orleanians enjoy having a parade for just about any reason.

The New Orleans funeral marches and second-line parades have a deep history. One of the most famous early examples followed the 1863 Civil War death of black Union officer Captain Andre Caillon, who was killed at the battle of Port Hudson. An estimated ten thousand mourners attended his ceremonies.

Brass bands, which are the musical heart of the second line, were a high-profile characteristic of the Union occupation of New Orleans and naturally continued their popularity, especially in the black community, during Reconstruction. The brass band became in a very real sense the sound of emancipation.

However, backlash against the emancipation of black Americans began to take hold in the ensuing years, and insurance companies would not provide death benefits for African Americans. Even a basic, proper burial of the dead was risky in that environment, and the only safe way for members of the community to conduct funerals was to enlist the help of a Social Aid and Pleasure Club (SA&PC). These clubs, such as the Golden Trumpets, formed in 1873, and the Young Men Olympians, formed in 1884, were exclusively black organizations. By the early twentieth century, 80 percent of the black population of New Orleans belonged to an SA&PC. As all of the early New Orleans jazz players had connections to the clubs, the jazz funeral was enabled by the SA&PCs and became an integral part of the brass-band tradition.

Though New Orleans is known for its brass bands, the tradition did not start there. Brass bands were a European invention that became a staple of military marching music. The bands also became popular concert attractions during the nineteenth century in Europe and America. The tradition took hold in New Orleans and became infused with African elements, a development that helped influence the development of jazz. All of the early jazz brass players had connections to the brass-band tradition; it was their bread and butter, just as ragtime and the blues were to contemporary piano players.

"As they go to the cemetery, they play in a funeral march; they play 'Free as a Bird,' 'Nearer My God to Thee,' and they express themselves in those instruments, singing those notes the same as a singer would, you know," Louis Armstrong told legendary newsman Edward R. Murrow in his 1956 television documentary *Satchmo the Great:*

> And they take this body to the cemetery, and they put this body in the ground. While he's doin' that, the snare drummer takes the handkerchief from under the drum, from under the snare, and they say, "Ashes to Ashes," and put him away and everything, and the drummer rolls up the drum real loud. And, outside the cemetery, they form, and they start swinging "Didn't He Ramble." And all the members, the Odd Fellows, whatever lodge it is, they are on this side. And on this side is a bunch of raggedy guys, you know, old hustlers and cats and good-time Charlies and everything. Well, they['re] right with the parade, too. And, when they get to wailin' this "Didn't He Ramble" and finish, seems as though they have more fun than anybody because they applaud for Joe Oliver and Manny Perez with the brass band to play it over again, so they got

to give this second line, they call it, an encore. So, that makes them have a lot of fun, too, and it's really something to see.

Somewhere along the way, that second line became more than just a street party accompanying the return of the mourners from the cemetery; it turned into a celebration of its own. At first these parades were used to promote membership in the SA&PCs, but they eventually took on a unique identity. In the wake of the depression and World War II, the tradition, still exclusively practiced in black neighborhoods, was in danger of dying out.

"Back then, there wasn't a lot of organizations," said sixty-one-year-old Larry Ward in the oral history *Coming out the Door for the Ninth Ward*, a book sponsored by the Neighborhood Story Project:

Only certain people participated—it was street people of a lower socioeconomic class. Middle-class black people, bourgeois black folks didn't embrace that. They were trying to emulate the white culture, you know, so that was too Africanized...During that time, the second-line organizations didn't allow women to participate as far as dance. They could follow the second-line procession and dance, but you really had to be somebody like my sister [Doris] who was antiestablishment...You only caught a second line two or three times a year. We had to find out through the grapevine. It wasn't publicized.

In 1965, in celebration of the centennial of the Thirteenth Amendment to the Constitution, the abolition of slavery, Congress passed the Voting Rights Act, effectively granting black Americans the right to vote. Along with the Civil Rights Act of the previous year it marked the beginning of the end of racial segregation in New Orleans. In the 1970s the African American culture was gathering strength, and the modern second line began to become a more regular feature of New Orleans street life, so much so that the city council actually tried to outlaw parades as "a cultural eyesore" in 1979. Largely through the growing popularity of the New Orleans Jazz and Heritage Festival, the SA&PCs and second-line parades became even more popular than the jazz funerals themselves, and a growing audience of white tourists began attending. The attendant confusion about what actually constitutes a second line became a twisting labyrinth. In the 1990s the Sunday afternoon second lines and Mardi Gras Indian parades were bona fide tourist draws, and groups of white revelers were organizing their own parades, which fell somewhere between second-line celebrations and outright Mardi Gras street parades.

We might well wonder whether many Orleanians got their definition of a second line from New Orleans soul queen Irma Thomas, who broke it down during her rendition of "Done Got over It" during a Voodoo Fest performance. "There's a dance that we do in New Orleans," said Irma, "called the second line. It is a dance we do in this city whenever there is a reason to celebrate. And we find a reason to celebrate everything." Irma then urged her fans to wave their handkerchiefs in the air and follow her instructions to "put your backfield in motion."

By the first weekend in December, while the city was still without power and basic services in many areas and few businesses had reopened, nearly all of the most important music venues that had been operating before the storm were back in business. This small miracle indicates how crucial to the city's identity live music is and how much of a motivating force it had been since the storm. House of Blues was in high gear, the Howlin' Wolf moved to a larger space in the warehouse district, and the Louisiana Music Factory resumed its free Saturday-afternoon concert series. The Frenchmen Street corridor reopened in force with live music everywhere except the Blue Nile, which was structurally damaged in the storm and needed extensive repairs.

Tipitina's not only reopened but turned its foundation, which had been raising money for student instruments and internships before Katrina, into the Musicians' Community Center. The club offered musicians office space and equipment and even provided feathers and other materials for Mardi Gras Indian members looking to fashion new garments. The Tipitina's Foundation was one of several relief agencies, along with MusiCares, the New Orleans Musicians' Clinic, and Sweet Home New Orleans, that joined in the relief work being done by organizations like the Red Cross and Habitat for Humanity. As the dreadful year of 2005 drew to a close, a city that had been broken in every part except its spirit looked to its musicians to show the way forward. The musicians were more than willing to shoulder this burden, but with very little additional support, the effort they exerted was taking its toll.

CHAPTER 6

Let It Go

The new year of 2006 brought Orleanians hope along with the mountain of frustration at the lack of progress and anger at the authorities, who absolved themselves of responsibility for the mess. There was also a deep wellspring of unresolved grief and utter sorrow, emotions that revealed themselves at the unlikeliest moments. An elderly cabdriver who took me from Bywater to Canal Street began the trip with feisty comments on the recovery and ended up sobbing over a statement he had heard on television by House of Representatives majority leader Denny Hastert that New Orleans was not worth saving.

Only two days after the disaster, when people were dying in the floodwaters, Hastert said in an interview with the *Daily Herald* of Arlington Heights, Illinois, that New Orleans was not worth rebuilding. "It looks like a lot of that place could be bulldozed," the Illinois Republican observed. This public statement of no confidence by one of the country's political leaders framed the debate about the city's future for months and created anger and disillusionment in New Orleans. It was a musician, songwriter and virtuoso Cajun violinist Gina Forsyth, who stepped up to respond with the witty protest song "Talking Hurricane Refugee Blues."

> *Of all things*
> *The Speaker of the House [is] wondering if New Orleans is worth saving.*

On January 7, 2006, James Andrews brought his band to the Jazz National Historic Park's Visitor Center in Dutch Alley, a narrow, cobblestoned passage next to the river levee off of Saint Philip Street. The cozy museum and bookstore had room for fewer than a hundred people but staged free afternoon concerts featuring various New Orleans performers, and this was the first one since the flood. Andrews's quintet was anchored by keyboardist Joe Krown, who'd been Clarence ("Gatemouth") Brown's musical director before Katrina. Brown died shortly after the deluge engulfed his Slidell home. The room was packed with a mixture of local musicians and tourists, so many people that a crowd gathered outside on the North Peters Street promenade. Even though they couldn't see the band, they danced to the music, which blared out of an external sound system. Andrews kept the program simple, playing a number of New Orleans R&B classics and an intriguing take on Sonny Rollins's "Saint Thomas." After giving Krown a solo spot for a Professor Longhair tribute, Andrews performed the perennial crowd-pleaser "What a Wonderful World," an appropriate tribute to Louis Armstrong from a man nicknamed "Satchmo of the Ghetto." Andrews had the crowd second-lining for "Mardi Gras in New Orleans," which showcased all his strengths—affable vocals, a biting trumpet solo, and that innate ability to get a party rolling. "We're gonna rebuild New Orleans note by note," he vowed.

In early 2006 James also recorded what he hoped would become an anthem for the city's recovery, "New Orleans, New Orleans," a song that reflected his new role in post-Katrina New Orleans as an organizer of musicians and a kind of spiritual cheerleader for the local music scene. That role was codified in the title track of the CD single, "New Orleans, New Orleans (the Anthem)." The uplifting spiritual took the listener through the storm experience in the first verse, lamented the aftermath in the second verse, when the city "couldn't get a helping hand," and then, in true gospel ballad tradition, promised a glorious future: "With the music and the laughter/we'll be happy ever after." The other tune on the CD was a slinky R&B groove, "Katrina, Katrina." The assembled "friends" backing up Andrews on this session were members of an all-star cast of New Orleans greats, including John Boutté and "Big Chief" Alfred Doucette on vocals, Kevin O'Day on drums, Jon Cleary on piano, Gina Forsyth on violin, and Tom Fitzpatrick on tenor saxophone.

Saturday, January 21, 2006, was the day I finally realized that New Orleans could fully regain the festive spirit of its past. That afternoon the Zydepunks played a live performance at the Louisiana Music Factory, a set that was immediately followed by an all-star lineup of local musicians across the street at the House of Blues. The occasion was *OffBeat*'s annual music awards show, which featured more music than awards because the procedure for voting on the awards was disrupted by the flood. Instead of the usual awards, New Orleans R&B icons Allen Toussaint and Irma Thomas topped a list of lifetime-achievement award winners, which also included "Uncle" Lionel Batiste of the Treme Brass Band, singer Wanda Rouzan, and New Orleans jazz promoters George and Nina Buck. Performers included James Andrews, Coco Robicheaux, Davis Rogan, Cowboy Mouth, Walter ("Wolfman") Washington, Papa Grows Funk, Shannon McNally, Theresa Andersson, Quintron, and John Boutté.

Rogan flew through a set of songs from *The Once and Future DJ*, exhorting the crowd to sing along and throwing in outrageous anecdotes in between songs. He went past his allotted time, and the stage manager was fuming in the wings. He had his moment in the spotlight, and he wasn't letting go of it even if it got him into trouble. He was brilliant and funny, a defiant oddball in the tradition of New Orleans characters like Jessie Hill, Ernie K-Doe, and Chris Kenner.

There was James Andrews once again, flying the flag for New Orleans music and performing as if his very life hung in the balance. Mardi Gras Indian Chief Alfred Doucette and the Treme Brass Band joined him for a raucous version of his grandfather Jessie Hill's iconic R&B tune, "Ooh Poo Pah Doo." Andrews then joined Cowboy Mouth's Fred LeBlanc and Paul Sanchez during their acoustic set.

Both Toussaint and Thomas were inspirations to everyone there that night. Despite the fact that they had both lost everything in the flood, they each arrived in an upbeat mood and expressed confidence in the future. Toussaint held an emeritus position in New Orleans culture before Katrina, but in its wake he seemed positively energized by the challenge of overcoming the tragedy. He would go on to produce some of his best work in the coming years, including his outstanding collaboration with Elvis Costello, *The River in Reverse,* and showed how strong his creative currents were flowing that night by leading the audience in an impromptu composition built around the line "Everybody must come home."

The spirit of cooperation was rampant at the show. Violinist Theresa Andersson played with World Leader Pretend, while Anders Osborne and saxophonist Tim Green jammed with Papa Grows Funk, and Fred LeBlanc took over the drums with PGF and friends for a wild version of the Beatles' "Come Together."

LeBlanc and Sanchez, who took the stage like a New Orleans rock 'n' roll version of Laurel and Hardy, really tore things up during their acoustic set. The stout, effusive LeBlanc demonstrated his dangerously surreal charisma by singing "Over the Rainbow," which might have fallen flat in other circumstances but fit the hopefully optimistic mood of this fingers-crossed crowd. When he followed it with the homecoming anthem, "Take Me Back to New Orleans," he sealed the deal. By the time LeBlanc and Sanchez harmonized the chorus of the band's best-known song, "Jenny Says," LeBlanc had the crowd totally under his spell:

> *Let it go, let it go, let it go!*
> *When the world is coming down on you, let it go.*

The catharsis in the room was palpable.

"All of a sudden that song is pretty relevant around here," LeBlanc later told me over a lunch of fried chicken livers, greens, and red beans at the Praline Connection:

We played at Voodoo Fest, and we had about ten thousand people watching us. People in New Orleans have been hearing that song for thirteen, fourteen years, but that day every hair on my body was standing completely on end. I just remember getting the audience to sing "Let it go, let it go." Those people just needed to be screamin' 'Let it go." People have to let go of a lot of really hard crap that's gone down in the last few months. Having our music used as a catalyst for people to feel better even for a moment is a great thing to be part of.

A few days later I met Paul Sanchez on a late January morning so impossibly beautiful it seemed almost like nature's apology for the terrible storms of the previous summer. We sat on an old porch in the Vieux Carré, surrounded by silence except for the mule-drawn carriage that rattled past us. In what had become an even smaller town than usual, friends stopped to chat as they passed down the street. Sanchez, who wore his trademark well-worn fedora and a black jacket with a Meher Baba button on the lapel, tried to come to terms with the mixed feelings churning inside him—pride at what he'd achieved with Cowboy Mouth, inexpressible grief over the loss of all of his possessions and a life's worth of music, and an overriding dread about where he was heading.

The band had just about finished making a record that all the members felt finally represented them accurately over the summer. They were in Atlanta with producer Russ-T Cobb, putting the finishing touches on the recording when Katrina hit New Orleans. "We were all in shock," said Sanchez:

> The flood hits, and Russ-T has got to finish the record with people who are literally sobbing, glued to the TV, glued to the Internet, watching our city being destroyed, and then we would have to go on the road to do gigs, and we came back, and Hurricane Rita hit.
>
> My wife and I were online at a site she jokingly called yourhouseisunderwater.com, and you could see a satellite picture of your house. We just got a new roof put on which was supposed to be hurricane proof. It was perfectly intact, but the rest of the house was under water. We sat there every day for three weeks, looking at the house. I was down to all my possessions in a suitcase. We came back in December. It was weird; you see people going through the ruins of their house, and you say, "Don't go through it. It's useless." But when you're there, it's your house, so we stumbled through it and started going through all this wet stuff we couldn't keep, and then we realized you just have to say goodbye to your stuff. My house sat in sewage for three weeks, and every inch of the place, where you laughed and ate and made love, it's covered with shit, and you never want to see it ever again.

Sanchez tried to figure out another place to live but knew he couldn't survive for long away from the culture that's nurtured him over a lifetime. "It's really cool to be home," he said. "The people are really beautiful, and they make me very hopeful about the future. The politicians are useless; it's the same old business." Sanchez wrote "Home," and LeBlanc "On the Avenue" immediately after the storm, and both songs made it to the album they were recording when Katrina hit, *Voodoo Shoppe*. Playing live after Katrina was difficult for Sanchez at first. Cowboy Mouth stopped playing one of its most popular songs, "Hurricane Party," which Sanchez had written in 1992 about deciding not to evacuate during Hurricane Andrew. The song's repeated chorus, "Hurricane party, out of control/Lyin' in the gutter eating Tootsie Rolls" took on a new, unwanted meaning.

"It was almost impossible for us to play," Sanchez said, his eyes brimming with tears:

> I just couldn't do it. The kids like to throw Tootsie Rolls during that song, and those Tootsie Rolls landing on stage sounded like nails in my heart. I just couldn't sing the song, but kids just kept holding up their New Orleans driver's license and calling for it. Finally we got home, and we were doing the reopening of the House of Blues show, and we put it back in. It was cathartic because that's the nature of live performance, but they were the most difficult shows I've ever played in my life. The best thing about music is you can disappear in the moment.

The title track, "Voodoo Shoppe," is an R&B-influenced song inspired by Sanchez's good friend and sometime songwriting partner John Boutté, who used to live upstairs from a botanica. Boutté sang on the album and would soon prove to be a bigger partner in Sanchez's career than he realized at the time.

CHAPTER 7

Don't Let Them Wash Us Away

In the chaotic months after the storm, tensions ran high in New Orleans as the priorities of the recovery were the source of often bitter arguments. One of the biggest cultural hurdles New Orleans had to face was how to stage Mardi Gras. In 2006 Fat Tuesday fell on February 28, but the Mardi Gras season begins on the Feast of Epiphany, in early January, and the parades traditionally begin three weekends before Fat Tuesday itself. With many of its displaced citizens still unsure of how to get home, there was a real debate about whether the city should go forward with a 2006 Mardi Gras celebration at all. However, regardless of the official position, the remaining locals would have celebrated anyway. The city agreed to stage a truncated version of the festival, with several parade groups not participating and others forced to alter their routes.

Cowboy Mouth was enjoying its highest profile in years, and *OffBeat* used the band as its Mardi Gras cover story. Cowboy Mouth took to heart its responsibility of waving the New Orleans flag. "It's never been more important than now to be in Cowboy Mouth," said Sanchez. "When you stand up there on that stage and say you're from New Orleans, it means something."

LeBlanc was even more effusive. "This Mardi Gras counts and I plan on raising as much hell as I possibly can," he vowed:

> I intend to have the greatest time of my entire life this Mardi Gras. Everyone who's in New Orleans now, we're in charge of saving the city. We're in charge of saving Mardi Gras. We're in charge of the culture of the city. It's up to us whether the city goes on. I'm not talking about my band or myself. I'm talking about everybody who lives here. That's why we need people to come visit this Mardi Gras, this Jazz Fest. It's not just about putting money in our pockets. It's about saving the culture, saving this creative musical celebratory way of life. If we don't do it, it won't get done. Period.

LeBlanc's bravado was far more than mere rhetoric. The soul and character of New Orleans were at stake. Because the ties to the past had been cut so cleanly by the depopulation of the neighborhoods that nurtured the city's music, the only way to restore the culture was for those musicians to come home and return to doing what they had always done. The musicians understood this better than anyone as their periodic road trips would show them. Those who were exiled to Texas and Georgia and New York understood it best.

When the Krewe de Vieux parade rolled in mid-January, brass bands accompanied the satiric revelers through the streets of Marigny and the French Quarter. Sporting themes such as "The Corpse of Engineers Presents a Day at the Breach," the floats took humorous potshots at political leaders and institutions. The blue FEMA tarps covering roofs all over the city became raw material for an array of creative attire. The most popular costume was the dead refrigerator, easily assembled from boxes and perfect for wearing antigovernment slogans.

The news media had been covering New Orleans extensively since the flood, and Mardi Gras was an obvious target for wall-to-wall electronic voyeurism. The week before Fat Tuesday, network newscasts showed scenes of Bourbon Street revelers as proof that the city had returned to its peculiar version of normalcy. More than eight hundred media organizations applied for credentials to cover Carnival 2006, and most of them were looking for shots of drunken young women baring their breasts for a handful of plastic beads.

Still, there was a palpable air of desperation in that 150th anniversary of Carnival in New Orleans. The weeks of celebrations, parties, and street parades leading up to Mardi Gras had always been the time of year when New Orleans earned its nickname of the Big Easy, but nothing had been easy for the city's beleaguered residents since August 29. Many locals were unhappy about the media coverage of this Mardi Gras. With three-quarters of the city still in ruins, sporadic electricity, postal service, and traffic lights, hospitals and schools closed, and only the most limited public transportation available, the few residents who'd been able to return to New Orleans bristled about media reports that life had returned to normal.

"The fact that underage suburban tourists can puke on Bourbon Street without fear of going to jail doesn't mean that things are all right with New Orleans," noted Terry Fredericks, a cook at Verdi Mart. The asthmatic Fredericks was one of the people who stayed in the city throughout the storm. Days later he suffered an attack, but with the stores abandoned and looted, the only way he could get his medicine was to see whether there was anything left at the drug store. As he was picking his way through the rubble, he was confronted by an armed guard who told him, "Leave now, or I'll shoot you."

Of course, everyone in town knew that, unless the tourists returned, New Orleans was finished. After Katrina, the city lost several big events, including the Sugar Bowl, the Bayou Classic, and the Essence Festival, along with virtually all of its convention business. Without a healthy festival season, the small businesses that had managed to reopen wouldn't last out the following summer. "We know we have to have a good Mardi Gras to survive," said Jesse Paige, manager of the Blue Nile, the Frenchmen Street club that reopened its doors for the first time since Katrina the Friday night before Fat Tuesday. "We've got everything on the line. The bands have all agreed to play without guarantees. We're counting on this weekend's business to generate enough cash to keep us operating."

The celebration is unique in that it's not a corporate or municipally sponsored event but a series of parades and balls organized by private citizens who are members of various secret societies, or "krewes." Each organization charges its members annual dues and requires them to commit to buying a minimum amount of beads and other "throws." The members keep their identities secret when riding on their krewe's floats by wearing masks. The all-woman Krewe of Muses, which rolls on the Thursday night before Mardi Gras, charged $850 in dues and a commitment to buy $500 worth of throws, thereby ensuring that all of the parade goers got a wealth of trinkets. The Muses drew a huge crowd that was heavily populated with children, who were lavished with stuffed animals and flashing beads, all bearing the Muses' signature.

John Gros, leader of Papa Grows Funk, had a full work schedule during Mardi Gras but made sure his daughters, Rachel and Emily, got to see as many parades as possible. "I do it because I remember when I was a kid how special Mardi Gras was," said Gros. "My grandfather used to take me to all the parades. We would watch the beginning of the parade at Napoleon Avenue, then jump into the car and drive to another spot, where we could watch it again."

Each parade had a theme, and the anonymous nature of the krewes allows for plenty of political satire and outright protest dating back to the Reconstruction era following the Civil War, when masked dissidents assassinated a federal official during the confusion of Mardi Gras revelry. In 2006 the Knights of Chaos rolled one of the most devastatingly satiric parades ever just before the Muses' parade. It was titled "Hades—A Dream of Chaos." Organizers drew a direct parallel to the nineteenth-century dissidents. "This tableau could be called 'Reconstruction II,'" read the krewe's proclamation, which was printed on small cards thrown from the floats, "as we look with both sadness and humor at events and individuals involved in the devastation of New Orleans."

The floats all depicted harrowing, flame-engulfed scenes from hell, with themes like "The Headless State," "Carpetbaggers," "Homeland Insecurity," "The Pigs of Patronage," "The Corpse of Engineers," and "Ministers of Misinformation." There was a withering caricature of New Orleans Saints' owner, Tom Benson, "Boogieman." The Saints, New Orleans's beloved National Football League franchise, had a particularly tough year without their home field, the ruined

Superdome, and Benson had enraged fans by saying he wanted to move the team to San Antonio.

The most dramatic float, "The Inferno," showed Governor Kathleen Blanco, Mayor Ray Nagin, and FEMA director Michael Brown as infernal cooks brewing a giant cauldron of human gumbo in the Superdome as members of Congress forced people into the boiling pot with pitchforks and a leering George W. Bush presided over the whole scene as the horned Satan incarnate.

The parades and pageantry went off without a hitch, although Mardi Gras also demonstrated how much of the city's culture was damaged in the storm. With no functioning school system in place since the storm, the city's vaunted marching bands were crippled or sidelined completely, which left gaping holes between the floats during the parades. New Orleans high school institutions like the Saint Augustine Marching 100 were known throughout the country for their extraordinary rhythms, which were at once influenced by the parade beats of the second lines and foundations of the city's unique funk drumming style. Those bands, notorious for their stamina, which was built up over a series of long marches along the parade routes, were conspicuously absent for most of the 2006 Mardi Gras, but the musicians and artists who played the soundtrack and built the elaborate floats for Mardi Gras delivered the goods, and the parade schedule went on with few hitches, while the clubs were filled with great music all over town.

Frenchmen Street was particularly vibrant that Mardi Gras. The Blue Nile's reopening was a tremendous success and allowed the club to get back on its feet and resume its role as a mainstay of the city's music scene. One of the most anticipated shows was a Mardi Gras Indians jam session at the music club d.b.a., which was headlined by Big Chief Monk Boudreaux and included a John Gros–led group as the backing band. It also featured guitarist Anders Osborne, who had collaborated with Boudreaux on two memorable albums for Shanachie Records.

Gros began the set, fronting a band with Jeffrey ("Jellybean") Benitez on drums, Donald Ramsey on bass, and Robert Maché on guitar. Though the songs were all pre-Katrina, they seemed to reference the tragedy. The angry funk rocker "Rat a Tang Tang" was originally written about punishing someone who did Gros wrong, but in this instance it sounded like a musical curse on Katrina. Osborne began chanting, "Indians, here dey come!" and Boudreaux approached the microphone. Sousaphone player Kirk Joseph stepped up and began honking away an accompaniment to the groove. Monk, a stone-faced elder offstage who turns into a dynamo when the music swirls around him, picked up the chant, and, with Jellybean rolling a second-line drum rhythm, the moment was pure New Orleans, a mixed group of black and white musicians hammering out a monster beat that had everybody in the place moving.

At the height of the piece the PA and all the house lights cut out, but the instruments still had power, so the guitars and drums continued in total darkness, breaking into a wild jam as the crowd picked up the chant: "Indians, here dey come!" After about fifteen minutes of this, the band took a break, and hasty repairs were made to the power system. New Orleans had been dealing with frequent blackouts since the storm, so this one did nothing to dampen the spirit of the moment. Eventually the PA came back on, and the show, now lit by candles, resumed with Boudreaux chanting an incantation and other Indians moving toward the stage to answer his exhortations. "Mardi Gras morning, well, here it come," Monk bellowed over a hectic pulse. "We're gonna get together and have some fun."

The words seem simple on the page, but in this context, the lines—repeated over and over with variations—took on a magical vibe as Monk transformed into the shaman, an elemental force that seemed to invoke the furious moment of the storm itself. Then Monk went into another Indian chant, the refrain invoked when creating the magical Indian suits themselves, the sacred vestments worked on all year and finally revealed to the world on Fat Tuesday. "Everybody got to sew, sew, sew," Monk moaned. Osborne's guitar line soared, the music took wing, and just as it hit another peak, the power went out again. The crowd erupted in excited cheers and whistles, and the call-and-response went on for half an hour with the band wailing in the darkened room and the audience continuing the chant. Monk later dismissed the technical problems with a wave of his hand. "I don't need no 'lectricity once the spirit takes hold," he said.

"Monk said his voice knocked out the power, and he was just getting warmed up," a still-smiling Gros said after the show. "He would have gone all night long." However, the important thing is that the show still happened even without power, and none of the audience members left unfulfilled.

Big Chief Boudreaux of the Golden Eagles Mardi Gras Indians was still trying to cobble together his outfit for Fat Tuesday, the day before Ash Wednesday begins the forty days of atonement known as Lent in the Catholic liturgical calendar. Every Mardi Gras morning Boudreaux assembles his gang, one of dozens of these secret societies representing the various African American neighborhoods around the city, to parade in their feathered costumes and follow the rituals of their tradition.

In the destruction and chaos following the storm, the Mardi Gras Indians were one of the most endangered of the city's cultural institutions. The African American neighborhoods where the Indians lived were among the hardest hit by the flood, and many of the Indians hadn't returned to the city. Lost among homes and possessions were Indian suits that were being made for 2006, costumes that required hundreds of hours of work and great expense to create. The few Indians who had returned, struggling to find housing and employment, had little time to finish their outfits.

Offering aid to the Indians was particularly difficult due to the insular nature of the societies. Even the name "Mardi Gras Indians" is a kind of misnomer, a handle coined by white New Orleanians who traditionally saw these African American men only on Mardi Gras day, when they paraded all over the city. In the black neighborhoods, where they practiced their songs and sewed their costumes all year, they were known as Black Indians, and their traditions were seen as much as a tribute to their African tribal ancestors as to the Native Americans they met when they were brought to America as slaves.

Mardi Gras was a satisfying renewal of the city's mythic culture, a demonstration of its ability to get back on its feet and support a major event despite all of the problems people were still facing. However, an even greater challenge loomed in April, when another season of festivals brought enormous numbers of music fans from all over the world to hear New Orleans music. Of all the music-based cultural events on the city's calendar, the French Quarter Festival, celebrated shortly before the New Orleans Jazz and Heritage Festival, was probably the easiest to mount since the Vieux Carré was one of the sections of town untouched by the flood, and all of the performers were local New Orleans musicians. One of the festival's main events that year was the reunion of John Boutté with his older sister, Lillian, who was responsible for getting him to sing professionally.

Lillian had been living and working in Europe when Katrina hit and watched in dismay as her hometown was destroyed. With many family members unreachable, Lillian feared what she would find as she traveled home to see what had happened. When she finally got to New Orleans, those fears were confirmed. "When I came off the highway onto Louisiana Avenue, I was driving on my own," she recalled:

> I thought I was tough. Closer to the house, I saw the trees and the playgrounds that we played in and Our Lady of the Sacred Heart, the church we went to, the grocery store that has been there for generations. Then I started to go down Roman [Street], and I was getting sick, but I had to pull myself together, and when I came to my mom's house, it just took me to my knees. Everything was washed away. I just had to let the rest of it go and be happy that everyone's okay. I couldn't drive. I was shaking. The tears wouldn't allow me to drive. I couldn't see. It was just overwhelming. You just want to get out and do something. What can you do? You can't do anything but get mad and pray. You don't let it go this long, not like this, not in America.

Though the house she grew up in was gone, Lillian Boutté consoled herself with the fact that her family members had survived the flood. Then she thought of her father. "I went straight to the foot of Canal Street by the cemetery and

Figure 4. Satiric George W. Bush costumes proliferated during Mardi Gras 2006. Photo by Barbara Mathé. Used by permission of Barbara Mathé.

Figure 5. Flamingos at Mardi Gras. Photo by Barbara Mathé. Used by permission of Barbara Mathé

Figure 6. T-shirts with flood themes were everywhere in the shops during Mardi Gras 2006. Photo by Barbara Mathé. Used by permission of Barbara Mathé.

Figure 7. Moldy refrigerators were another common theme at the first Mardi Gras after the flood. Photo by Barbara Mathé. Used by permission of Barbara Mathé.

Figure 8. Zulu Grand Marshal Harold Dudley. Photo by Barbara Mathé. Used by permission of Barbara Mathé.

Figure 9. Zulu 2006 rolls on Canal Street. Photo by Barbara Mathé. Used by permission of Barbara Mathé.

Figure 10. Rebirth Brass Band marched with the Zulu parade. Photo by Barbara Mathé. Used by permission of Barbara Mathé.

Figure 11. Zulu featured some of the most colorful Mardi Gras floats. Photo by Barbara Mathé. Used by permission of Barbara Mathé.

Figure 12. The gilded coconut is the most coveted Mardi Gras throw. Photo by Barbara Mathé. Used by permission of Barbara Mathé.

Figure 13. At the Zulu parade. Photo by Barbara Mathé. Used by permission of Barbara Mathé.

Figure 14. Kermit the Frog gets into the act. Photo by Barbara Mathé. Used by permission of Barbara Mathé.

Figure 15. After the parades, revelers danced on Frenchmen Street. Photo by Barbara Mathé. Used by permission of Barbara Mathé.

checked if my daddy was still around, to make sure he hadn't floated off because nobody had been able to check on him yet. He was right there, not a rock off it. My mom was happy to know that he had not been desecrated. It was something for me to hold on to." Lillian and John started off the French Quarter Festival on April 21 with an emotional performance that included John's tribute to their dad, "At the Foot of Canal Street," a song he wrote in collaboration with his buddy Paul Sanchez. Sanchez and Boutté were spending a lot of time together in the months after the storm, developing a creative collaboration that would evolve into one of the most important music developments in the city in the wake of the flood.

New Orleans didn't have much of a corporate presence before the flood but had much less afterward, as even fast-food chains were reluctant to reopen. That didn't prevent vultures from attempting to move in on whatever was left of value, and one of the most coveted prizes was the city's signature music culture event, the New Orleans Jazz and Heritage Festival. I spoke with one high-placed advertising executive who assured me that the deal was done to move Jazz Fest to Los Angeles. Austin, Memphis, and Atlanta were other locations mentioned as possible alternate sites. Even producer Quint Davis acknowledged after the storm that Jazz Fest 2006 would take place, but he didn't know where.

It was easy to see why people doubted whether Jazz Fest could take place in New Orleans that year. The grandstand at Fair Grounds racetrack, the site of the festival, was severely damaged by the one-two hurricane punch of Katrina and Rita, and the flood left the track itself and the infield a fetid sewer that looked more like a toxic-waste dumping ground than a park. Fixing this mess in time for the last weekend of April, the traditional opening of the festival, appeared to be a hopeless task.

Churchill Downs, Inc., the Kentucky-based horseracing company that had purchased Fair Grounds from the Krantz family in 2004, had the deep resources and political connections to accomplish the task of refurbishing the plant. Although Churchill was forced to move the fall horseracing meet elsewhere, the Fair Grounds were miraculously restored to working order in time to hold the Jazz and Heritage Festival in 2006. It was an example of what New Orleans was capable of and, perhaps more important, a reminder of what the city was unable to accomplish. A massive racetrack and casino complex with the right connections could be refurbished in months, but the city's hospitals, schools, infrastructure, and affordable housing stock remained in ruins for years.

Having seen the Fair Grounds after Katrina, with its roof shaved off and giant plate-glass windows shattered, I was astonished to walk through the Gentilly Avenue gate on the first day of the 2006 Jazz Fest and discover a setting that looked more or less the same as ever. The majestic live oaks had been ravished, and scaffolding covered the inside of the upper floors of the grandstand, but the first floor of the grandstand and the paddock area were back in action. The Allison Miner stage, named for one of the festival's founders, moved from the second floor of the grandstand to the paddock and was a hot spot all weekend, with a nice warm-up from zydeco star and Mardi Gras Indian Sunpie Barnes before his fais do-do stage performance, an intimate set from the versatile and talented New Orleans vocalist Ingrid Lucia, and the most talked-about event of the weekend, an unscheduled acoustic duet by British rocker Elvis Costello and New Orleans songwriting legend Allen Toussaint.

Opening Friday had a tentative, laid-back feel, that kind of pinch-me-to-prove-I'm-not-dreaming quality that perfectly suited the mellow afternoon and the reverent, happy crowd. People came in large numbers, and the lines at most food booths and particularly the poster booth were huge. Work was continuing on the grandstand, and there were two fewer stages and one less day, yet the 2006 New Orleans Jazz and Heritage festival reopened right on time at 11:15 A.M. on Friday, April 28, when the New Orleans Jazz Vipers began playing at the Economy Hall tent. The acoustic swing septet played a new song written for their displaced neighbors, "Hope You're Coming Back."

The music was restorative on that fine spring day, with several of the city's best musical institutions delivering memorable sets. On the main stage Dr. John headlined with a sparkling set of New Orleans R&B that had the crowd on its feet and dancing. Anders Osborne and Bryan Lee turned in virtuoso electric-guitar performances. Ninety-four-year-old trumpeter Lionel Ferbos, the featured player in the Palm Court Jazz Band, showed that traditional New Orleans jazz was still alive and well, while nineteen-year-old pianist Jonathan Batiste proved that New Orleans jazz had a future as well. Trumpeter Irvin Mayfield, who lost his father in the flood, led the New Orleans Jazz Orchestra through an emotional set, which opened with two pieces from Duke Ellington's New Orleans Suite, "Second Line" and "Portrait of Louis Armstrong," which became a showcase for Mayfield's trumpet playing and Evan Christopher's outstanding clarinet work.

The festival organizers did a remarkable job of assembling New Orleans brass bands, Mardi Gras Indian groups, Social Aid and Pleasure Club second-liners, and local musicians of all categories for the six-day bash. The R&B legend Eddie Bo summed up the spirit of the event after an exultant rendition of "Check Your Bucket" by saying, "If you haven't had a drink today, go get one. You gotta get something to drink today. Today is celebration day!"

The eccentricities inherent in the New Orleans scene were in full force. Fird ("Snooks") Eaglin, a blind black guitarist known as "the human jukebox" due to his encyclopedic songbook and penchant for switching from one song to another in the middle of a performance, played a characteristically unpredictable set backed by bassist George Porter Jr., along with John Gros on keyboards and Jeffrey ("Jellybean") Alexander on drums from Papa Grows Funk. Eaglin burned his way through an eclectic program that ranged from Professor Longhair's classic "Mardi Gras in New Orleans" to the Isley Brothers' "It's Your Thing."

The blues tent was abandoned that year, but the other stages had blues galore, from Bryan Lee on the Gentilly Boulevard stage to J Monque'D at the Fais Do-Do stage. Some kind of special magic hung on that Fais Do-Do stage all weekend, and Monque'D wasted no time channeling it in the hottest set he'd ever turned in at Jazz Fest. Raful Neal Jr. and Marc Stone on guitars were just chomping the stomp out of a hard-edged set of classic blues, pushed on by one of the city's greatest R&B drummers, Willie Cole. With Nelson Lunding pounding away at the keyboardist and Monque'D grunting and strutting and delivering those blurting harp solos, this unit sounded like nothing less than the Muddy Waters band in its prime. Monque'D may have been pumped by the desperation that followed the loss of his new album, which had been near completion when it was lost in the flood.

Monque'D repeatedly referenced his experiences with the Baton Rouge blues tradition. "When I was a kid, we were scared to death of Slim Harpo," he said of the Louisiana bluesman made famous by the 1966 hit "Scratch My Back." "He had the red devil–looking eyes." He then launched into an apocalyptic "Raining in My Heart" and followed with a tribute to Earl King and Professor Longhair, a merry, lurching "Big Chief," where he really nailed the whistled melody, and the crowd danced ecstatically. The show ended with an apoplectic hammering of Muddy's "I've Got My Mojo Working," Monque'D signifying with his gold teeth glittering through a wicked mustache grin under his tan fedora and wraparound shades. He shook his jowls, and those cheeks did some serious moving. Then he nailed it all down with a driving harp solo.

Katrina's emotional impact on the musicians playing at Jazz Fest was clearly evident as many of them made some direct reference to the flooding and its aftermath before revving up the celebration. Cowboy Mouth was a subtly different group in the wake of the hurricane. Drummer/frontman Fred LeBlanc, who could always be counted on for some outrageous stunt in past Jazz Fests, directed his energy in a far more abstract sense this time around. "Despite the best efforts of some *bitch* named Katrina," he bellowed, "this year we had Mardi Gras and Jazz Fest. This song is a love song to the greatest little city in the world." LeBlanc proceeded to sing the sentimental ode to his beloved hometown, "On the Avenue," and the usually raucous CM crowd was respectfully silent. This new, subdued, reflective LeBlanc finished the tune with an affirmation: "This will not be the end of the Avenue." The band started to spit its old fire on the next tune, "Hurricane Party," but the systemic failures that continued to plague the city returned when the power went out. In previous years LeBlanc might have reacted by climbing the scaffolding or throwing himself into the crowd, but instead he sang "Over the Rainbow," which was as effective a moment as that at the House of Blues OffBeat party.

By contrast, Bob Dylan was careening away on the other side of the infield, smiling broadly as he cranked his way through a set that avoided any direct political or social comment unless you want to read something into his choice of "Maggie's Farm" to open the set. Dylan had a perfect opportunity to make some Katrina reference on the chilling "High Water (for Charlie Patton)," but he deliberately expanded the context. After all, the song was written well before Katrina. This nightmarish, near-metal riffing "High Water" was totally devoid of sentimentality. "It's rough out there," he sang in a tone of deepest, almost mocking irony, emphasizing the idea that the high water is not just in New Orleans but everywhere. Dylan doesn't need to make his songs literal or reactive to current events. In Dylan's art, the hidden truths are always more important than the slogans that drive the anthems. He didn't have to play to the gallery because he'd already tipped them off. Look around you, he was saying to the crowd. The high water isn't just in New Orleans but everywhere. New Orleans was symptomatic of the trouble waiting down the road for the rest of the country, the rest of the world. Dylan didn't need to pound the literal meaning or tie his lyrics to current events—they worked outside the timeline of history, which made them perfectly suited to the secret world of New Orleans, where events take place in sacred, renewable time, a calendar defined by the ritual of the city's music.

In the run-up to Jazz Fest, rumors swirled around the city that the Rolling Stones and U2 would be surprise performers. As it turned out, at least some members of U2 were indeed prowling around town, and the Edge even made a brief onstage appearance with one of the groups James Andrews cofounded, the New Birth Brass Band. The U2 guitarist also sat in with the Dave Matthews Band. In the final reckoning, most of the headliners were locals. Some national acts did perform—along with Dylan, Lionel Richie, the Dave Matthews Band, Paul Simon, Herbie Hancock, and Elvis Costello also played—and Bruce Springsteen chose Jazz Fest to debut his acoustic orchestra playing *The Seeger Sessions*.

Springsteen's gesture was magnanimous. By showing up on a stage like this, with the whole world watching, he drew attention to a body of work by Pete Seeger that was always self-effacing, more about those who were listening (or preferably singing along) than performing. However, Springsteen, a natural politician, played to the audience's sense of betrayal and frustration and manipulated those emotions brilliantly while backed by a band whose arrangements coaxed previously unrealized nuances out of the material. "The guy has amazing charisma," marveled Radiators front man Dave Malone, a charismatic fellow in his own right. The Radiators, who traditionally close the Gentilly stage on the final day of the festival, sent out a "relief kit" to the visiting bands.

At that historic Jazz Fest the drama was high right up until the last minute. The final day's headliner, Fats Domino, backed out of his performance amid reports that he had been in ill health. In the immediate aftermath of Katrina,

Domino, whose house was among the buildings in the lower Ninth Ward swept away by the flood, was thought to be among the missing. He had in fact been evacuated to a shelter but suffered from severe stress and was still not himself months later. Domino's inability to take the stage at Jazz Fest was a dramatic example of the physical and psychological toll the stress of the flood put on the city's musicians.

The performance John Boutté turned in at Economy Hall midway through the last day was the emblematic moment of Jazz Fest '06. Boutté and Paul Sanchez had been writing songs together and talking about the performance. Sanchez played Randy Newman's "Louisiana 1927" for Boutté and suggested some new lyrics for the song. Boutté loved Newman's heartfelt lament about a flood from another era. Times and circumstances had changed, but the results were still about human tragedy. The 1927 flood was caused by a rain-engorged river system, not a hurricane, but with help from Sanchez, Boutté rewrote some of the words to fit the current occasion.

Boutté's set at Jazz Fest included a version of the Annie Lennox song "Why?" which he had performed on the *Sing Me Back Home* project. In that recording and at Jazz Fest, he turned the question of the song's title into an accusation. Boutté went on to electrify the crowd with a hair-raising update of Neil Young's "Southern Man," urging the people to "scream like you're in the Convention Center...scream like you're in the Superdome!"

The short, slender Boutté was a vortex for the crowd's surging emotion as he stood implacably on the stage with his head cocked aloft and his face expressionless, a monument to African American dignity in the face of the greatest hardships. He waited until the mayhem subsided, and an eerie quiet crept over the congregation as everyone listened intently to hear what would come next. Boutté then unveiled the new lyrics to "Louisiana 1927," creating what would stand as one of the great moments in Jazz Fest history. Rewriting a Randy Newman epic is a move that would've sounded foolish if it weren't so powerfully appropriate. In the Boutté version the clouds came in from the gulf, and when Boutté transformed Newman's line into a reference to the deadly flood that followed the collapse of the Industrial Canal by singing "six feet of water in the streets of the Lower Nine," the screams of recognition from the crowd nearly drowned him out. By the next verse it was "twelve feet of water in the streets of the Lower Nine," and people were out of their chairs, lamenting and moaning like worshipers at an ecstatic church service. "President Bush say, 'Great job, great job what the levees have done,'" Boutté sang. "Don't let them wash us away."

CHAPTER 8

Reality Check

As the summer of 2006 moved along, people in New Orleans were filled with both dread at the prospect of another major storm and relief that one hadn't come yet. Everyone knew that another hurricane of Katrina's magnitude could finish the city off. If there was one overriding feeling at this point it was anger—anger at political leaders, the lack of a coherent recovery plan, the flimsy and poisonous FEMA trailers provided as temporary housing, the intermittent power outages, and water main breaks. There was even anger at some of the charities that collected money intended for New Orleans.

The city and its people may have been left for dead, but many of its cultural institutions and particularly its music had survived in the midst of this morass and now led the way to whatever shape the recovery was going to take. All of the major festivals except the Ponderosa Stomp and the Essence festival, which temporarily moved to other cities, were renewed. In addition, musicians were able to make some powerful recorded statements about what New Orleans was going through.

Juvenile, the one major hip-hop artist who kept close to his New Orleans identity after Katrina, recorded a strong album titled *Reality Check*, which included his searing Katrina commentary, "Get Ya Hustle On," a nihilistic message of hopelessness addressed to his followers in prison and the people who lost everything in the storm. "Man, I'm tryin' to live, I lost it all in Katrina," said Juvenile, whose house was damaged in the flood. The video, set to an ominous, doom-evoking beat, depicted three kids in George Bush, Dick Cheney, and Ray Nagin masks walking through the devastated lower Ninth Ward past signs with slogans like "2005 = 1905," evoking the era of American apartheid. When the three kids arrived at the Saint Claude Avenue bridge, they dropped "relief" parachutes down to the ground holding empty tin cans and water bottles. The symbolism was stark and clear, and Juvenile commented darkly about government betrayal and media voyeurism.

The most controversial lines in "Get Ya Hustle On" addressed the $2,000 relief checks FEMA sent to displaced citizens, suggesting they should use the money to buy cocaine. Some people thought the line was in bad taste; others that it was a clever Katrina-inspired verse. However, if you look at it as a metaphor for government response to the tragedy, it makes the most sense. When the official reaction to people's losing their homes and possessions is to cut them a check for $2,000 and send them on their way, the residents might as well go out and buy cocaine for all the good it will do them. Of course, the ugly downside of this reality check was that the drug trade brought back the gangs who sold the drugs, and those gangs brought the culture of cold-blooded murder back to the city with them.

But out in the street, where the Cash Money artists originally came from and all New Orleans music was formed, locals were still turning out astonishing music against all odds. Though the poor neighborhoods were depopulated and the biggest names had left town, the returnees brought back their music bit by bit. A vacuum was filled by the only-in-New-Orleans genre called sissy bounce and its major practitioners, Big Freedia and Katey Red, who performed tirelessly. Hip-hop made by the gay and transgender MCs was the ultimate outsider culture considering the deeply sexist and homophobic strains that characterize mainstream rap.

New Orleans didn't really develop a distinctive hip-hop scene until the latter part of the 1980s. In 1987 Gregory D recorded "Buck Jump Time" with DJ Mannie Fresh, who would go on to create the Cash Money beats, taking cues from what the Rebirth Brass Band was doing with its reinvention of brass-band music as a hip-hop hybrid. "Here we go with a brand new style," rapped Gregory D, who went on to quote the Mardi Gras Indian chant "Hey Pocky Way," gave shout-outs to various New Orleans locations and tapped the ubiquitous audience-participation chant "Wave your hands in the air like you just don't care." Gregory D went in a different direction after that, but bounce was on the map even though it still existed more in the streets than in the marketplace. The first all-bounce album, from DJ Jimi, didn't come out until 1992.

Though there was a widespread misconception that all New Orleans hip-hop was bounce, the best-known New Orleans rappers eventually dropped the form in order to appeal to a national audience. Juvenile contributed extensively to the DJ Jimi material, but by the time he signed with Cash Money records and became part of one of that label's signature groups, the Hot Boys, along with Li'l Wayne, B.G., and Young Turk, he was already moving away from the simple chants, dance cues, and neighborhood shout-outs that characterize bounce.

That connection to the neighborhoods and to a past that is part of a cyclical timeline that is always renewing itself and is often confused with the New Orleans nostalgia music played for tourists explained why so much New Orleans music was linked to common sources. Shrewd observers have been pointing out for years that New Orleans musicians have been rapping at least as far back as Louis Armstrong. Bounce emerged out of the same elements that inspire all New Orleans street music—Mardi Gras Indian chants and second-line marching rhythms.

Ricky B used a sousaphone on the rhythm track for his early bounce release, "Y'all Holla," which included brass-band chants, along with neighborhood tags like a tribute to the Ninth ward's Desire project. In addition, K. C. Redd's "Hot Girlz on Fire" quoted "Iko Iko," making a direct connection to Mardi Gras Indian culture, as well as the classic New Orleans R&B, which shared many characteristics with bounce—nonsense lyrics, nursery-rhyme chants, local dialect, explicit sex themes, catalogs of dances, and a goofy sense of humor. Another similarity hip-hop shared with classic New Orleans R&B was the treatment of women subjects as either commodities or the brunt of jokes. Nevertheless, New Orleans hip-hop also had female voices who didn't hesitate to turn the sexual objectification table on their male counterparts.

In the wake of the flood, the local bounce artists took over the hip-hop scene. Gotti Boy Chris created a local buzz with "Cut It Up," an exciting track that showcased Chris's Jamaican-influenced rapid scatting over a torrid rhythm track. The accompanying video showed Chris and a large posse dancing in front of various New Orleans scenes, including a boarded-up housing project and the ruined, abandoned Circle Supermarket made famous in post-Katrina media coverage. Even as the city burned and their relatives were cut down by gangland violence, Chris and his crew cut it up among the ruins.

Other important recordings came out in Katrina's wake. The Dirty Dozen Brass Band (DDBB) put out its reimagining of the Marvin Gaye classic *What's Going On*, a daring and creative record that avoided being too reverential to the original, using Gaye's songs to make contemporary political points and arranging the charts to accommodate collective improvisation. The band used hip-hop MCs' Chuck D and Guru to deliver potent contemporary comment on Gaye's songs. On "God Is Love," Ivan Neville responded to Rev. Pat Robertson's claim that Katrina was sent by God to punish New Orleans for its wickedness. "Don't go and talk about my father 'cause God is my friend," Neville charged in an emotional rap with the DDBB backing him up. The album was a departure from the Dozen's trademark second-line, brass-band rhythms, but it was true to the band's vision of expanding this music into a lexicon that can interpret a wide range of styles. Bettye Lavette and G. Love also contributed to the project, with an August 29 release date that marked the one-year anniversary of Hurricane Katrina's landfall.

Ivan Neville, son of Aaron Neville and leader of one of the city's best funk bands, Dumpstafunk, which includes his cousin Ian Neville on guitar, was displaced by Katrina and migrated to Texas, where he played with the New Orleans Social Club before returning home. Just as Ivan's performance on *Sing Me Back Home* was charged with post-Katrina emotion, Neville delivered "God Is Love" with the sting of the storm palpable in his voice. "Ivan nailed that. He really felt it," said DDBB saxophonist Roger Lewis, one of the countless musicians who lost his home in the flood. Lewis expressed outrage at Robertson and other public figures who appeared to exult in the suffering of New Orleans's poorest. "It was a kind of immature statement for a reputed man of the cloth to make," said Lewis, who, after the flood, took visiting journalists on tours of the devastated lower Ninth Ward, where he was born. "We're looking at the total demise of a neighborhood," said Lewis as he drove through debris-ridden blocks of devastated houses. "Everything out here was under twenty feet of water. It was like a lake. A lot of people's lives got lost. A lot of people's history got lost. It will take thirty years to clean up this mess." Lewis also expressed frustration about the recovery's slow and inefficient pace. "It's all about greed," he charged, a sentiment that a growing number of local residents shared.

"I'm mad, I'm tired, and I'm salty," said Dr. John, who recorded the inspirational *Sippiana Hericane* after Katrina was followed a week later by Hurricane Rita, which devastated western Louisiana:

> They try to shuffle us under a rug, but when you look at the bottom line of all of it, there still ain't been no federal help. Basically FEMA's been a disaster, [and] the Corps of Engineers has been a disaster. They need to put dikes in there and save the wetlands. Unfortunately, it's something they could have done anytime in the last fifty years, and it would have cost them nothing, but everybody, true to form in politics, pockets all the money they can. It always happens. The city, the state, the feds— everybody does the same thing. We lost another 150 miles of wetlands last year. Bobby Charles, who wrote "Walking to New Orleans"—the whole town he was livin' in is gone. He used to call me at least twice a year and tell me he's gettin' closer and closer to havin' gulf coast property, which he never wanted.
>
> You got a city where the workforce, the people that makes [*sic*] New Orleans what it is, are [*sic*] basically stuck elsewheres. My band members are all over the place. My bass player's in Michigan, my drummer's in Baton Rouge, and so on and so on. I was talking to Henry Butler. He's got no place to go back to. He was trying to find a place in Dallas or Colorado.

Butler, the virtuoso pianist and vocalist who was also part of the *Sing Me Back Home* project, had relocated to Boulder, Colorado, and was adopting a wait-and-see attitude about returning to New Orleans. "I'm keeping my options open," he admitted:

> I'm not in a rush to make a quick decision. I wanna see what they do. They don't always make wise choices in terms of how the politicians deal with the general citizenry. I'm totally saddened by the fact that there's not really a school system in New Orleans at this point. You've got forty or fifty chartered schools, all operating on different standards. I don't know how you can call that an educational system. If you can't educate your children, I don't think you can claim to have a real city. I love New Orleans, and I don't want that to get lost in all of this, but as long as I've been conscious of it, I've never liked what the politicians have been doing, and I've never appreciated that the politicians truly cared about the arts. I know that the current mayor, for instance, could [sic] care less about music in particular. I know people he's hired as consultants, and they've basically just been ignored.

Irma Thomas, the fabled "Soul Queen of New Orleans," was wiped out by Katrina. Her house and nightclub, the Lion's Den, were both destroyed. It was the second time Thomas has been displaced from New Orleans by a hurricane— she was forced to move to California for a few years after Hurricane Camille hit back in 1969.

"This isn't the first disaster I've lived through, and I'm sure it won't be the last," she said defiantly. "Camille was nothing compared to this one. That time I only lost my work, but this time around I lost everything. I'm working on getting my home rebuilt, but I'm getting out of the nightclub business." Thomas reacted to the disaster like a number of other local musicians—by going into the studio and making an outstanding recording, *After the Rain*, an R&B classic imbued with the spirit that has made New Orleans music central to the city's identity.

Trumpeter Terence Blanchard recorded a kind of requiem for New Orleans, *A Tale of God's Will*. These beautifully orchestrated tracks expand on themes Blanchard composed for the soundtrack of Spike Lee's moving documentary, *When the Levees Broke*, which ended up unexpectedly starring Blanchard's mother, whose unrestrained grief at her loss, as well as her son's tearful attempts to comfort her, became a powerfully dramatic metaphor for the tragedy.

Lee's tale of New Orleans may become one of his most important works. This was a story that needed to be told from the black perspective, and Lee knew how to present that point of view accurately without patronizing the voices he was documenting. Lee was careful to make the point that the devastation hit people of all colors, but the African Americans he interviewed knew of Lee's work and understood that they could talk directly to him about their concerns without resorting to the carefully considered language delivered to "official" sources.

The depth of the anger and sense of betrayal felt by the black community can be measured by the certainty of those who believed they heard the levee being blown up. The undisputable physical evidence of the barge that crashed through the wall on the Industrial Canal and sat in the Ninth Ward for months didn't deter that belief because it was based on a generational memory more than physical observation. The same land was flooded when it was farmland worked by black sharecroppers in 1927. Back then the levees below New Orleans were dynamited to save the city. The grandparents of the people who drowned or were displaced by the post-Katrina federal flood of 2005 told them the stories of political betrayal by the white establishment in 1927, and when the waters rose, these folks knew who to blame. They still knew who to blame for what was hard not to call the systemic political attempt to keep these same people from return-ing to their homes on a massively uncoordinated federal, state, and local level. A deadly combination of incompetence, personal vanity, political expedience, and greed on the part of a host of politicians betrayed all of New Orleans, but the poorest communities, the heart of what was a black city before the storm, took what appeared to be mortal blows. Does it really matter whether it was dynamite or political corruption that caused all those people—and the world they created in New Orleans—to die?

Lee's documentary ended on a decidedly positive note, however. Lee recruited Glen David Andrews to sing what was becoming his trademark version of the spiritual "I'll Fly Away." On the last verse, according to Lee's instructions, Andrews changed the words and sang "New Orleans will never go away."

One of the oddities about New Orleans albums released in 2006 is that some of them were recorded before the storm, yet many of the songs on them sounded like they had been written in anticipation of Katrina. One of the records, by the subdudes, was even called *Behind the Levee,* a title that had been agreed upon before the levees broke.

I visited Tommy Malone, one of the cofounders of the subdudes, at his Mid-City home, which had taken fifteen feet of water in the flood. Every house on the street had suffered similar damage. In front of each one was a mound at least ten feet high, composed of ruined possessions and gutted sheet rock. Malone and his family were living on the top floor while the rest of the house was restored. "It's heartbreaking to look around," said Malone:

> No one knows what our future's gonna bring. The politicians are all crazy, running around like chickens with their heads cut off. Everybody's trying to just make this come back to the place it was. I'm just doing my little part of bringing some attention to a place that was beautiful and

special. It's not like these are songs that are linked to an event. Often those things come out not sounding so genuine, if you will. I know their intentions are good, but it's dangerous territory. It's almost like I'd rather talk about it than write about it. So I don't think we're presenting this as a reaction to Katrina, but it's at least our little way to make people aware that... God, it's hard... I just want them to feel what they used to feel about New Orleans when they hear this.

As he spoke, the band was planning to play its first show in the city since the flood.

"I think it's gonna be very emotional," said Malone. "We know some of the diehard fans will be coming in for the shows. I hope people show up to help celebrate coming home. It's a hard thing to talk about. We're grateful to have fans, period. We're grateful just to be able to play music. I'll know the faces when I see 'em, and I think we're all gonna be very emotional. It really feels like a homecoming. It will be interesting to see who's here." The subdudes played that show at Southport Hall with tarps covering the stage area to keep the leaky roof from dumping rainwater on the band.

Susan Cowsill's *Just Believe It* was officially released the same day Katrina hit New Orleans. Cowsill's voice sounded like tragedy, loss, hope, and revenge—all in the same song. Her hushed articulation of the word "sin" could stop you in your tracks. The way she sang the line "I can smell the sugar in the air" brought the dance, and her simple plea, "I don't wanna leave this world," smiled through tears of joy. The latter song, written for an older relative who was looking wistfully yet defiantly at the prospect of death, revealed Cowsill's roots in her family band from the 1960s, a band that had a huge single, "Hair." The Cowsills also recorded the eerie, unforgettable "The Rain, the Park, and Other Things," a song that evoked the central image of the time, the flower child. "I love the flower girl," they sang. "Flowers in her hair... Flowers everywhere." Susan, the youngest of the singing family, literally was that flower girl, the symbol of the 1960s' embrace of nature as a saving grace, of "flower power" as a quixotic antidote to the horrors of the Vietnam War. That pensive moan she plied on *Just Believe It* carried a sense of the lost possibilities, grief, and postresignation defiance.

The adult Cowsill was already a cult legend for her amazing vocal collaboration with once and future Bangles member Vicky Peterson in the Continental Drifters. The battle of the sexes that took place within the Drifters had people calling them the Fleetwood Mac of New Orleans, but it also gave Cowsill great material. "Talkin'," an acerbic barb hurled at her ex from the Drifters, Peter Holsapple, was almost shockingly hard edged in its anger, but Cowsill's bittersweet observations about life and relationships were more tender the rest of the way.

After the flood, Cowsill's mood was much darker. Her brother Barry, once a sex symbol in the Cowsills and a formidable songwriter in his own right, perished in the bleak days after the flood. His body was found weeks later, wedged into pier moorings in the Mississippi River. Barry's friends had a New Orleans funeral for him in February. A brass band played for the mourners on the banks of the Mississippi, then led a second line to the Kerry Irish Pub, where Susan had organized a musical tribute to Barry. Many of his friends played, and the family band played. Susan performed with her band and played a new song written in the months since she'd become a Katrina refugee, "Crescent City Sneaux." The song detailed Cowsill's sense of displacement and her longing to return home. In a wistful final refrain she delicately asked in a slow, mournful cadence:

> *Who dat?*
> *Who dat?*
> *Who dat say they gonna beat them Saints?*

The refrain became a sing-along that took its cue from the proud hometown chant for the city's professional football team, the New Orleans Saints. The fans loved to root for the Saints even though the team rarely offered much to cheer about—at that point they were one of only three NFL teams to never win the league championship. That season was a particularly rough one for the Saints, who were homeless themselves, while the severely damaged Super Dome was being repaired. Cowsill's sad and sweet recasting of this beloved fight song as a lament was a perfect metaphor for the emotions the people of New Orleans were feeling in early 2006.

Local groups made a number of recordings down the block from my house at Piety Street Studios, the old building across from Markey Park where owner/producer/musician Mark Bingham, a sonic auteur and amateur philosopher, held court. Bingham watched Elvis Costello and Allen Toussaint make their record, ran the mixing board as the Radiators cut *Dreaming Out Loud,* played on the debut album of the Happy Talk Band and John Mooney's outstanding electric blues record, *Big Ol' Fiya,* and helped Morning 40 Federation develop from a ragtag group of eccentrics into a great contemporary rock band on *Ticonderoga.*

"We were back in operation by Halloween [of 2005]," said Bingham. "Then, on the tenth to the eighteenth of December, Allen Toussaint and Elvis Costello were in here. I'd just been in New York doing the Katrina benefit album with Hal Willner and Joe Henry, so they knew we were open. It helped that the engineer had worked here a couple of times before."

The Morning 40 Federation became the unofficial band of the young bohemian enclave in the Bywater, where Cofféa and Piety Street Studios, Vaughan's, Markey's, the Saturn Bar, Quintron's Spellcaster lodge, various art galleries, and Elizabeth's restaurant were all clustered around the nineteenth-century creole cottages, which were among the few houses in this part of the city not completely destroyed by the hurricanes. Though their music, a cacophonous amalgam of boozy laments and grandiose sonic gestures alternately reminiscent of the Rolling Stones and the Stooges, bore little relation to traditional New Orleans jazz and funk, Morning 40 still managed to embody the sound of the city's streets.

"I don't think you can fake that," said saxophonist Josh Cohen:

And the reason is because we wrote those songs as we were out getting drunk at the bars in New Orleans, hanging with the people in New Orleans. Of course, Morning 40 Federation is influenced and inspired by traditional New Orleans music. How can you not be? The syncopation of the rhythms, the repetition of riffs, hitting the flatted fifth every now and then for that blues impact. I think Katrina hitting New Orleans gave us a renewed sense of purpose and reaffirmed that what we're doing is significant—if nothing else, just to give people an outlet to relieve stress through going out and seeing a show and dancing and forgetting their problems. If we were a bunch of wimps, we could've moved out of New Orleans for convenience's sake because it's inconvenient to live there now. There's a series of inconveniences associated with living in New Orleans, but we're like spokespeople of New Orleans to some degree, and we realize that it wouldn't send a good message if we left. It's also because we have a deep love and affinity for the city. I've traveled around the country, and there's no place as friendly as New Orleans.

Bingham had watched the city's music evolve in his twenty-plus years producing local records. He'd seen the New Orleans scene change to reflect the eclectic tastes of young music fans who flocked to the city in the years before the flood and only seemed to multiply in 2006. Those young musicians were a key element in the future of a New Orleans music scene that will inevitably be somewhat less rooted in traditions and more in keeping with the innovations that originally created those traditions. "To my mind New Orleans has been a transplant scene for the last fifteen years," said Bingham, who records all kinds of music at Piety Street:

The only new stuff coming out of New Orleans music really has been hip-hop, and the local-music power structure ignores that as much as possible. People are still gonna come to New Orleans because it's a free zone, and there's still going to be hundreds and hundreds of musicians here. The people who are still here will still play Jazz Fest and play the second-line stuff at brunches if tourists come back. There will always be a traditional scene because it's fun music to play, and there's an ever-modern audience for it.

"Trombone Shorty is brilliant. Those kids are all playing great," Bingham added. "I saw him at the Blue Nile about a month ago. It was incredible. It had something to do with New Orleans, but it also had something to do with Bombay, so the thing is [that] if that stuff is allowed to grow like that, we're gonna hear some very interesting songs. A lot of these bands from my neighborhood, I wouldn't even know they existed if I didn't live and work among them. To have the Morning 40s and Moose Jackson and the Radiators and John Mooney all in the same camp, Shannon McNally and Jim Dickinson working together—I love this whole weird mix-up of things."

CHAPTER 9

Don't Take My Picture

The cost of the flood continued to take its toll on New Orleans residents as 2006 wore on. People lost jobs, slid into chemical dependency, and fought bitterly for no apparent reason. Katrina exiles in Houston cemented deep connections to that city's drug cartels, which connected directly to Mexican narco gangs. Hard drugs returned to New Orleans in greater amounts than local police had ever seen. Suicide and murder rates soared.

People feuded, sometimes for no good reason. But everyone knew the overriding reason. One of the most public feuds was between *Times-Picayune* columnist Chris Rose and Big Chief Alfred Doucette of the Flaming Arrows Mardi Gras Indians. Rose, who had written in a Dave Barry–like humorist style before the flood, was changed overnight by the post-Katrina realities of life in New Orleans. His personal style allowed him to talk openly about the raw, conflicting emotions people were feeling and to ask simple questions about what he saw while driving around town in the wake of the deluge.

One of the things Rose saw was a feathered Mardi Gras Indian staff saved from the ruins by Doucette and nailed to the front door of his totaled creole cottage at 2608 North Rocheblave Street. Rose used the photograph of the staff on the cover of *1 Dead in Attic,* his book of post-Katrina essays. The beauty of the Mardi Gras Indian regalia in the midst of the devastation led Rose to wonder about the people behind the costumes. Rose admitted he had always taken the Mardi Gras Indians for granted, but now that they were gone, he was burning with questions about them. "Who are these guys?" Rose asked. "Are [they] coming back?"

Doucette, who had seen all the members of the Flaming Arrows leave town, including his nephew, Kevin Gooden, who relocated to Austin, was in no mood for publicity, especially when the staff on his door was stolen shortly after the original column was published. Doucette blamed Rose. "That's my house on the cover," said Doucette:

That's my Indian staff on the front of the house. I felt used. Like I told him, a long time ago when a white man come in and try to take our picture, we'd say, "Don't take that picture," and we had no problem. The Wild Man would go up to him and say, "Don't take my picture," and if he took that picture, [the Wild Man] would take the camera and smash it on the ground and break it. Maybe we should go back to that because they come in there and use my picture to make money and don't even say who I am. That's my home. Everything I owned, all my equipment, I had a nice little studio in there, all my stuff, it was all under water, all ruined, my whole life.

Rose said he was unaware of the homeowner's identity when he wrote the piece. "Back then, there wasn't anybody around to ask," he said:

In the fight for the survival of our city, our art, and our culture, I get the feeling he thinks I'm on the wrong side of the battle, and he says I have cursed his house. I don't know how to respond to that other than to say I am engaged—heart, body, and soul—in this thing. We have used words and pictures to try and get a story out in the public—a story that honors our city and its people.

Since Katrina, the Flaming Arrows gang has no longer been a New Orleans institution. "Most of the people associated with the Flaming Arrows are scattered all over the country," said Doucette. "My nephew is over in Texas, and he's hooked up with Cyril Neville to do a Mardi Gras Indian thing up that way. If my nephew doesn't keep it alive, I don't know if there is a future for it."

Doucette was one of the last people I saw performing in New Orleans before the storm. A few days before Katrina made landfall, drummer Kevin O'Day played his weekly show at Ray's, a glass-walled club atop the World Trade Center right on the Mississippi River. The first set was a pleasant display of well-crafted music in a formal setting, so the tone was fairly subdued. Then, at the close of the second set, Doucette's tall, lanky frame snaked through the crowd, and he proceeded to electrify the proceedings with his signature tune, "Marie Comin' Out," a second-line invocation of voodoo queen Marie Laveau sung to the unforgettable folk melody "Little Liza Jane."

That song led off Doucette's post-Katrina release, *Rollin' wit da Legends & Marie Laveau*, which remarkably was his debut recording at the age of sixty-seven. He sounded like he'd been doing it all his life, and in a sense he had, chanting and singing as a member of the Flaming Arrows. The album felt like it was conceived as the soundtrack to a Mardi Gras party, with its up-tempo pulse, frequent references to Indian parades and Carnival themes, and careful mixture of original material with party classics from the New Orleans canon. Doucette avoided the lethal trap of relying on this material's familiarity to carry him, taking care to draw the listener's attention to the singer, not the song. It was a tightrope walk on the cover of Bill Withers's "Use Me," a standard cover tune for New Orleans bands, but Doucette pulled it off with a riveting vocal over a mesmerizing rhythm track. Similarly, the Nevilles' "Fire on the Bayou" posed the nearly insurmountable task of not sounding like a copy, but Doucette managed to subtly emphasize its celebration of Mardi Gras Indian culture in a way that allowed him to lay claim to the tune.

Doucette's most impressive work with familiar material placed him in the realm of local musicians who don't just do covers but also delight in treating the New Orleans canon as a series of tropes that can be morphed into a myriad of musical shapes. His version of Jessie Hill's classic "Ooh Poo Pah Doo," one of the most powerful songs in the canon, avoids the overstatement that can accompany its performance. There's no improving on the joyful expression condensed into Hill's powerful original performance, and Doucette played it close to the vest, using a dramatic vibrato at certain points in the contours of the melody.

Rose and Doucette eventually resolved their dispute in the simplest manner— Rose stopped using the photograph on future editions of the book. The conflict was a classic illustration of the kind of misunderstandings that were plaguing a population stretched to the emotional breaking point after the flood. Rose, a middle-class white guy, thought he was doing his job of reporting what he saw. Doucette, one of the leaders of the black community, a man who had booked New Orleans greats such as the Meters and Deacon John when he owned and operated the Nite Cap, saw the dispute against the backdrop of New Orleans's history as an apartheid city in which African Americans were freed from the direct exploitation of slavery but not from the subtler and more indirect exploitation of their culture.

Elsewhere old alliances frayed and broke apart. Cowboy Mouth, in the midst of one of its biggest years, lost cofounder Paul Sanchez, who suddenly decided to leave the band and go out on his own in November of 2006. The band had sold more records at the 2006 Jazz Fest than any other local group, but the stress of surviving Katrina had taken its toll. Sanchez was making a decision that would turn out to be savvy. As a solo artist he went on to become a major player in the revival of the city's music scene.

The Fair Grounds racetrack resumed its thoroughbred-horseracing meeting in November 2006 after losing its 2005–2006 season to the flood, which destroyed the grandstand and swamped the racetrack and infield with a brackish goo of salt water and toxic waste from ruptured service station tanks and ruined oil refineries. The grounds crew had to spread tons of gypsum over this mess to extract the poisons and make the land safe for humans and animals to walk on again.

I covered the thoroughbred-racehorse meeting at Fair Grounds as a reporter for the *Daily Racing Form*. Part of the job was listening to the stories of displaced backstretch workers, trainers, and owners. All of them had been adversely affected by the flood, which had compounded the normal hardships of working on the backstretch. However, the job also entailed documenting the fairytale seasons of apprentice jockey Joe Talamo, a local kid from across the Mississippi in Marrero, who won the riding title that season, and of trainer Al Stall Jr., the product of a family of Louisiana horsemen who came tantalizingly close to winning the Louisiana Derby, the meet's premier race with his plucky chestnut colt Ketchikan.

I really liked the job because I could watch the horses on the cool mornings as they worked out, then write my stories for the *Form* as the horses raced over the course of the afternoon. I watched everything from the best seat in the house, the press box atop the refurbished grandstand, right next to the steward's box. Bill Hartack, one of the greatest jockeys ever, was one of the Fair Grounds' stewards, and he liked to come into the press box to argue the fine points of racing with *Times-Picayune* racing reporter Bob Fortus and me. Hartack was also a bit of a music fan—he liked '50s rock and rockabilly—and we'd chat about that as well.

In New Orleans, horse racing is considered an important part of the local culture. Just about everybody goes to the track, and on the traditional opening day of Thanksgiving, going to Fair Grounds is a major social event. People dress up and wear fancy hats. You're likely to see many local musicians at the track on Thanksgiving. When Fair Grounds reopened after the storm, Irma Thomas sang the national anthem. She didn't stick around for the races, though. "I've got to get home and cook Thanksgiving dinner," she said as she headed for the exit after her performance.

The racing was over by 5 P.M. every day, and I would walk out of the Fair Grounds onto Esplanade Ridge to enjoy the golden evenings as dinner and the perennial New Orleans nightlife beckoned. Between Esplanade Avenue, with its stately homes and giant live oaks, their limbs wooly with Spanish moss, hanging over the road, and the cool, still waterway of Bayou St. John, the ancient Native American portage point between the Mississippi River and Lake Pontchartrain, was a quiet residential neighborhood. Ed Volker, a songwriter, poet, and artist who is a founding member of New Orleans's notorious rock band the Radiators, lives on the second floor of one of those houses. On some days during my evening wanderings after the races I would see Volker sitting on his porch drinking a glass of wine. Invariably he would invite me up to listen to his latest collection of songs.

Volker's Bayou St. John digs evoke the spirit of a nineteenth-century poet's cottage, a repository of occult knowledge, and meticulously archived secrets. In addition to his notepads, dream diaries, rare books, and collection of dictionaries, Volker has a treasure trove of music—his own small recording studio, racks of CDs, a wall of vinyl LPs crammed into shelves, and hundreds of hand-marked cassettes with secret music on them that even his band mates have never heard. However, the most remarkable piece in Volker's collection is a box of 45-rpm records with no labels, survivors of the inevitable water damage that accompanies a lifetime lived below sea level in New Orleans. It's all local music from the 1950s and '60s, rhythm and blues, and rock, much of it obscure. Volker reaches into that box with a wicked smile and identifies each one before he plays it, as if he's reading the fingerprints of the grooves themselves.

In addition to the two thousand or so songs he's written for the Radiators, the prolific Volker constantly writes for his own projects, particularly the band Jolly House, as well as for his own amusement. Over the years select friends would receive cassette tapes of private Volker recordings, but until the digital age he was content to keep this material, composed on an old system in his music room, to himself. These days Volker has begun to make some of these recordings available on the Radiators' website as digital downloads. They come with his quirky illustrations, which are often spiraling pen-and-ink constructions based on found text from newspapers or magazines.

Volker spent several months away from New Orleans after the flood, exiled to Austin, Texas, where he even played with an ad hoc group of New Orleans transplants at the Continental Club on Tuesday nights. However, the native New Orleanian couldn't stand being transplanted from his watery home to the dry, dusty Texas hill country. "It was nice, but it wasn't what I was used to," he mused. "When I would go out to a restaurant, they were always playing country music, not Louis Armstrong."

Volker clearly cherished his home in the days after his return and spent a lot of his energy on an extensive project organizing his life's work, research that unearthed treasures, including the career Radiators' retrospective, *Wild & Free*, and a great early studio recording, *The Lost South Lake Sessions*. But the material he was writing privately was extraordinary. The first of these recordings to be released as a download, *Prodigal*, issued under his pseudonym of Zeke Fishhead, is a haunting and painful piece of self-expression that Volker began writing just before Katrina and finished while he was in exile.

Volker is a poet and visual artist interested as much in the raw sensuality of sound and word-as-word as the literal velocity of his compositions, so his home-studio productions, with their quirky one-man-band immediacy, are like a series of postcards from a wandering friend lost out along the interstate highways of America. He chronicled his exile from New Orleans after Katrina in a mixture of Felliniesque theme music and songs that ruminate on the nuts and bolts of his life post-K, including a lamentation on the absence of Fred Neil records.

He spoke about it most directly in the hair-raising "K," with its haunting, dead-pan refrain:

> *Where were you when the lights went out?*
> *When the water rose and the souls froze*
> *Where were you when the lights went out?*
> *When darkness fell and the bodies swelled*
> *Maybe you couldn't run or fly*
> *Maybe your body just floated on by*
> *Where were you when they came back on?*
> *In the stinking ghost town without a ghost around*

"A song is real," Volker explained, "because of what the music says. I'm kind of a word guy, and every now and then you might hit on something, but really I'm usually more for incantation rather than exposition. I'm trying to conjure things. The words and the music work together, but the music is where all the spirits reside."

Volker's songs are all crafted from aspects of the dream world inhabited by lyric poets and musicians mining ancient folk traditions from bards to griots, from shamans to Mardi Gras Indians. He conjures the spirits who populate his music by accompanying himself on an electric keyboard with various rhythm settings and a percussion table that includes shakers, bells, and cardboard boxes he strikes with sticks for an eerie, otherworldly sound. His songs resonate with symbolic representation. He is deft at taking one idea and transforming it into another or using it as a building block in a separate construction. The song "Clementine," a dirgelike love ballad, has a spooky resonance that comes in part from the contrast to its sing-along cousin, "My Darling Clementine," a song that was translated via different lyrics into the seemingly innocuous "Found a Peanut," which becomes a child's warning that death can lurk in the most unlikely places.

Violent crime, a perennial problem faced by poverty-stricken New Orleans, had dropped dramatically during the curfew months but returned with a vengeance in 2006 as drug gangs returned to the city and fought bloody turf wars. The murders started happening in earnest in June 2006. Grisly stuff, gangland execution-style rubouts. Young men shot in the head walking down the street, sitting on a front porch, driving in their cars. Drive-by shootings, turf-war retaliations.

On June 17, 2006, five teenagers in a sport utility vehicle were driving in the Central City neighborhood of New Orleans at about 4 A.M. When they reached the corner of Josephine and Danneel streets, a hail of gunfire rained down on them. The driver lost control of the vehicle, which crashed into a telephone pole. Dead at the scene were brothers Arsenio Hunter, 16, and Markee Hunter, 19, as well as Warren Simeon, 17, Iraum Taylor, 19, and Reggie Dantzler, 19. Three victims were found inside the SUV. The other two escaped the vehicle only to die in the street. The massacred boys were involved in what New Orleans Police Department superintendant Warren Riley described as a turf war between rival drug gangs. Police later said three of the five victims had been involved in a drive-by shooting on May 1 in Jefferson Parish.[1]

Louisiana governor Kathleen Blanco issued an emergency order for three hundred National Guard troops to join the local police in patrolling the city's streets. A new juvenile curfew was installed. "It's going to be a long, hot summer," Riley promised. However, the killings continued—and not just as a result of drug-gang disputes. Tourists in the French Quarter and locals inside their homes were also at risk. Just about every day throughout that summer and fall the *Times-Picayune* had another story about another local murder.

On the afternoon of November 26 John Boutté, Susan Cowsill, and other local musicians performed for free at Woldenberg Park next to the Mississippi River at the Second Annual Down by the Riverside: A Concert of Thanksgiving event. The concert was organized by the Jazz and Heritage Foundation as a thank-you to the volunteers from around the world who contributed to the city's recovery. Later that night, just a few blocks away, an eighteen-year-old man, Frank Boudreaux of Carriere, Mississippi, was stabbed to death at the corner of Bourbon and Canal. He staggered down Bourbon and collapsed at Iberville Street in front of a frozen daiquiri stand, surrounded by horrified tourists.[2]

December 25 is Christmas Day, one of the most cherished events in a city with deep roots in European Catholicism. In early December actor Brad Pitt offered an early Christmas present to the slow-recovering city when he unveiled an ambitious rebuilding project in the lower Ninth Ward, which more than a year after the hurricane still looked like it had been carpet bombed. Pitt's Make It Right Foundation instituted a project, nicknamed "Pink Houses," which began as a kind of environmental art installation, with pink tarps hung on every proposed housing plot. However, on Christmas evening in the 2400 block of Josephine Street in Central City, the deadly presents being distributed were bullets, and the holiday spirit was ruined by two more brutal deaths.

The *Times-Picayune* headline called it the "Christmas Shooting," a street massacre that left two dead and four wounded. According to the police report, the victims were inside or near a house in the middle of the block. One of the dead was killed by a spray of bullets from an assault rifle. Another man who'd been shot was slumped up against the house with his head down and his chin against his chest. The Emergency Medical Service reported that the wounded included a 22-year-old man with gunshot wounds to the neck and leg; an 18-year-old man shot in the leg; a woman, 19, shot in the knee; and a man, 17, shot in the arm.

Times-Picayune staff writer Brendan McCarthy detailed the anguished responses of dozens of local residents, who called for divine vengeance as they were prevented by police from entering the crime scene. "Man, this is Christmas, this is bullshit," screamed a bystander. A middle-aged woman collapsed in the street after screaming "I just want to see my baby, I need to see my baby."

Musicians were among the victims of this violence. On December 28, Dinerral Shavers, snare drummer for the Hot 8 Brass Band and director of the L. E. Robinson Sr. High School Marching Band, was shot in the back of the head as he drove his black Chevrolet Malibu up the 2200 block of Dumaine Street. The bullet was intended for his fifteen-year-old stepson, who was involved in a deadly rivalry between warring factions from different New Orleans neighborhoods.[3]

Shavers wasn't the first New Orleans musician to be victimized by street violence, and, unfortunately, he wasn't the last, but the circumstances of his death froze the blood of the city's tightly knit music and arts community. At first people were in shock, numbed by the stupidity and worthlessness of the killing. Some of the patrons of the Sound Café began talking about putting together a formal protest march on City Hall to demand an end to the violence.

CHAPTER 10

Musicians Strike Back at Violence

Glen David Andrews says he was one of the last people to see his friend Dinneral Shavers alive. "I talked to him five minutes before he was killed," said Andrews. "He said 'I'm working on my house over in the Musician's Village. When are you coming to help me?' I told him I'd be there Saturday. I got a gig that day, and I'ma come a little early. He pulled off, drove three blocks, and the next thing I saw was his car running into a pole."

"Dinneral was my first drummer in my own band," Andrews said. "When Dinneral was killed, it was so bad because it was just getting to the point where it seemed like musicians was being slaughtered. Dinneral wasn't a drug addict. He wasn't a bad person. He had never been to jail. He was a beautiful, honest, young black male trying to make things happen."

Andrews had been part of a music-education program at Sound Café, and the coffeehouse owner, Baty Landis, asked Andrews to participate in a march on city hall to protest Shavers's killing and the culture of street violence that caused it. However, even as a formal protest of the murderous atmosphere that resulted in Shavers's death was coalescing, the killings continued. On January 4, 2007, a week after Shavers was murdered, another regular Sound Café patron, filmmaker Helen Hill, was killed. Hill was in the backyard of her home on North Rampart Street at 5:30 A.M. feeding her pet pig, Rosie, when she was surprised by an intruder, who shot her in the neck. Hill's murder was one of six in a twenty-four-hour period.[1]

Helen Gillet was a friend of both Shavers and Hill. She had taken care of Hill's pig when her family was out of town and had gone to numerous social events at her house. "I definitely knew her from my first year in New Orleans," said Gillet:

> I knew her and her husband, Paul. I was a patient at their clinic. At one point I lived pretty close to where she lived. Actually I was in charge of babysitting Rosie, their pig, when they were out of town. I would go in and feed her. I remember Helen putting me through the ropes of how to feed her. I had a fear of pigs, so I was sort of afraid of the whole ordeal,

but Helen was so great, her personality is really upbeat—very creative and reassuring at the same time. She just showed me how to feed Rosie, so I did that. And I would go over there for her little cupcake social tea party gatherings and things. They were really great people. She was one of the women who really inspired me to do a lot artistic wise.

Gillet will never forget the day she found out about Hill's death:

I was at the Sound Café, [and] my brother was in town for the holidays because it was right after New Year's Day. We were just having coffee over there, just having a regular day at the Sound Café. Somebody said, "Did you hear about that terrible shooting on Rampart Street?" which unfortunately was not an unusual enough thing for me to jump up right away. Then I heard somebody else say, "It's so sad. She had a baby," and then somebody said the word "Helen," and I thought, "There aren't too many Helens." It's an old-school name. And then I was struck. It was like I didn't want to know, but I had to ask, "Who's the father?" and the father's named Paul. I couldn't believe what I was hearing. There I was at the Sound Café, and my whole world sort of… everybody knew Dinneral as well, and everybody who knew both of them, both of these amazingly lovely people… it was like your whole world has crumbled.

Instead of falling apart with grief, Gillet was seized with a passion to do something about these tragedies. "I just became somebody else," she said:

I think I felt a lot of anger. I also felt a sense of urgency because so much had to be taken care of after the storm. You could become obsessed about copper plumbing; you could expend all your energy on one aspect of what the city needed and go there for years. For me it was safety. They say you don't kick into high gear until somebody you know is affected. I would be a hypocrite to say that that wasn't true. I'd known it was a problem, and I'd certainly signed petitions before, but I had not gotten involved like this until it hit really close to home.

Gillet joined Baty Landis and writer Ken Foster to form a group called Silence Is Violence, based out of the Sound Café, and organized a march on city hall. "A lot of us got together," Gillet recalled:

I was sort of out of my mind with grief and not being able to understand it. We all got together and helped organize this march. Really, Baty is an amazing part of this. She kind of organized this march, and I mc'd the event. As the performer of the bunch I was able to envision what the flow of the speakers at city hall was gonna go like. I got to know Glen David Andrews and the Hot 8 a lot more through that event.

The closest thing I'd ever done to political involvement was before I moved here. I worked with the Wisconsin Alliance for Arts Education, lobbying and stuff like that. Coming from playing music full time and being involved in politics for three months, my phone kept ringing, and it was like CBS News calling me. It was super stressful for me, actually. I made it through, but it was taxing on my mental and physical state. We shared all the duties, but I took a fair amount of TV and radio interviews.

The Sound Café's protest mushroomed into a mass march on city hall on January 11, 2007, where five thousand people chanted demands for the ouster of Mayor Nagin and the district attorney, Eddie Jordan. The Hot 8 Brass Band led the march under a banner that read "March for Survival, Walk with Us." Glen David Andrews marched alongside with a determined gait. Others held placards emblazoned with the slogan of the march: "Silence Is Violence." Some held posters lamenting the deaths of Shavers and Hill. One sign had a picture of a child with the slogan: "Born in New Orleans . . . Murdered in N.O."

"That march, it was just unbelievable working with and meeting all these beautiful people," said Gillet:

> It really helped me to meet all these active and amazing minds that were way more experienced in politics. I was just maybe a little bit of a facilitator and MC and just somebody to take in all this energy. People were looking toward me all of a sudden, and I just had to keep reminding myself that you don't have all the answers, but just keep forwarding along, getting together in a group of people. As a cellist's personality I kind of take things in.
>
> I was amazed at how many people ended up involved. The day of the march we had no idea what the real crowds were gonna look like. We had three starting points, one from midcity, one from central city, and then the Ninth Ward contingent. We all came from different spots, and by the time we got to city hall it was clear that there were thousands and thousands of people that came out. People were just coming out onto the street out of the workplace, and you just had the sense that the whole city was involved, and it was very beautiful.

The most remarkable thing about the crowd was that it included people of all colors. In a city with a long history of racial polarization the crowd composition recalled the makeup of the interracial protest marches at the height of the 1960s' civil rights movement.

Gillet's crucial moment arrived when the crowd gathered in front of the city hall steps and spilled across the street into the park. The podium was only about a foot off the ground, and Gillet was surrounded by people pushing and yelling at her, demanding to address the crowd. Mayor Nagin was only a few feet away from Gillet, and though his aides demanded a forum, he was never allowed to speak. "I had Mayor Nagin's people poking me to get up on that podium," Gillet recalled. "I had to politely keep saying no to all these people who wanted to speak because we had a roster of speakers, and it was my job to make sure they got to speak."

Clad in a black sweater with a giant red paper heart pinned to her chest, Gillet determinedly kept the speakers to a predetermined program of appearances, summoning up a strength she didn't realize she possessed before that moment. "I wore a heart," she explained. "Helen liked to do these little animations, and she would cut out hearts, little hearts, so I cut out a red heart, and I pinned it on my chest to remind me of my humanity. I don't know if this is a normal thing. When you're dealing with politicians, you tend to think 'Oh, my god, am I still human?' At this point I was just so freaked."

Speaker after speaker railed against the violence that was tearing New Orleans apart and the lack of effective response from city officials. "We have come to declare that a city that could not be drowned in the waters of a storm will not be drowned in the blood of its citizens," bellowed the Rev. John Raphael Jr., reflecting the sentiment of the crowd but also avoiding the overriding issue that those citizens were killing each other.

It took a musician to speak the naked truth. "Young people, shame on you," Glen David Andrews charged, aiming his anger at the killers and the endless cycle of violence they created. "You know better!" Andrews's speech was an act of courage and leadership, but most of all it was a sign that the violence in his city had spurred him to rethink his own choices in life. Before the storm he had been thick with the bad-boy crowd and had written "Knock with Me, Rock with Me," which coined the popular drug-deal chant "Gimme a dime . . . I only got 8." He had been an integral part of the ongoing cross-pollination of the city's brass-band and second-line rhythms with hip-hop MCs, who borrowed freely from those genres. Nonetheless, in the wake of the flood, Glen David Andrews struggled to recast those musical values in a more positive way, his personal tribute to what he understood was a precious gift from his ancestors.

Andrews did not spare the other targets of his ire. He spoke eloquently about his fear of a police force whose members routinely harassed black musicians. He expressed particular anger at the mayor. "Mayor Nagin," he shouted, close enough to Nagin for him to take it personally, "Get on your job!"

When I interviewed her years later, Gillet looked back on the day of the rally with wonder and realizes that those events at the beginning of 2007 became a turning point in her life and her direction as a musician. It was the kind of transformation that a lot of people in New Orleans were undergoing at the same time.

"I was on this adrenalin rush," she said:

> It felt really beautiful to see all these people come out. I hadn't cried yet since I heard the news about Helen. It had been a week. We pulled all of this together in a week. Everybody was ready for this. Baty and Ken are geniuses, but they knew I was much better at crowd management, and they were nervous about that part of it. I was like, "Well, I'm used to dealing with drunken people at bars, [so] I'll help you with this." There were reverends insisting that they go up and speak, [and] my elders looking at me, going, "What do you know? Get out of my way." I was just doing my job, and it was just all caught up in the moment. I don't think it was until after the speaking was done and we had our moment of silence that I was able to relax.
>
> I was in a daze, walking by myself back to my car, and my friend Ben Shank, he just came and gave me a hug, and I remember just losing it at that point. I cried and cried and cried in his arms. I let it all out at that point. He said "Thank you for doing this." I guess I felt pretty moved, and I was finally able to begin my own individual mourning process. It was three months later when I finally realized I had to let go of this. I had to go back to concentrating on my music. I wasn't sleeping very much. I became this impossibly obsessed person. I definitely wasn't taking care of myself throughout all this. It took a toll on me. I gave it my all while I was in there, but I realized I have to be a musician, and I have to focus in on that. I was just talking to a couple of improvisers about this, and I think it did influence my music quite a bit, this whole period.

The rally was an important moment in the history of the city's recovery. Musicians played a key role in the planning and execution of the event, and the general agreement was that Glen David Andrews was the most inspired speaker that day. Andrews showed character that was built through a family structure deeply ingrained with the values of self-respect and regard for tradition. Those values are shared with the many relatives of Glen David Andrews who populate New Orleans bands, including the brothers James and Troy ("Trombone Shorty") Andrews.

By 2007 Trombone Shorty had outgrown his name. Now in his twenties and at the brink of stardom, Troy set a perfect example of how music can provide a life focus that leads to the freedom of creative expression instead of the volunteered slavery of a life working street corners on the hustle. Shorty is a part of one of the proudest legacies of New Orleans culture—the musical family. The Andrews brothers and cousins are continuing a long tradition of great music, a style taught hand to hand from one generation to another. The family name stands alongside those of many great New Orleans musical families—Neville, Marsalis, Batiste, Lastie, French, Ferbos, Barbarin—and as Shorty himself is also nephew to both the Lastie and the Batiste families, his place within this great legacy is firmly founded.

Shorty's immediate family is filled with musicians. Along with James and Glen David, another cousin, Revert ("Peanut") Andrews, plays trombone with the Rebirth Brass Band, as well as in Glen David's band. More cousins play with Rebirth and Dirty Dozen brass bands, while a whole new generation of nephews performs as the Baby Boyz Brass Band.

It's not difficult to be steered into a life of music when you're literally surrounded by it from childhood. The house where James and Troy grew up, by the intersection of Dumaine and North Robertson in Treme, was constantly filled with music. The boys' grandfather, the New Orleans R&B giant Jessie Hill, is best known for the 1960 hit "Ooh Poo Pah Doo," a staple of both James Andrews and the Andrews Family Band sets. Hill was a master during the time that R&B was noted for its wit and brevity. "Ooh Poo Pah Doo" was a party anthem that coined a memorable beat with the unforgettable climax:

Whoa-OH-oh-oh/whoa-oh-oh.

"Our family *was* the music of the Treme," said James Andrews, the oldest of seven siblings. "We came from a musical family, and a lot of people in the family were in the Social Aid and Pleasure Clubs all over Treme." Though their father, James Sr., wasn't a musician, he was a member of the Bayou Steppers Social Club, and many of his musician friends visited the Andrews home. "A lot of musicians came by the house—Tuba Fats, Milton Batiste, Efram Townes from the Dirty Dozen," said James. "My dad was friends with Danny Barker, so he'd come to the house all the time. My grandfather Jessie Hill was a big presence in the house. When we was kids, he used to take us on the gigs with him. We would play, tap dance. He took us to Tipitina's, Jazz Fest, and we'd meet different musicians. I always thought it was a cool thing, going places to make music."

Troy always struck a more serious demeanor than his loquacious older brother. A child prodigy on various instruments, Shorty learned to express himself through his playing. Cousin Glen David Andrews, nearly six years older than Shorty, was born a decade after James. Glen David was always the most mercurial of the three musicians, a great, enthusiastic storyteller and an extremely emotional conversationalist who could take you on a roller coaster of expression even during a brief exchange. A natural songwriter, Glen David is the most complex of the three men.

James and his brothers also met Dr. John at their grandmother Dorothy Hill's house. "He and Jessie came by my grandmother's house a lot," recalled James. "That was the Nelson family, which is Prince La La and Papoose. My grandmother is their sister. The music in our family goes back to my great-grandfather. He was Papoose's daddy. His name was Walter Nelson. He used to play the guitar outside the supermarket they called the Treme Supermarket."

Danny Barker was a key element in teaching the Andrews kids about traditional music. He initiated Andrews along with a whole generation of players into the world of traditional New Orleans jazz. Barker is one of the most important figures in the city's music history. Born in 1909, Barker was the grandson of bandleader Isidore Barbarin and nephew of early jazz drummer Paul Barbarin. After playing New Orleans jazz during its early incarnation, Barker went to New York, where he played rhythm instruments in swing bands and built a solid reputation in the jazz world. Barker returned to New Orleans in 1972 and formed the Fairview Baptist Church Marching Band, members of which eventually became the Dirty Dozen Brass Band.

James Andrews was one of dozens of young players influenced by Barker, who also formed the Roots of Jazz Brass Band, which included another young New Orleans trumpeter, Nicholas Payton. James went on to lead the All-Star Brass Band and later played with the Treme Brass Band. In 1995 James became the lead trumpeter and singer of the New Birth Brass Band, which included members of the Rebirth, Young Olympia, Dirty Dozen, Li'l Rascals, and Treme brass bands.

One of Barker's greatest pupils was Anthony ("Tuba Fats") Lacen, who took the traditional jazz and brass-band influences he learned from Barker and passed them on to younger players. Though they were aware of Barker, both Trombone Shorty and Glen David Andrews talked of learning about the tradition from playing with Tuba Fats in Jackson Square. "When I first learned about sustaining a solo by using the circular breathing technique, I picked it up right away," said Shorty.[2] "I went down to Jackson Square where Tuba Fats was leading a jam session and played for twenty-two minutes without stopping. Tuba Fats liked it. He took a nap. He would do that. He'd fall asleep while the music was going on, and someone would call his name or play a loud note to wake him up, and he would come out of it playing the right note for the part as if he'd been listening the whole time."

While Danny Barker taught them about traditional music, James and his brothers David, Buster, and Bruce also played with the school band. The brothers played in Barker's Roots of Jazz band before forming their own group, the All-Star Brass Band. They played in Jackson Square in the afternoons, then watched the masters of the craft at Preservation Hall in the evenings. Ever since his uncle Lionel Batiste gave James his first horn, Andrews had always been attracted to traditional music, and Preservation Hall was his favorite place to hear it.

"We used to go to Preservation Hall and listen to Kid Thomas and Willie Humphrey, Percy Humphrey, Frog Joseph, Kid Sheik, and all those guys," said James. "What struck me was the way they played the music. It just had that New Orleans energy. They could control the crowd through the music. One style of jazz is for dancing, and one style is for listening. New Orleans jazz is more for enjoying yourself and reacting with the people. The reflection of the crowd is part of the music. It's got that fire."

Given such a background, it's easy to understand why James chose the trumpet as his instrument. Before long he even adopted Louis Armstrong's nickname, calling himself "Satchmo of the Ghetto," the title of his 1997 debut recording for Allen Toussaint's NYNO label. James became the organizer of his generation of Andrews family musicians. His gregariousness made him a natural leader, and he managed to include the array of brothers and cousins all participating in the second-line parades, Jackson Square sessions, and impromptu performances by what would eventually become the Andrews Family Band.

Naturally James was among the first to recognize the musical talent of his youngest brother, Troy, who began playing whatever he could get his hands on even as a toddler. "It was obvious when he was like three," said James. "Maybe even when he was one."

There were plenty of old musical instruments around the house, where Tuba Fats stayed for a time and taught Troy to play an instrument so much bigger than he was that he had to play it on the floor to reach the mouthpiece. Troy played his first show outside of New Orleans when he was four years old. "We took him on the road with us," said James. "His first gig was in Arizona. He couldn't even reach the full slide position on the trombone, but he had it in him." James began introducing Troy as "Trombone Shorty," a nickname that took hold.

As a child, Shorty was well known in Treme for playing with "the 5 o'Clock Band," an informal, after-school group of kids playing their instruments and beating on cardboard boxes and soda bottles. The group included his cousins, trumpeter/tuba player Travis Hill and trombonist Glen David Andrews. By the time he was seven, Shorty was leading his own group, the Tiny Toones Brass Band, and playing for tips in the French Quarter. They sometimes joined Tuba Fats for his Jackson Square jam sessions. On Sunday nights Shorty played at Donna's, the North Rampart Street showcase for brass bands.

The Andrews family and the Neville family had strong ties due to Cyril Neville's close friendship with James Andrews, which led to Troy Andrews's playing in a band with Cyril's son Omari. "James' brother Trombone Shorty and Omari became good friends," said Neville:

Omari started out when he was three years old playing with Def Generation, which was a band we put together. It was the Caesar brothers, Ricky and Norman, with Jason Neville, Cyril Neville Jr., Carlos Neville, and a couple of other little kids from the neighborhood. It was the first time that brass-band music and hip-hop was put together. They had a song called "Runnin' with the Second Line." There was a DJ called DJ Davis playing it, and the song became a kind of hit in New Orleans even though they didn't have a record out. The guys who were playing horns on it wound up becoming the Soul Rebels. He was playing with them at Jazz Fest when he was six or seven years old. Omari and Shorty were in another band together. Me and James put them together with other little kids and with another friend of mine, Alonzo, his two sons, and they formed a group called New Orleans Jazz Babies. At the time we had a little place that everyone was calling the New Orleans Cultural Conservatory, where people like Tuba Fats and Fred Shepard and James and other older musicians would come in a couple of times a week and get with the kids, not just teaching theory but actually playing.

The Andrews family decided to open a music club called Trombone Shorty's based on Troy's growing fame. This is where U2's Bono and the Edge got their first glimpse of the child star. Troy's primary recollection of the club was that he wasn't allowed to play there. "My mom actually had that place," he said, "and she used to let me come in every once in a while and play but only for like ten minutes because I was way too young to be in there. They still named it after me, which surprised me."

Shorty's careful remarks, when contrasted with Glen David's more florid observations of the same events, go a long way toward defining the differences between the two. "He was playing every time the band struck up," laughed Glen David:

> It was the world-famous Caledonia ballroom, and my auntie bought it and named it after Troy. There was even a drink called the Trombone Shorty. "We'd get out of school at 3 o'clock, me and Troy go back to the house. Okay, it's after school, we gonna play basketball, but not Troy. There's a limousine there to take him to the airport. I'm talking about he's seven, eight years old, and there's a limousine to pick him up. We all looked up to Troy even though he was younger.

Troy's peers remember him playing other instruments as well when he gathered them together in the Trombone Shorty Brass Band. "Three or four of us cousins really knew how to play," recalled Glen David. "So we teamed up with

Figure 16. Left to right: Glen David Andrews, James Andrews, Troy ("Trombone Shorty") Andrews. Photo by Elsa Hahne. Used by permission of Elsa Hahne and *OffBeat* magazine.

Figure 17. Troy, James, and Glen David Andrews surrounded by family and friends. Photo by Elsa Hahne. Used by permission of Elsa Hahne and *OffBeat* magazine.

Figure 18. Passing by Tuba Fats Square (right rear corner), where Glen David was arrested for playing music in public. Photo by Elsa Hahne. Used by permission of Elsa Hahne and *OffBeat* magazine.

Figure 19. Glen David, James, and Troy Andrews stroll through their Treme neighborhood. Photo by Elsa Hahne. Used by permission of Elsa Hahne and *OffBeat* magazine.

Figure 20. Standing in front of Ruth's Cozy Corner, where Grandma Ruth cooked for all of the Treme musicians. Photo by Elsa Hahne. Used by permission of Elsa Hahne and *OffBeat* magazine.

Figure 21. Trombone Shorty jumps for joy. Photo by Elsa Hahne. Used by permission of Elsa Hahne and *OffBeat* magazine.

Figure 22. The Andrews Family: Where the past and future of New Orleans music meet. Photo by Elsa Hahne. Used by permission of Elsa Hahne and *OffBeat* magazine.

Figure 23. Trombone Shorty poses for the cover of *OffBeat*. Photo by Elsa Hahne. Used by permission of Elsa Hahne and *OffBeat* magazine.

Troy in the Trombone Shorty Brass Band. Troy played the tuba. He played tuba for a long time. He played trombone, too, but there was no instrument that he couldn't play fluently except I never saw him playing reeds, but piano, organ, drums, any kind of brass instrument."

Glen David and his older brother Derek Tabb, the drummer in the Rebirth Brass Band, lived a stone's throw away from James and Troy at Ursuline Street, right across from their grandmother's place, Ruth's Cozy Corner, which later became Joe's Cozy Corner. The cousins all bonded as children.

"Everybody born and raised around there hung out at Troy and them's house," said Glen David:

> We all was all raised together. Whenever I went to my grandmother's house, whether it was my grandmother or James's grandmother, every-body was equal. That's why we all still so close to this day. You need to be close with your grandmother. Troy and them's house is the founda-tion for our family. Jessie Hill was around, but as a young kid I didn't recognize who he was. I didn't realize who Fats Domino and all these people was who was sittin' in our house.

Glen David's experience of Jessie Hill was different from the one James described. "I would see him, and he'd have a pocket full of money, a brand-new tuxedo, and a brand-new limousine," said Glen David:

> Then the next time I saw him, it looked like he got hit with that same lim-ousine, like it ran over him in that tuxedo. But he was a professional and a very great musician. Jessie Hill was one of the few black musicians from that era to own all his music. I learned from James anything you sing, any-thing you write down—copyright it. And don't steal nobody's material.

Glen David's gift for songwriting manifested itself early. He said he wrote the anthem "Knock with Me, Rock with Me" while he was with the Trombone Shorty Brass Band even though it wasn't recorded until years later. "I had been writing all my life," he said:

> I always liked to write music. I like to write, and I like to imagine other people singing my thoughts. "Knock with Me, Rock with Me"—we made that on the corner of Dumaine and Robertson. Everything in that song is what was going on in that block. Music playing, to drug selling, to second lines, to Indian suit making, to crime, to after-school homework—there was so much going on on that fucking block. That's why all our records is named after the Sixth Ward—Orleans Avenue,

Dumaine Street, everything's named after the Sixth Ward. That's like everything for us.

The Andrews family suffered a deep tragedy when James and Troy's brother Darnell ("D-Boy") Andrews was murdered. The experience may have deepened the family's desire to nurture Troy's musical prowess. He went to live with Susan Scott, who was James's manager. Meanwhile, Shorty did well at school, attending McDonough 15 in the French Quarter through the seventh grade, then winning early admittance to the prestigious New Orleans Center for the Creative Arts (NOCCA) as an eighth grader. At NOCCA Shorty went beyond his natural ability to become a polished technical player, sight reader, and student of jazz history. Shorty's playing improved by leaps and bounds. "We knew he was special," said James. "We groomed him to be what he is. He had the best of the best. The best of the best. Am I right?" For a family that specialized in the music of the streets and churches of Treme, training at NOCCA was a new direction.

When Troy started out at NOCCA, Glen David started thinking about his own career. "I was about sixteen, seventeen, and I realized this is what I'm gonna do, but I have to make a living at doin' it," said Glen David. "I wasn't into school. I had fun freelancing with James and everybody, but it was never a real reflection of who I was trying to become. It was about a year before Katrina when I decided to take a real stab at being a professional."

However, Glen David ran into addiction problems that threatened to curtail his career. "There were some things in my life that I needed to tackle," he admitted. "In a way I think Katrina was a blessing in disguise because it made me take a long look at myself. I was pretty much finished with playing with New Birth before the storm. I'm not good at following. I'm only good at leading."

The members of the Andrews family knew they had something really special going for years, but it wasn't until after Katrina that the rest of the world started to find out. "I ain't counted how many in the family," says James. "And we got so many parts of the family—the Andrews, the Hills, the Lasties, the Nelsons. We got Halls now. I got at least a few hundred cousins. Family's the most important thing to me. Family and friends are everything. I cherish that. I could be living in a tent, but if I got friends, I'm okay. Am I right?"

CHAPTER 11

I Am New Orleans

Trombone Shorty was on the verge of stardom in the year leading up to the flood. Though he was still a teenager, Troy Andrews demonstrated his range of talent in early 2005, when he released two albums simultaneously—one that showed off his chops as a jazz trombonist and trumpeter, the other as a funk/rock bandleader.

Lenny Kravitz had invited Shorty to join his band as a featured soloist on a world tour, so when the Andrews Family Band played the 2005 renewal of Jazz Fest, Troy wasn't able to be part of the group. His cousin Glen David Andrews rose to the occasion, giving a strong indication of the great things that were in his own future. "We hot like fire...somebody scream!" Glen David sang that day as he dominated the sixteen-piece Andrews Family Band. He worked the crowd like a young James Brown, pitting one section against another and shouting "Is the party on the left?" over and over while pointing to the screaming fans. He switched to right, center, front, and back, each time eliciting ecstatic responses until he built the crowd to a fever pitch, getting them to stand and chant "Trombone Shorty" over and over again. After a call-and-response romp through his signature tune, "Knock with Me, Rock with Me," Glen David started a boasting chant as he beat his chest and enumerated the brass bands who wanted him to perform with them: "The Hot 8 tried to get me. The Soul Rebels tried to get me..." At the height of Glen David's performance James leaned into the microphone and said, "Trombone Shorty ain't here. Send the checks to *me!*"

When Shorty returned from the first leg of his world tour with Kravitz, he was no longer on the verge—he was ready for the big time. Mayor Ray Nagin declared May 26, 2005, "Trombone Shorty" day "for his outstanding contributions to New Orleans music and its legacy." Before this, Troy had relied on his musicianship and had been under his older brother's wing, but the experience of playing before large rock audiences and watching how Kravitz worked the audiences gave Shorty a sense of how to be a front man addressing huge crowds.

He was also improving daily as a musician whose trumpet playing was becoming even more impressive than his trombone work.

Troy Andrews was advised by music-industry insiders to relocate from New Orleans to pursue his career either as a jazz artist in New York or as a rock band leader in Los Angeles, the thinking went. However, especially after the flood, Troy felt it was his destiny to remain a New Orleans-based artist. "I never thought of going somewhere else to do this," he said, slouched over a wrought-iron table in a French Quarter courtyard under the shade of a magnolia tree on a humid afternoon in 2007. "If you have your city behind you, everyone else will pay attention. You have to build out that way."

Trombone Shorty understood that there was something about New Orleans itself, about the Treme streets he had grown up on and the musical culture handed down to him by his ancestors that sustained his art and informed the passion at the heart of his performance. He also sensed a responsibility to his home city. If all of the talented young musicians of New Orleans went to LA or New York or Boston, Chicago, or Austin, Texas, as many of them have, what future would their hometown have as a music center?

"I *am* New Orleans," he concluded. "I grew up in one of the richest musical neighborhoods in the city, the Treme neighborhood. Music was everywhere, always surrounding me. I can't leave New Orleans any more than it can leave me."

When the television cameras turned their attention to New Orleans culture after the storm. Troy burst onto the national music scene with a series of high-profile performances on America's biggest stages. Shorty stole the show at the New Orleans Superdome when he joined U2 and Green Day for a celebration of the reopening of the famed stadium. Executives at the NBC television network were so impressed with the public response to his performance of "O Holy Night" on a Christmas-season broadcast that they featured the clip on the network website. And on festival stages across the country Andrews won over countless new fans with his electrifying shows.

Shorty was not content with developing a reputation as one of the city's most important jazz musicians, though, and set out to create his own musical brand with his band, Orleans Avenue, a high-powered, electric-funk outfit that blended elements of heavy metal, hip-hop, R&B, and New Orleans brass band music into a heady mix of James Brown, AC/DC, George Clinton, and New Orleans sounds from traditional second line to bounce. He handpicked the members of Orleans Avenue from friends who had played in his childhood bands and the ranks of fellow students at NOCCA. He spent most of his energy developing this band, and they took their music to another level, getting wild reactions from young festival crowds and coining a new kind of dance music in the process.

New Orleans rapper Juvenile often joined Andrews on stage for his popular dance tune "Back That Azz Up." Shorty acknowledged affinities with hip-hop but pointed out, "It's not really hip-hop although there are hip-hop elements in it. It's more of a rock & roll band. I selected these musicians to play with because I felt we could grow together as a group," he explained. "I wasn't trying to get the person who was necessarily the best at his instrument. It was where they were headed as musicians and what I thought they were capable of for that material. My goal is to keep learning from every experience, to keep growing as a person and an artist. I might learn about how to do something from talking with you."

Trombone Shorty was well versed in the many traits and quirks that make up the eccentric and often occult nature of New Orleans music, and the idea of shared repertoire lies at the center of that nature. The songs of New Orleans that all native musicians who grow up there learn make up a kind of sacred liturgy unique to the city. While party anthems and Blues Brothers–style covers of 1960s' R&B tunes are rampant in the city, often descending to the banality of Bourbon Street tourist clichés, there are touchstone songs of New Orleans whose meanings contain cavernous emotional depths adeptly plumbed by local musicians who understand how they work as archetypes. "Saint James Infirmary" is an ancient lament whose imagery of identifying the dead body of a loved one is chillingly contemporary in light of the thousands who drowned in the 2005 flood. This is one song that, in the right hands, can't be overused, and it was a featured element in Trombone Shorty's post-Katrina performances.

The rendition of "Saint James Infirmary" he delivered during the 2007 Jazz and Heritage Festival was the perfect illustration of the song's power. Shorty had an enormous crowd stretched out in front of the Congo Square stage, jumping up and down with their arms in the air as he launched into the song, playing it not as the slow, funeral dirge most performers choose but as a fierce rave-up with a series of corkscrewing climaxes that exploded into fifteen choruses of a circular breathing solo on a single trumpet riff. When Troy finished the trumpet solo, the MC prompted the crowd: "If y'all want to hear Troy play higher, stick your fingers in the air and SCREAM!!!" Andrews then played an Armstrongesque ascending run on trumpet beyond high C, ran to the front of the stage, and waved his arms, urging the ecstatic crowd to scream even more loudly. It was a performance as athletic as it was musical, and the crowd rocked like it was at a football game. The line between music and sports was blurred even more when Shorty finished the show with an intense version of "When the Saints Go Marching In," urging the crowd to chant "*Who dat* say they're gonna beat dem Saints...*who dat? who dat?*" over and over.

A major theme that members of the Andrews family have always stressed is how important local educators are in passing on the tradition. One of the most important of those teachers, clarinetist Alvin Batiste, died the night before his scheduled appearance at the 2007 Jazz and Heritage Festival and demonstrated how closely knit the city's musical community is. On the morning of May 6, the last day of the festival, the musicians' grapevine was burning with the news of Batiste's death. Batiste was scheduled to play that day at the jazz tent in support of his new album, *Marsalis Music Honors Alvin Batiste,* and many of the musicians who'd known him over the years had planned to be there to visit him. Now they were suddenly changing plans, preparing instead to mourn his death and celebrate his life.

"I got calls from a whole bunch of people at the same time, five people called within five minutes," recalled trumpeter Maurice Brown, who played the opening set at the jazz tent that day:

> It was overwhelming. I was preparing for my gig at Jazz Fest, and the phone wouldn't stop ringing. I remember it was like time stopping for a moment. I mean, that was going to be one of the highlights of Jazz Fest for me to see Mr. Bat and catch up with him. Once I got to the festival and all the cameras were there and people wanting to interview me, it hit me that this was really happening. It's funny, on Saturday I was playing with Roy Hargrove, and I saw Al's picture at the jazz tent, and I was looking at the picture, and I felt like a little kid getting ready for Christmas.

Brown, who studied with Batiste during the thirty-five years Batiste taught at Southern University in Baton Rouge, decided to play a new song he'd written for his mentor, "Bat's Ordeal." "I had been working on it over the last year and hadn't had a chance to play in front of people, so I decided to do it at the last minute after I'd learned what happened," said Brown.

He returned to that jazz tent stage later that day to pay tribute to the late master along with other former Batiste students—from his latest class of NOCCA seniors to jazz stars such as Branford Marsalis and Harry Connick Jr. An atmosphere of anticipation filled the tent as the crowd buzzed and musical luminaries hugged each other backstage. The tribute opened with a set from three of Batiste's teenage NOCCA students—pianist Conun Pappas, bassist Max Moran, and drummer Joe Dyson. On "Clean Air," a song from Batiste's album, the band's crackling rhythmic poise and collective dexterity as an ensemble, along with vocalist Ed Perkins, was fitting testimony to Batiste's talent as a composer and effectiveness as a teacher. Branford Marsalis joined the group on alto saxophone for the spirited "Salty Dogs."

The emotional high point of the tribute came early in the show, when Batiste's niece and nephew, vocalist Stephanie Jordan and trumpeter Marlon Jordan, came on the stage. Earlier, there had been no plans for the two to perform, but when

Branford Marsalis heard that Batiste had died, he arranged for the Jordans and other family members to attend the event and encouraged them to perform. "It was a sad time," said Marlon Jordan, "but we decided to go out there and play for Uncle Alvin. We were supposed to do 'Skylark,' which is on his last record, but Stephanie didn't feel like doing that. She wanted to do [Shirley Horn's] 'Here's to Life' because she thought it was more fitting to welcome him to the new place he was going." The band played the opening theme, and when Stephanie half-whispered the words "No complaints," musicians and listeners alike lost it and began weeping.

"I was so emotional," said Marlon, "I was just trying to maintain my composure. He was my Uncle Alvin. He's known me since I came out of the womb. To me he was more than Alvin Batiste, the educator. To me he was Alvin Batiste, my uncle, who could make me laugh. I was just thinking about how he's not here anymore. I don't know what to do to get over that loss."

Marlon spent four days after the flood stranded on his roof in the broiling sun, unable to move because he had broken both his ankles. Meanwhile, his family had collected at Uncle Alvin's place in Baton Rouge. With no word from Marlon, they feared he had been lost in the deluge. "I felt bad for my mother because she didn't know where I was," he recalled. "When I saw everybody, they were so relieved I was still here. It was a bad experience, but it showed me that the human spirit can rise above everything." Marlon Jordan said Batiste's teaching helped him survive those hopeless days of pain, hunger, and desperate thirst as he clung to that roof. "It's life lessons, so many things I learned from Uncle Alvin," he said:

> Every time we would get together, every Sunday we would talk, even when I was like eleven. Our family is very creative, very strong, and we always get together. He taught me lessons about being a man, taking care of your kids, trying to survive. There's a thin line between being a jazz musician and being a homemaker, and a whole lot of things that go with that.

Batiste's influence and reputation resonated far more deeply with the New Orleans musicians than it did with the general public. Although Batiste was underrecognized and rarely heard outside the immediate community, his legacy was nonetheless extended to thousands of students during his four decades of teaching. In recognition of his inestimable contribution, Batiste in 2004 received *OffBeat*'s Best of the Beat Award for Lifetime Achievement in Music Education.

Randy Jackson of television's *American Idol* fame is one of Batiste's most famous students. "Probably other than my parents, [he was] one of the biggest influences and mentors in my life," said Jackson. "His inspiration and teachings truly helped me to get where I am today. I love him and will miss him, and I am sure he is dancing with Miles Davis and John Coltrane right now, as he should be because he was one of the greatest educators spiritually and mentally."

Batiste, who remained a powerful performer right up until his death, had a singular approach to harmonics and a unique emotional breadth characteristic of great poetry. One of the most remarkable moments of his career came when he stepped on stage with Ornette Coleman at Jazz Fest in 2003 and inhabited the strange, beautiful angularity of Coleman's dimension with complete familiarity, in marked contrast to the uneasiness other famous musicians have demonstrated when exposed to Coleman's uncompromising vision.

Batiste's method, called the root progression system, was as brilliant in its novel approach to improvisation as Coleman's celebrated harmelodic system. "Everything evolves from the root, the bottom of the chord," Maurice Brown said of Batiste's technique. "It's an approach to improvisation. It was a revelation to me. It's a way to make progress. If you practice the root progression seriously, it expands your vocabulary because you're playing everything every possible way. It's like a puzzle. You play an idea every possible way it can be explained."

Alvin Batiste left a modest legacy of recorded music and a number of compositions that may yet come to light in the hands of his students. To Batiste's great joy and our good fortune, Branford Marsalis produced what would become the clarinetist's epitaph, an album that covered much of the musical ground he traveled over the course of his career. However, like all the great New Orleans musicians, Batiste's ultimate legacy could never be reduced to a digital recording. His impact on the city's culture was human, as strong a bond as a handshake, as fleeting a gesture as a smile. "He was one of the greatest people to ever teach jazz," said Marlon Jordan, "and all of the jazz musicians he affected that will go on to affect the world, people like myself, my brother Kent, Branford, Donald Harrison, and all the people who come out of that line. They will go on to share that information that they've learned with new generations. That's the way the music is going to continue."

Jordan's observation was particularly salient in light of the work Donald Harrison was doing to keep the spirit of New Orleans music burning brightly in the young musicians who were just learning the craft. Harrison, the great alto saxophonist, extended his career as a jazz musician into the world of Mardi Gras Indians, following in the footsteps of his father, Guardians of the Flame Big Chief Donald Harrison. Harrison was also an educator, mentoring numerous musicians, most famously the rapper Notorious B.I.G. Harrison came out of New Orleans at the same time as trumpeter Terence Blanchard. The two played in Art Blakey's Jazz Messengers together, then formed their own group, the Harrison-Blanchard Band, and made several albums before going their separate ways. Since then Harrison has pursued many different musical avenues, from the neobop work of his early years to the crucial recording *Indian Blues,* which combined Mardi Gras Indian music with jazz and R&B, to smooth jazz, including his chart-topping *The Power of Cool* album, to the amalgam of jazz, R&B, second-line and hip-hop music he calls nouveau swing, epitomized by the dance-oriented *Free Style.* His nephew, trumpeter Christian Scott, has worked with him on several updates of jazz material, including *For Art's Sake, Kind of New,* and *The Chosen.* Harrison has also tutored scores of young New Orleans musicians in the traditions of their culture. His most important work in this realm may be his role as artistic director of Tipitina's Internship Program (T.I.P.), which offers internships to New Orleans–based high school musicians. The program is designed to improve skills in performing, recording, and producing by involving students in numerous recording sessions. Finally, the students make a recording of their own, produced by Harrison.

All the best efforts of jazz educators would be for naught if the music didn't have venues to present it to the public. However, Preservation Hall's grand reopening on April 28, 2007, indicated that the music would continue to have a place to grow. Preservation Hall, one of the key remaining links to New Orleans's history as the birthplace of jazz, reopened its doors for the first time since Katrina that day, celebrating its forty-fifth anniversary in the process. It was a hard-fought victory for the Preservation Hall Jazz Band, an organization that had been forced to operate as a contemporary version of the wandering minstrel since the storm. Ironically, when the levees broke, the band was in the process of a daring and creative update of its profile by adding a young white saxophonist and vocalist, Clint Maedgen, and players from his group, The New Orleans Bingo! Show, to the lineup.

The idea to adjust the band's focus to appeal to more contemporary listeners came from Ben Jaffe. Jaffe had inherited the stewardship of Preservation Hall from his parents, Allan and Sandra Jaffe, who opened the club in 1961 as a living tribute to New Orleans jazz history. Jaffe called the new approach the New Orleans Revue and promoted it as a combination of traditional New Orleans Jazz and Mardi Gras revelry. New material, including songs written by Ray Davies of the Kinks, was added to the repertoire, and the Bingo! cast members would second-line through the audience, throwing confetti and beads and handing out parasols to the dancers.

Jaffe realized that if the members of Preservation Hall did not receive immediate help after the storm, the group would cease to exist. Its members were stranded in various spots around the country, and several were in ill health. With help from his wife, Sara, Jaffe founded the New Orleans Musicians Hurricane Relief Fund. The organization quickly raised $500,000 from donors to help New Orleans musicians return home.

Part of that fund brought trumpeter/vocalist John Brunious, leader of the Preservation Hall Jazz Band (PHJB), back to New Orleans after his evacuation to Florida. But Brunious's stay in a French Quarter apartment was a temporary arrangement. He was grateful for the help but didn't feel he had really returned home. "I love New Orleans," Brunious told me after the PHJB played a stirring set on the back lawn of New York's Gracie Mansion to kick off the JVC Jazz Festival. "But there's nothing left there." Brunious has seen the neighborhoods he grew up in reduced to rubble and his friends scattered across the country.

"The musicians in the PHJB all grew up within a mile of each other, playing together and listening to the great musicians of the past," said Jaffe:

> Now the banjo player is living in Houston, the drummer is in Georgia— we're gonna lose a tradition that's been part of our heritage. We've got to get these musicians back to New Orleans to teach these kids about their heritage. I hate to say it, but New Orleans jazz has been on the endangered species list for a while. There need to be some red flags going up. We only have a small window to do this because we're losing musicians every day... It's tragic that the city could lose the Neville Brothers. There's no way to put a dollar value on the cultural significance of someone like Cyrille Neville or Aaron Neville living here in New Orleans. Those guys participate in Mardi Gras Indian practices, their children are a big part of the hip-hop community, and they participate with the Tipitina's Foundation in teaching young kids recording techniques.
>
> New Orleans is the cultural spine of the United States. We are the epicenter. We're not the South. We've never been the South. We were settled by the French; we were settled by the Spanish. We're an African city, the northernmost point of the Caribbean.

Jaffe has dedicated his life to keeping this music alive, and the only hopes for the culture's survival are the singular efforts of people like him and other small-business owners who'll buck the odds and stay in New Orleans no matter what the future holds.

CHAPTER 12

Shorty on the Block

Trombone Shorty's influence on the post-Katrina music of New Orleans began to extend well beyond the music he was making with his own group and with the family band. His thirst for finding new musical contexts reflected a subtle shift that was taking place in the city's postflood music community. With the shuffled populace changing the city's demographics, new neighborhood alliances were forming. Mardi Gras Indian music and brass-band culture had been almost exclusively African American before the storm, but in its wake musicians were cooperating based more on musical affinity than ethnicity. Shorty epitomized this trend by ensuring that his band, Orleans Avenue, was a balance of black and white musicians. He also played a key role in the comeback of one of the city's most important funk rock bands, Galactic.

Saxophonist Ben Ellman was sitting on the Galactic bus at it made its way into Missoula, Montana, on July 8, 2007, when he heard the news. The NAACP had laid the N word to rest during its national convention when it ceremonially put the word used to demean African Americans throughout U.S. history in a pine box. Ellman had just coproduced the new Galactic album with hip-hop mixmaster Count, *From the Corner to the Block*. Unlike just about every other hip-hop-related recording of the year, *From the Corner to the Block* made no reference to the N word.

"We've never done that," said Ellman. Ellman and the rest of Galactic are Caucasians, but they have always been deeply influenced by and respectful of black culture.

From the Corner to the Block features Galactic's infectious dance grooves behind a densely layered revue of hip-hop MCs, including Lyrics Born, Juvenile, Ladybug Mecca from Digable Planets, Boots Riley from Blackalicious, Mr. Lif, and Lateef the Truth Speaker. Each of them delivers lyrics describing scenes on their particular corner, giving the record a powerful theme that underscores its musical coherence and making it nothing short of a masterpiece from both a sonic and a lyrical perspective.

The album's release was the culmination of three years of struggle as the band tried to determine its direction following the 2004 departure of R&B vocalist Theryl ("Houseman") DeClouet, a black man who fronted a white band. Back in 2003 Galactic released *Ruckus,* a song-oriented album that featured Houseman more prominently than any of its previous efforts. During the ensuing tour to promote the album, Houseman developed complications from diabetes that forced him off the road. Galactic was faced with a huge question mark about its future.

"When the band first started, it was all about Houseman," Ellman said. "The whole band obviously was not from New Orleans, so when we got to New Orleans and we started playing with Houseman, it was what we were all into—still are. Especially when the band first started, he was a huge part of it and a big influence. We've always been an instrumental band, and Houseman was like a permanent special guest."

Bassist Robert Mercurio and guitarist Jeff Raines were steeped in the Washington, D.C.–area go-go scene when they started Galactic after moving to New Orleans to attend college. The band developed its identity as a Meters-like funk outfit after native New Orleanian Stanton Moore took over on drums and then Rich Vogel began playing keyboards. Ellman had been playing saxophone in local brass bands, which is how he met Trombone Shorty. He brought the brass-band dimension to the lineup in yet another direction when he joined. The group's live shows became legendary for lengthy sets of hard-edged funk capped off by Houseman's old-school R&B vocals.

"Every time we go into the studio, it's like the next step for us," said Ellman:

> We do all the live shows, which are based around improvisation, trying to do something new and interesting with the songs, capturing the spirit of the moment. But when you go into the studio, it gives you a chance to redefine yourself in more of a controlled setting. I always feel like, after we make a CD, it's another step. *Ruckus* felt like that. It was very much structured for us. We toured the record pretty heavily before Houseman found out about his diabetes. It came down to just being on the road was not good for him [because] it was hard for him to take care of himself or eat right out there. He's certainly a lot healthier right now than he would have been had he stayed on the road with us.

Galactic kept touring, first with guest vocalists, then just as an instrumental group. "The idea for this record was always in the back of our minds," said Vogel. "Since parting ways with Theryl, we were playing instrumentally, and that was going good in terms of the live shows, and everybody was playing well, but making records is a different animal, and there wasn't a lot of inspiration in the idea of just cutting an instrumental record."

Galactic has often paired its bills with progressive hip-hop acts, and it was during one tour with Lyrics Born that the idea for *From the Corner to the Block* began to take shape. "We've worked with Lyrics Born on the road, and we're big fans," said Ellman:

> We love performing with him. Stylistically, it was a really good mix, as it was with all the MCs. Originally we were talking to Lyrics Born about producing the whole thing. We had this even crazier idea at the beginning—a concept album which involved a lot of MCs playing different characters with a narrative running through the whole thing. Lyrics Born got really busy, so he didn't have time to do it, but in the end we started working with all these MCs, and it kind of changed the concept around a little bit.

Vogel noted that the concept was based on a book called *Intersection/New Orleans*. "A lot of the music that influenced us as a band is a lot of the same stuff that the first generation of hip-hop was about," said Vogel:

> We wanted to model ourselves on the great funky rhythm sections— Booker T and the MGs, the Meters, James Brown's band. That was our school, learning to play the stuff. So this was such a natural idea. Here we are a funky groove band, [so] it makes sense for us to work with interesting MCs. One album we talked about when we were coming up with the idea for this project was the Brand New Heavies' record that they made with all the MCs, *Heavy Rhyme Experience*. We wanted to make a record on that model for the current generation of underground hip-hop artists. We came up with the corner idea based on *Intersection/ New Orleans* to give the album thematic unity.

Work began on the album at the band's New Orleans studio during the summer of 2005, when Moore went in and recorded drum parts: "I would lay down drum tracks. Then Ben would take what I played and put effects on it," said Moore. "He would maybe lilt it up, slice and dice it, start it in a different place, and just do different things with it to make it interesting. Ben has been getting into a lot of production over the years, and he was actually starting to make some tracks, so when it came time to do this record, he had already developed some skills in this area."

Before the band could take the next step in the recording process, Hurricane Katrina destroyed the studio. Moore's drum tracks were safe, but suddenly the band had nowhere to live, let alone record. "We went away just for a weekend totally unprepared to be gone for months," said Ellman:

We didn't have a chance to properly evacuate. We left town with nothing but a backpack, so it was like "What's gonna happen?" Our first instinct was: "Let's book a tour. We need to work right now. Let's go on the road and start playing shows if we can't go home." We did do a couple, and we realized it was not a good idea. It wasn't time to go provide the party. We were not in the right headspace to do that. Our first show after the storm, we were all crying onstage. It was really difficult. We felt an obligation before we started playing to talk about it a little bit to the audience. It was so fresh. But we couldn't just get onstage and play. We just weren't ready; it brought us all to tears. We needed some time. We were scattered, and we were trying to figure out what we were gonna do personally. People had families, and it was too difficult. We ended up working on the CD, which was good.

The band also recorded two tracks with Robbie Robertson for another project, *Goin' Home: A Tribute to Fats Domino,* a benefit record for the Tipitina's Foundation.

Galactic holed up in a studio in Pennsylvania—in the Poconos—and wrote instrumental pieces based around Moore's recorded drum passages. After a month of this they'd come up with enough material to send to the MCs and ask them to add their verses. "They gave me a concept," said Lyrics Born:

They said, "We want you to write a song about what happens on a corner. This is your corner." Basically I drew on my experiences growing up in the flea-market scene out here. I grew up in Berkeley, California. Anybody from Berkeley knows in those days everybody tried to sell you something or sell you on something. So it was a really easy song to write and a lot of fun because I had a lot of personal experiences to write from. I don't get asked to do this kind of stuff that often.

Coordinating the performances of the MCs was a painstaking process that required organization, trust, a lot of patience, and some luck to pull off. "We kept asking ourselves, 'Is this a good idea?' " said Vogel:

We know how hard it is just for the five of us to get something accomplished. So to have this collective project with so many different artists who all have careers, they're working on their own shit, and that's obviously their prime concern. There was a point where we said, "Oh man, what were we thinking?" But once you get one or two on board, you start to relax a little bit. There was a snowball effect.

Once the band had the lyrics in place, Count, Ellman, and Moore convened to put fresh drum tracks on the whole record. "Count had this studio in Dallas, so we drove a bunch of my drums over to Dallas," said Moore:

> We brought like three bass drums, a bunch of snare drums, and about twenty mikes for different miking situations. I went back, and I rere-corded everything we had done, whether it was me originally or a breakbeat or whatever it was. On some of it I just played wacky percussion on top of it. We would decide what situation worked best for the track, whether it was me or a breakbeat or whatever, and Count would decide which microphone situation was working the best for that. It was a fun process. During that process Count would ask me, "Can you swing this a little more?" or "Can you straighten that out?" and I would do it really easily, so he was pleased with that.

Trombone Shorty came in and recorded an orchestrated instrumental track, "Tuff Love," which was a key to the album's flow. "It was kind of the Trombone Shorty horn section because all those horns are just me and him," said Ellman. "We had talked about actually putting together a brass band, which we have done since then, called the Midnight Disturbers, but before that me and Shorty had talked about it. I really wanted him on the CD, and he came in with this song, and he and I just sort of laid out all these parts and put it together in the studio. He played trombone and trumpet, did all the brass arrangements. It's unbeliev-able—the solo on that track was really one of the only solos on the record. It was a one-take thing. The dude is amazing. He's a true prodigy. I've known him for years. When I first came to New Orleans, my first job was with the Li'l Rascals Brass Band. I was the oldest guy in the band and the only white guy. At the time, Shorty was, like, five or six."

Ellman marveled at the strides Troy had made since the storm. "Being on stage just to see what he's doing," he shook his head:

> I just say, what am I going to play after that? The crowd's going crazy, and now I have to do a solo. Man, how am I going to follow *that*? It's very important to realize that I don't have to be like Troy. I can be my own person. I can be my own player, very distinct from what he's doing. So I think that kind of allows me to be a fresh sound and not have to play the same kind of thing Troy does on stage. I've learned a lot from him. I've learned from just standing next to him on stage and watching him play. Since he was a little kid he knows me as the white kid in a brass band.

Once the record was complete, the group had to figure out how to play it live. They jumped into deep water by making the Bonnaroo festival the debut showcase, but the gamble paid off. "The toughest track to figure out how to do live was 'Second and Dryades,' with Monk Boudreaux," said Moore. "We would meet for two hours every day before the rehearsals. We had about four eight-hour rehearsals for Bonnaroo, then a fifth one with the MCs."

The band finally settled on treating Monk's vocal as a sampled element in the performance.

"On the Monk thing, Ben and I had to figure out who was gonna play which part, which loops would go through whom," said Moore:

> We actually sampled some of the effected drums and put them into different samples. Ben has one, and I've got this Roland SDBS (sample pad computer), which I hit with sticks, so I'm playing a combination of things. We actually vary it live, but we've gotten it to the point where it can sound exactly like the record if we want it to. We wanted to add a little live element to it. On some of the other tunes, I have two bass drums there anyway, so I can switch back and forth from a smaller bass drum to a bigger bass drum, and I'm also switching between different snare drums for different tracks. Bonnaroo was fun. It was kind of a lot for us to bite off musically because we had to learn three or four new songs for each MC we played with, but during rehearsals we figured out a way to do it.

With *From the Corner to the Block* Galactic expanded its audience and pointed toward a new direction for New Orleans music. "We're hoping to bring these two audiences together who may seem to be disparate but actually have a lot in common," said Vogel:

> There's definitely an overlap between alternative-rock kids and hip-hop hipsters. We've already seen a little bit of it in our club gig at South by Southwest and on a larger scale at Bonnaroo, where it felt like we had the best of both worlds going on. It had the intensity of a Galactic show with some great MCs who are dynamic performers. I don't know how many people were in that tent, but it looked crowded to me, and people were jumping up and down the whole time.

CHAPTER 13

The Armstrong Legacy

All of the trumpeters that come from New Orleans—whether we know it
or not, or whether we acknowledge it or not—we live in the echo of Pops.
—Wynton Marsalis

Jazz traveled the technological and aesthetic passageways of the twentieth
century to a point where it has millions of faces around the world. But in New
Orleans, Louis Armstrong stands out as the face of jazz. His music defines the
contours of traditional New Orleans jazz and the swing era, yet it continues to be
a direct influence on the city's young musicians. In the starkly recontextualized
post-Katrina New Orleans, Armstrong's influence is one of the cultural realities
that was not washed away and doesn't need public money, charitable institutions, or political rhetoric to sustain itself.

Most of all, Armstrong's influence lives in the musicians themselves, in
Leroy Jones, in Kermit Ruffins, in James and Troy and Glen David Andrews, in
Irvin Mayfield, in Shamarr Allen, and in all the other trumpeters who summon
Armstrong's spirit in the annual birthday celebration for "Pops," the Satchmo
SummerFest. The festival is renewed every year on the first weekend of August,
roughly corresponding to Armstrong's birthdate of August 4, and it never fails
to be one of the most joyous and characteristically New Orleans festivals of
the year. Different stages concentrate on traditional and contemporary jazz,
brass-band music, and a children's stage that showcases young people playing
Armstrong's music. Satchmo SummerFest always ends with an exciting cutting
session called "Props for Pops" at the finale of Kermit Ruffins's set, a friendly
rivalry between several trumpeters that features a high-intensity exchange
between Kermit, Allen, Mayfield, Troy and James Andrews, and any other
trumpet players on the bill. "A lot of trumpet players have a beginning, a middle
and an end when they play," said Ruffins. "Louis, right off the bat he was playing
like it was the last note he was ever gonna play in his life." The 2006 edition of
Satchmo SummerFest took place in the alleyways around the French Market,

but in 2007 the festival returned to its traditional site on the grounds of the U.S. Mint.

Though there are no recordings to document the influence, the younger Armstrong clearly heard Buddy Bolden, who by all accounts played in a style that influenced him. Armstrong codified the concept of a jazz soloist and the rhythmic Rosetta Stone of swing on his 1920s' recordings, the legendary Hot 5 and Hot 7 sessions. In later years, he became even more famous for his singing. Cutting across all of these accomplishments was the fact that he was arguably the first twentieth-century pop musician, a man whose sense of how to sing and play influenced every musician who's ever heard him.

"Louis Armstrong was a rock star," Shamarr Allen argued. "He was a star. He wasn't like how we think of jazz musicians, kind of underground, be-bop people. He was like a real national pop star. Think about it. Louis Armstrong created a certain style of music, and he took it all around the world. Everybody talks about him like he was a traditional player, but back then he wasn't traditional. He was pop music."

Though each trumpet player in the jazz tradition has had a unique way of paying tribute to Armstrong, in New Orleans Kermit Ruffins probably resembles him most completely in his performances, and, in fact, Kermit also resembles

Figure 24. Shamarr Allen solos during Satchmo Summerfest jam session. Photo by John Swenson. Used by permission of John Swenson.

Armstrong in his lifestyle. Ruffins enjoys himself publicly, tacitly inviting his audience to join him. He's always toted a cardboard suitcase of cold beer cans around with him like it's an essential piece of music equipment and sung the praises of smoking reefer. He has also become noted for always having a grill going so his fans can enjoy some of his barbecue between sets. Armstrong displayed remarkably similar habits. A thoroughgoing bon vivant, he advocated pot smoking, New Orleans cooking—famously signing letters, "Red beans and rice-ly yours"—and other indulgences.

James Andrews also bears an uncanny resemblance to Armstrong in his stage performance—an influence he maintains is hereditary. "Louis Armstrong, that's the magic for me," said James. "I think every musician in New Orleans is some kind of influenced by Louis Armstrong. When I was a kid, everybody was talking about him. My family goes back to the beginnings of jazz. They played this music before it was called traditional jazz. Papa Celestin was my grandmother's godfather. She'll tell you Louis Armstrong was her cousin. Tad Jones told me that, too. He said, 'You related to Louis Armstrong.' "[1] Andrews continued, "Around the house they were always playing his music. That's where I first heard him. They would say, 'That's Louis Armstrong. He's your cousin.' "

Given such a background, it's easy to understand why James chose the trumpet as his instrument and why he called himself "Satchmo of the Ghetto."

Trombone Shorty's nickname obscures the fact that he's also one of the top trumpeters in town, and he can move a large crowd the way Armstrong did. Shorty calls to mind all of Armstrong's dazzling technique, but what really stamps him as Armstrong's heir is his stage presence. If Kermit and James embody Armstrong's spirit, Trombone Shorty has demonstrated the sheer technical and emotional brilliance that characterized him. Shorty can voice every note on the horn (and even some that aren't) with authority. He has a quicksilver style that can climb the scale to hit impossibly high notes just as Armstrong did. He merges musical excellence with personal charisma.

When he was growing up in the lower Ninth Ward, Shamarr Allen was a student of Ruffins. Kermit used to drive his pickup truck to Allen's Jourdan Avenue home and teach Allen and his band, Wolfpack, the rudiments of traditional jazz. Allen decided to play the trumpet after his father, a saxophonist, played him a Louis Armstrong record.

"My father, Keith Allen, played saxophone, but he wasn't a professional sax player," said Allen:

> He did it for the fun of it. He wanted me to play saxophone. I played around on the saxophone, but I never took it serious. I just fiddled around with it because my dad played it, and every little kid wanna be like his dad. I was home, and he was playing me some records, Herb

Alpert and some other guys, and he said, "Listen to this." He played an Armstrong record, and I was shocked. I was like "Dad, whatever he playing, I wanna play that." It seemed like he was having so much fun with his singing and his playing, the way the band played, it was so much fun that it made you just want to have fun, too.

Trumpeter Leroy Jones appeared in a "Young Louis" role back in 1972 during the half-time of Super Bowl IV, when the Dallas Cowboys played the Miami Dolphins in Tulane Stadium. "I performed on two numbers with the Onward Brass Band, 'High Society' and 'Hello Dolly,' on the latter accompanying Ms. Carol Channing," Jones said. "She was the main attraction of the half-time show. My role was to play as little Louis Armstrong. The half-time theme was Carnival or Mardi Gras, and it was a tribute to Louis Armstrong, who had passed away in July of 1971."

Jones released a new album, *Soft Shoe,* just before the 2007 Satchmo Summerfest and performed twice, playing with the Hurricane Brass Band and New Orleans' Finest, a traditional jazz combo. "My roots are grounded in brass-band music," said the forty-nine-year-old trumpeter, who was another one of Danny Barker's pupils. "That began back in 1970 with the Fairview Baptist Church Brass Band, which later became the Hurricane Brass Band. New Orleans' Finest is the name I chose for my quintet back in 1980, when we had our first Bourbon Street gig at a nightclub called Frenchy's."

Jones first heard Armstrong as a child because his parents had a few of his albums. "I remember one of the LPs was a live recording of Louis and his All-Stars," Jones said:

> Louis' cadenza at the end of "Ain't Misbehavin' " gives me chills to this day. I listened to that track so much until I was able to play the solo pretty much like Louis when I was thirteen years old. In later years, when I played with the Louisiana Repertory Ensemble, I was introduced to the earlier recordings of Armstrong, the Hot 5, Hot 7 sessions and those great recordings he did with his orchestra from 1929 through 1933. Louis Armstrong will always remain my first mentor.

Jones admitted that he had to get past the dominance of Armstrong's influence in his playing to find his own voice on the trumpet. "When I was younger, like most young brass players, I played very loud," he said:

> Later, after developing a different technique, I discovered the difference between volume and intensity. I did have a more big-voiced, brassy tone when I was younger. Every trumpet player has his or her sound, be

it brassy or mellow. Nowadays, I reckon I fit into that mellow category. Armstrong had an unmistakable, unique, and tremendous sound all his own. To possess a distinct and individual sound is the goal of every musician or vocalist, particularly within the jazz genre.

Although Jones has worked to establish his own artistic persona and make his own music, he also paid tribute to Armstrong when he recorded *Props for Pops* in 1996. Armstrong is a difficult subject for tribute albums; his greatest recorded work is so iconic that it can't be improved upon, and simply reproducing it, although a daunting task in itself, doesn't accomplish anything. Wynton Marsalis did an outstanding job of bringing the Hot 5s and Hot 7s to live audiences, and Kermit Ruffins can make people smile with the grace and ease Armstrong possessed, but with *Props for Pops,* Leroy Jones did justice to Armstrong and his own work simultaneously by including well-crafted arrangements of a number of Armstrong favorites and several strong original compositions in the Armstrong style. "I wanted to pay tribute to my first and foremost mentor," Jones said. "I wanted to approach the music in an honest manner, using the concept that worked best for the musicians on the session. I never want to find myself trying to copy someone else's playing. I don't think I really tried to make a conscious effort to avoid playing like Armstrong. The influences are obvious."

Over the course of Satchmo SummerFest, many aspects of Armstrong's enduring legacy trace a career arc that extends from the brass-band tradition he grew up in to his historic small-group recordings of the 1920s; his conceptually brilliant orchestras of the 1930s and '40s; the return to the small groups of his All-Stars period; his reign as "Ambassador Satch" during the 1950s, when he played U.S. State Department–sponsored tours around the world; and finally his dénouement sharing the wisdom of his years. However, the greatest example of that legacy will be the musicians who continue to follow the trail he cleared for them a long, long time ago.

Satchmo SummerFest is all things Armstrong for a weekend, but Armstrong's legacy may well be more obscured that it appears. Historical perspective is an optical illusion. Legacy turns into myth, and myth into an abstracted reality formed to the viewer's convenience. Armstrong is easily deconstructed into a series of faith-based gestures by well-meaning acolytes who deify him without understanding him, the ultimate fate of all mythic heroes. The smile, the handkerchief, the gravel voice, and a couple of familiar songs are all a Son of Satchmo needs to reanimate the myth. However, what of Armstrong, the ambitious young player in the streets of New Orleans who would hitch his wagon to the rival band's as they both attempted to promote that night's concert and cut his opponent to ribbons until he was properly humiliated? It's a vision of a young man most closely related in today's music world to the hip-hop community.

Figure 25. Street jam with young brass-band musicians during Satchmo Summerfest. Photo by John Swenson. Used by permission of John Swenson.

The young Armstrong boasted, talked bawdy, ridiculed religious hypocrites, promoted drugs, and called for the grisly demise of his enemies. It's all right there on the records, too. Louis Armstrong's legacy is obvious in the graduating classes of NOCCA and Louis Armstrong Summer Camp, where all of the well-scrubbed niceties of his history are adhered to. Nonetheless, his legacy goes far deeper than that. It extends to the jail cell where New Orleans gangsta rapper Mystikal sat in 2007, wondering what his future held.

"I think if Louis Armstrong was born in my generation," said Allen, who mixes hip-hop with traditional jazz in his performances, "his music would sound like the stuff that I'm doing now."

As the summer of 2007 wore on, the drumbeat of violence continued. One of the more senseless killings took place two weeks after Satchmo SummerFest, when a twenty-eight-year-old woman sitting at Pal's Bar in Mid-City was murdered by a stranger who walked up to her and slashed her throat while she was having a drink and talking with a friend.

Nia Robertson held her throat as she bled to death on the barroom floor and pleaded, "Why did he do this to me?"

The man who slashed Robertson, a white laborer named Erik Traczyk, had apparently gone to the bar to kill someone else. Robertson just happened to be in the wrong place at the wrong time.[2]

Six people were murdered over the course of a weekend in October, running the total number of killings to 163 for the year, one more than the 162 killed in all of 2006, with eleven weeks to go in the year. A week later three more people were killed in a single day. One of them, Shana Thomas, twenty-three, was shot multiple times in the face and left for dead on the side of the road in East New Orleans.

Since the flood, few murderers in New Orleans ever reach trial due to the thug's best friend, Article 701 of the Louisiana code of criminal procedure. It's a get-out-of-jail-free statute under which suspects cannot be held for longer than sixty days on a felony arrest without an indictment. With the police department understaffed and the DA's office in no hurry to prosecute after the flood, killers know that, in Louisiana, taking someone's life means a sixty-day "misdemeanor murder" jail sentence.

Before Katrina, a few hundred murder suspects were released every year under the statute. In 2006 nearly three thousand suspects were released by Article 701, and the Orleans Parish DA successfully prosecuted only one murder conviction out of 162 killings.

Nothing seemed to be able to stop the barrage of murders. In October 2007 six people were killed over the course of a single weekend, including an off-duty police officer killed in a home invasion. A bizarre development in this story came when police reported that a suspect in the cop killing had been involved in a robbery attempt thirty hours later and sought asylum in district attorney Eddie Jordan's house. Jordan resigned shortly thereafter.

One of the terrible by-products of this murder spree was that people who weren't familiar with the city's history interpreted every large gathering of African Americans in New Orleans as a potential source of more violence. Even funeral second lines and Indian parades were viewed with distrust, and city authorities seemed more interested in stopping these celebrations than in putting an end to the drug-gang gun battles that were taking place in the middle of residential neighborhoods.

On October 1 2007 the situation came to a head during a confrontation on the streets of Treme between the New Orleans police and musicians who were celebrating the memory of their departed colleague Kerwin James. Once again Glen David Andrews was in the middle of the action, but this time, instead of decrying the level of violence in New Orleans, he was singled out by the police and arrested along with his brother Derrick Tabb for creating a public disturbance. The arrest of musicians who were celebrating the life of a fallen colleague with a spontaneous second-line parade was originally covered in depth by the *New Orleans Times-Picayune* before it hit the dry tinder of the Internet. There it flared up into a media inferno that tapped the deep-rooted anger of a New Orleans African American community that had lost its neighborhoods to the flood and was now being prevented from restoring its culture to the city.

Kerwin James was a popular Treme resident, a tuba player with the New Birth Brass Band, and the younger brother of Rebirth Brass Band charter members Philip and Keith Frazier. "Kerwin was our biggest fan," said Philip Frazier. "He was always happy, and everybody loved him. A lot of musicians turned out to remember him."

The community of young brass-band musicians in New Orleans is very close. Many of them grew up and went to school together in the Sixth and Seventh wards. New Birth Brass Band founder James Andrews and his younger brother Troy were no strangers to these events. Both also played the jazz funeral for their brother Darnell "D-Boy" Andrews, another member of New Birth, who was murdered in 1995. New Birth's 1997 album, *D-Boy*, was dedicated to him.

Kerwin died on September 26, 2007, from complications of a stroke he suffered in the wake of Katrina. In the days and nights leading up to his funeral, his fellow musicians walked the streets of Treme, playing traditional funeral songs in his honor. As I have explained, the people who follow in the wake of the funeral marchers are known as the second line, but on the night of October 1 it was the third line, a score of police cars surrounding the marchers at the corner of North Robertson and St. Philip streets, that caused the trouble.

The large police force attacked the parade with guns drawn and snatched instruments away from the players. "One more note, and we'll arrest the whole band," Tabb remembers the police saying. Just as their African ancestors, deprived of their native instruments, took to song to express themselves, the marchers began to sing the traditional funeral hymn "I'll Fly Away." The police fixed on the most charismatic figure in the group, Glen David Andrews, and his brother and partner in music, Tabb, and arrested them both.

"It was crazy," said Philip Frazier, who would suffer a nonfatal stroke himself in 2009. "I told the police they were just respecting my baby brother, but they didn't care. What was so strange about it is I've been doing this all my life, and now this happens."

When Tamara Jackson, president of the New Orleans Social Aid and Pleasure Club task force, complained about the excessive force used to break up the march, the police spokesperson at District 1 responded that someone in Treme had called 911 with a noise complaint and that the police were required to respond. Jackson had fought for the second-line tradition before when she successfully sued the city to reduce the cost of street-parade permits and extend the length of the events from four to five hours. However, when it came to the impromptu jazz funerals and second lines that have been a longstanding tradition in Treme, the problems still loomed.

"The legal structure doesn't protect the social clubs," she said. "But we're working on securing an agreement that will protect the culture as a whole [and] that will include the jazz procession. I think the problem is the difference between the jazz funeral procession and the second line. The jazz funeral procession is not a second line, but when they see a bunch of us gather, they're frightened." The "they" Jackson is referring to were clearly the predominantly white new arrivals to the Treme neighborhood. "Us" is obviously the black community, which goes as far back as the city itself. The old battle along racial lines was being drawn once again.

It's easy to understand the outrage over the incident among African Americans. These were centuries-old funeral rites of one of the nation's oldest black American communities that were now under attack. And yet there were no police raids on Roman Catholic funeral masses; no handcuffs placed on Fundamentalist Christians who came to the city by the busload to disrupt Mardi Gras celebrations. The hypocrisy—and the racial profiling—were difficult to overlook.

"You need to protect the neighborhoods twenty-four hours a day, not just during the four hours of a second line," said Jackson, who also noted that the police need training "so the officers can understand the culture, what we do and why we've done it." The implication of Jackson's observation was that racial profiling was part of the New Orleans police department's standard operating procedure and that police officers actually need training to *not* profile.

Jackson spoke at a community meeting held in the Sound Café on October 25, called "Rebuilding New Orleans: The Second Line Model." Speakers talked about how second lines and the Social Aid and Pleasure Clubs were helping displaced New Orleanians return home and providing valuable networking services, but the agenda turned into speculation about how to save the second-line tradition.

"We have to contend with the invasion of the people coming into our community," said Ronald Lewis, president of the Big Nine Social Aid and Pleasure Club and curator of the Mardi Gras Indian and second-line museum he calls "The House of Dance and Feathers." "They say they love our culture, that's why they came here, but they lack education about it, and then they don't want it. They attack you, and then they justify it after the fact." Lewis is one of the New Orleanians that Dan Baum selected to represent the city in his book *Nine Lives: Life and Death in New Orleans*.

A few weeks after Glen David Andrews and Derrick Tabb were jailed for second-lining, I visited Sylvester ("Hawk") Francis at the Backstreet Cultural Museum in Treme. Francis, a slightly built, middle-aged black man, took the five-dollar admission fee and shoved it in his pocket, but he was not smiling. The man who has done more to document the jazz funeral and second-line tradition than anyone else in the city was having a bad day. His organization was unable to hold its traditional All Saint's Day parade on November 1, and his agitation was plain to see.

"I had to cancel the parade this year," he said vaguely—before providing a cursory fulfillment of his duty as Backstreet's curator. "That's the Indian room in there," he said, gesturing to his left, "and that room over there is for the second lines." He quickly disappeared down the hallway, leaving me alone to explore the exhibits.

The Indian room was filled with brilliantly feathered and beaded Mardi Gras Indian regalia, all worn by local "royalty." There was a shrine to "Chief of Chiefs" Tootie Montana and an honor roll of Indians who have been given jazz funerals under the heading "Live like Warriors, Die like Braves." Just outside the room was a photo of Native Americans with the caption "Fighting Terrorism since 1492."

The rest of the walls along the hallway were covered with artifacts ranging from a plaque for the "most humorous" entry in the Louis Armstrong umbrella contest of 1981, various framed articles and testimonials, a state-certified embalmer's license from 1927, a gallery of old Polaroid cameras, as well as a Bell and Howell 8mm movie camera Francis has used to photograph jazz funerals and second lines over the years.

"Hawk" Francis grew up in Treme alongside eighteen brothers and sisters. He became fascinated with jazz funerals at an early age, and in 1978 he bought a camera to start documenting these colorful events. After a few years doing it on his own, Francis was hired by the Rhodes Funeral Home to photograph their funerals. Francis amassed images of more than five hundred funerals, which he published in his book, *Keeping Jazz Funerals Alive: A Powerhouse of Knowledge*, which included a list of people buried with jazz funerals since 1980.

The Rhodes family also owned another Treme funeral parlor, Blandin's, which was located directly across the street from Saint Augustine church, the traditional starting point for most of Treme's funeral parades. Blandin's went out of business in 1990. Having been known for years in this neighborhood for photographing these events, Francis was offered the space for his archives. In 1999 he opened the Backstreet Cultural Museum.

Francis came back into the room, and I asked him about the trouble with the police at the second line. "I knew Kerwin, yes," he said cryptically, nodding his head vigorously as he walked out the front door and started pacing on the porch. I asked him where he got his parade permits. "I always get a permit," he said. "I go right up to the station over there. Five fifty." "That's what you pay?" I asked. "*I'll* give *you* one for five fifty," he responded.

The phone rang. "Yeah, there's one tomorrow," Francis wearily told the caller. "I don't have a route sheet yet. You'll have to call back." He hung up and then explained it was one of his club members, asking about a second line. Then he disappeared again into the back room. I spent a few minutes studying an autographed record album by Francis's grandmother Anita Thomas, an imposing woman who looked like she was capable of causing a few ships to be launched in her day. She was a female grand marshal when second-lining was still a predominantly male culture, the self-proclaimed "queen of the second line," and the album cover was inscribed in bold, sweeping script: "Keep on Second

Lining." Francis was clearly born to appreciate this tradition; hence, it's easy to understand his fascination with the jazz funeral and why he would come to curate this wonderful museum.

Suddenly he appeared from a side door, brandishing a yellowed newspaper clipping. "You wanna talk about the police and second lines?" he said. "This is from ten years ago." It was a front page of the *Times-Picayune* with a photo of the smiling, cherubic preteen faces of the Trombone Shorty Brass Band. Snare drummer Sammy Wilson proudly wore a sign around his neck, stating "I was arrested for playing music."

"See?" Francis said with courtroom finality. "People in this neighborhood are sick that this is still going on." Just as I was about to leave, Francis grew animated. "Let me tell you something, and you can quote me on this," he said, looking straight at me for the first time. "These kids gonna pick up a horn, or they gonna pick up a gun."

Francis was not issuing a threat but a cry for help. In a community where the foundation structures from housing and schools to hospitals and churches were either already gone or imperiled, where drug gangs ruled the streets with impunity and people are murdered in their cars and homes, where the very social structure was undermined by the loss of so many friends and neighbors after Katrina, the unifying element of a celebratory gathering like a second line was one of the few bright moments amid a gathering storm. In addition, the traditional brass music of the second line offered a healthy alternative to young people who might otherwise find that community elsewhere in the gang structure. Trombone Shorty, the eleven-year-old leader of the brass band in the clipping Francis showed me, truly resembled his nickname as he blew through an instrument bigger than himself. In 2007 Shorty was showing the way for a whole new generation of New Orleans musicians.

By the end of 2007 Mayor Nagin had developed vague plans for music in the city's new footprint, like the twenty-acre jazz theme park proposed by a downtown hotel conglomerate, but institutionalizing its cultural history as a museum piece without restoring the communities that supplied the young musicians is ultimately an empty, hypocritical gesture. "The people of south Louisiana, New Orleans and all, we all of the spirit," said Dr. John. "We got strong beliefs in that we ain't letting them bury us under the Gulf of Mexico. I'm hanging on to every little bit of our culture. The thing I most fear is I don't wanna see New Orleans become a shuck Disneyland or a shuck Las Vegas."

For too many, though, New Orleans had become a very real war zone. The murder rate had skyrocketed, and street violence had escalated to where the National Guard and state police were called in to restore order. At the same time, the city was desperate to keep bad news from reaching potential tourists even as at least one street gang had been mugging pedestrians in the French Quarter.

CHAPTER 14

Cold in the Trailer

Winter shadows shivered across the flagstones in Jackson Square on a late January afternoon in 2008 as a crowd of about fifty tourists bundled up in winter clothes passively watched an unlikely collection of musicians—a chubby, red-faced schoolboy trumpeter, a trombone player, a tuba player, a trap drummer, and a stand-up bassist—huff through a ragtag version of "Saints." Glen David Andrews, now twenty-seven years old, arrived with his trombone case slung over his shoulder, sat down on the bench next to the kid trumpeter, and proceeded to transform this tableau into an impromptu party.

During "I Have a Friend in Jesus," Andrews shouldered his trombone and sent a bolt of electricity through the crowd with a solo that corkscrewed in intensity as he threw in four- and eight-bar quotes from sources like horseracing's "Call to Post" or "C-Jam Blues." Andrews signaled the other trombonist to solo, then showed the trumpeter how to accompany the solo. Andrews got up off the bench, moving his gangling six-foot, four-inch frame in an elaborate, shambling dance as he started singing "My Bucket's Got a Hole in It," adding verses from "I Hear You Knockin'" and "Blueberry Hill." At every mention of his poor bucket, Andrews made a sad sack face, threw his arms to the side, and pointed to the tip tin.

Suddenly the tourists were doing an involuntary shuffle, and a handful of older men who'd been watching in silence and drinking 16-ounce cans of Busch light started dancing around and gesturing as if they were part of the entertainment. Andrews encouraged the kid trumpeter to sing "New Orleans Street Parade" and sang a scat vocal call-and-response, urging him to take another chorus. Andrews then played the opening strains of "Georgia," but when he started to sing, he changed it to "Louisiana." The crowd went nuts, filling the tip bucket with paper money, and Andrews took a bow.

I was impressed to see Andrews still playing on the street with whatever other musicians showed up even on a slow day. His commitment to the process of his craft went deeper than just personal discipline, though. He has been playing in this exact spot since he was younger than that red-faced trumpeter, learning from the legendary Tuba Fats. Though his career had taken him through spectacular ups and downs over the years with the Jazz Babies, the Li'l Rascals and New Birth brass bands, and the Andrews Family Band, he always came back to the hallowed spot in the square overlooked by Saint Louis Cathedral to keep in touch with the roots of his music.

However, playing in the street was also still a matter of survival for Glen David Andrews. In the year since he had stood in front of city hall and challenged the mayor to step up and do his job for the people at the Silence Is Violence rally, Glen David's fortunes had not kept pace with his notoriety. He was still sleeping on a cot in a FEMA trailer and kept his worldly possessions in a suitcase. Another year had meant more lifetime friends who'd passed away, more heartbreak, and more weary days and sleepless nights redeemed by precious moments of musical transcendence. He had been arrested for playing in a funeral second line honoring his friend Kerwin James in Treme just a few blocks from Jackson Square. You might think that would be a low point, but for Glen David Andrews it was a badge of honor, an act of civil disobedience in the service of the second-line tradition, which is so much a part of his identity.

"You have to just do it," he said of the jazz funerals and street parades. "They shouldn't even ask for permission. I've been second-lining all my life, and I'm going to keep on doing it. We paraded in the Treme yesterday for about three hours. Nobody bothered us."

Andrews walked across the square, past the equestrian statue of the charismatic general who won the first battle of New Orleans, Andrew Jackson. The trombonist and singer, an unlikely warrior in the latest battle for the city's survival, sat down in a wrought-iron chair under the eaves at the Cafe du Monde and talked about playing in Jackson Square.

"I like to play in Jackson Square," he said:

> I live for this. I'm not just doing it for the weekend. I like playing this music for people who've never heard it, and I like teaching young people how to play it. That's what I'm interested in doing, teaching people. I started out at the Sound Café teaching children how to play music. Give them a little direction. Nobody's teaching the traditional music. The only way you can really hear the traditional music is through the Treme Brass Band or at Preservation Hall.

Before the storm, Glen David was one of the bad boys of the new brass-band scene, which was evolving incestuously alongside the enormously popular New Orleans hip-hop style, bounce. He recorded the contemporary brass-band anthem "Knock with Me, Rock with Me" with the New Birth Brass Band. The song included a reference to his late cousin Darnell ("D-Boy") Andrews: "Who dat shot D-Boy, y'all?" However, after Katrina, Glen David devoted himself to playing music with his traditional New Orleans jazz band, the Lazy Six, and became a regular attraction at Preservation Hall.

"For me to earn a spot to play at Preservation Hall with my band is the ultimate honor," he said:

> When I saw the Olympia Brass Band for the first time—when I was like six or seven years old—I knew I wanted to be a part of that. I knew when I saw James Andrews at the [1984 New Orleans] World's Fair, I knew I was gonna be playing with him. I grew up with it in the Treme. It was all around me. Ironing Board Sam. James Black lived around the corner. I grew up with the Olympia, the Pinstripe Brass Band all my life, and I realize that's my niche. I love to sing the old tunes. Every Sunday when I get on the stand at Preservation Hall, I get a chill. They didn't used to do three sets, but now we're bringing in that many people every Sunday. The people at Preservation Hall saw what we were doing at Sound Café and said that would fit in with what they were doing at Preservation Hall. When I play there, I get to do songs by guys like Bunk Johnson, Punch Miller, and Red Allen. It's a dream come true.

A waiter strolled by in his green Café du Monde apron, and Glen David ordered a coffee. "I don't believe that stuff about all musicians do dope or you gotta do dope if you wanna be a musician," he said. He was talking from hard experience, as if he had to reassure himself on the point. "I don't believe that. People do it because they enjoy it. You take a chance on it, you're gonna like it. You're even gonna work with it for a couple of years."

He paused. His eyes widened. "You're gonna wind up broken by it," he said:

> I can't be doing any of that stuff no more. Welch's grape juice. That's it for me. If I didn't have the help of my family—because my family is very close knit—when I see 'em, I talk to them every day. If I was a weak-minded person, I'd be back on drugs. I'd most likely have killed myself by now. I look out the door of the trailer, and there's a woman across the street with her two babies, and they're sleeping on the street. Man, that shit breaks my heart.
>
> I watched the crack ravage Treme, man. I watched it. That crack came to New Orleans. It tore everything up. So many musicians got caught up in it. My grandfather Jessie Hill, he would get a royalty check, he'd be travelin' around in his limousine, doin' that crack. Then he'd be broke again. All the young musicians got into that dope, and they think

it makes them sound better. Meanwhile, you sweatin' like a dog, and your eyes is poppin' outta your head.

His struggle for sobriety mirrored his decision to move away from the brass band/hip-hop connection. "I did 'Knock with Me, Rock with Me' with the New Birth Brass Band," he acknowledged:

But that ain't what I want to do. I'm through with that. The new shit disses the old folks. And I just don't want to be part of hip-hop. I don't like all that "nigga," "bitch" bullshit. It's violence. It's not music. It's one chord over the same groove over and over. No offense to the Hot 8. No offense to the Soul Rebels. I like all those people as people. I don't want to listen to that. "That's the street thing," they say. "I'm trying to do something new." How the hell are you going to do that if you don't know where it came from? Do you know "Palm Court Strut?" Do you know who Danny Barker was? You need to find out about some of these things. You need to go by George Buck [owner of the city's biggest traditional jazz label and the Palm Court Jazz Cafe] and get you a couple of them records.

We just don't have nobody trying to play that good music. These bands, you can't tell them. You try to get them interested in the old stuff, they won't do it. I asked one of the Stooges if he'd play "Down by the Riverside," and he said, "I don't play that."

"I told a drummer last night from a brass band, he came to the Sixth Ward. He was sweatin' all over. He said, "I think I ought to go home," and I said, "I think you should, too." He called me up later and thanked me. "You a musician, man. Carry yourself like a musician."

Andrews said he learned how to carry himself from Tuba Fats. "Suits and ties," he said, shaking his head from side to side:

At Preservation Hall, if you don't come out there with a coat and tie, you can go home. You could be the tuba player, somebody I need. If you don't come with a suit and tie, you can go home. That's the way I learned it. Tuba Fats done told me that's the way you run a band. You gotta pay them, make sure everybody's looking good and professional and sounding good. Otherwise, it's gonna fall on you.

"They gave me a horn when I was a kid and said, 'Do this,' and I been doin' this ever since," he said:

I used to come by Tuba Fats, and he'd have me play the bass drum. He'd say, "Sit there and do this." I didn't realize it at the time, but he was training me. My cousins James and Troy Andrews, Nicholas Payton—they were my earliest influences. They all played together in brass bands. Kerwin James, who just passed away, he was there. I lived two houses from the Cozy Corner. My mother, Vanna Acker, sang opera. Eight of the younger kids are named James Andrews. You know the New Kids Brass Band? Well, that's all my cousin's and brother's children. Three of them in the band are named Glen Andrews. So the three of them and me and my cousin with the Rebirth, we went to Channel 4 about two months ago. Everybody is signing in as Glen Andrews. The security guard say, "Y'all come here. I don't know if you take security seriously or not, but this is not funny." So we all get to pullin' out our IDs, and he saw that we were all Glen Andrews. It all started there in the Sixth Ward."

The Sixth Ward is a long, narrow strip between Esplanade and St. Philip that includes the Treme neighborhood, where Glen David grew up. The city has slowly encroached on the neighborhood, beginning with the building of the I-10 overpass on Claiborne Avenue, which wiped out the heart of Treme's business district, then with the expanded Armstrong Park. Now, since Katrina, lifelong residents like Glen David Andrews find themselves locked out of their neighborhoods with little chance of returning.

"Cyril Neville was right to say what he said," said Andrews:

He said, "We didn't leave New Orleans. New Orleans kicked us out." You know, on one hand the city wants to use you to promote it: "Come to New Orleans to hear the great music," but on the other hand there's no place for you here. It's like the Musicians' Village, which I have a real problem with. And not just because they turned me down for a house. They turned down most of the musicians who applied, most of the brass-band members. The only people who are qualifying are people with good credit, older people with Social Security and folks like that. How does that help us, really? How are you supposed to have good credit when you're wiped out, lost all your possessions, and are living in somebody else's trailer? Even if I had good credit, if I could get a loan from a bank, what do I want to live in the Ninth Ward for anyway? I grew up in the real Musicians' Village, Treme. I wanna live in the real Musicians' Village, not in the Ninth Ward. But right now I'm living in a trailer.

Like Neville and many others, Glen David Andrews was evacuated to Texas after the storm. "I was in Houston for six months, but I left," he said:

I was stressed. They don't welcome us there. They have an ad campaign right now there, encouraging all the people in Houston to buy a gun to protect themselves from those people from New Orleans. "Those people." They did have that bunch of assholes that went out there killing everybody, but that doesn't represent the rest of us.

I tried to move back into my house in New Orleans, but it didn't pass the FEMA inspection, so we all had to move out. I could have cried. It was during Jazz Fest. I was kind of down because I was looking for a house, and I only had a week in town before I had to go back to Texas. There was only that one last gig. It felt like my final link to New Orleans. I was really discouraged until I played that first number. I've been feeling better ever since.

Without the neighborhoods like Treme, a big part of the social infrastructure that kept the traditional brass bands going is just gone. Not only that, many of the older musicians who played in those brass bands were unable to return to the city after the flood or were in such poor health they couldn't pick up where they left off. "They ran 'em off," Andrews insisted. "Earnest 'Doc' Watson and Mr. Smith, the only two active surviving members of the Olympia Brass Band, are outside New Orleans. I used to talk to Doc Watson all my days."

His voice began to catch, and I thought Glen David was about to cry, but he kept talking:

I would just call him and talk to him. He ain't here to do that anymore. There's no Tuba Fats left in the Sixth Ward. You do have the Backstreet Cultural Museum. Sylvester Francis is doing a good job of teaching them kids. Tuba Fats taught everybody—and not just about the music. He took us to London every year to play, and he took us to Amsterdam.

The best place you're going to hear traditional jazz on Bourbon Street is the Maison Bourbon. Jamil Sharif is there to commemorate the traditional music. That's the thing about the tradition. You've got to know "Sunny Side of the Street" before you can know "Gimme a Dime." You've got to know the tradition. And that's what's happening with these new brass bands. It's the same thing with these Indian chiefs. Everybody wants to be the Big Chief now. There's like twenty-three chiefs now; nobody wants to start off being the Spyboy.

Later that night Andrews traveled uptown to Carrollton Avenue to play his weekly gig with the Lazy Six at Mid-City Lanes Rock 'N' Bowl. The night was bleak, and even fewer people showed up than had seen GDA that gloomy afternoon at Jackson Square. When he finished playing, Glen David dashed farther uptown to the Maple Leaf, where two other cousins were playing with Rebirth. Maybe he would sit in for a couple of songs, maybe just hang. Andrews told me one of his cousins "went home to a little crappy hotel across the street. That's home. That's gotta be hard." Perhaps not as hard, though, as living as a guest in a relative's FEMA trailer. "I look at it that I am actually homeless," he said:

> I'm living in my uncle's trailer. I'm cold in the motherfucking trailer, sittin' there in my jacket. So I wrote a song about it at 3 A.M. this morning, "Cold in the Trailer." Little things get to you. I like to sit at the table and read the paper in the morning. But if I sit in that trailer I'll go crazy. I'm up and out of there by 8 A.M. It's hard.
>
> What pisses me off every morning is my suit that I have to wear has to be folded up and put away every night in a suitcase because there's nowhere to hang it. That's a psychological problem. It wears on you over time. FEMA gave me $4,700 dollars. I lost my whole life for $4,700. That's how people get strung out. I think I'm qualified to go crazy. We need mental health counseling here in New Orleans. Everybody here ought to see some kind of a psychiatrist. But I know God. And I know God is merciful. And I know he'll look down on me and give me the courage to keep going.

Exhausted, Glen David Andrews let his head fall into his hands. Even talking about what he'd been through took so much out of him he had to pause and take a deep breath before continuing.

"You've got to know what you want in life," he concluded:

> I know I want to own a house. I'm getting ready to have a family. I just have to be patient and wait. I'm gonna keep teaching the traditional stuff. I'm gonna keep it alive, man. I'm gonna party with the parades, second-line all the time. I'm gonna wear a suit to every gig. The last fifteen years of my career I've spent backing up. I backed Troy for five years. I backed James for seven years. I backed New Birth for years. The time has come for me to step out on my own. I'm a musician. I don't build houses. I don't paint. I don't know how to paint. I don't know nothin' about changing tires. But I can sing. And that's what I want to do.

Andrews understood that an overview of the New Orleans music scene post-Katrina would reveal that his beloved New Orleans traditional jazz and brass bands were imperiled. Clearly, the city's music community was among those that Katrina hit the hardest. Many of the music's elders, the keepers and teachers of the tradition, had passed away or been incapacitated. They didn't have to die in the federal flood to be mortally wounded by the loss of home and relatives, not to mention the city's poor post-Katrina health care.

A grim example of this trend was underscored shortly after my conversation with Glen David when trumpeter John Brunious, leader of the Preservation Hall Jazz Band for more than twenty years, passed away in Orlando, Florida, where he had been living since the evacuation.

Brunious's life was most likely attenuated by the physical battering he endured during and after Katrina. He remained in his home throughout the storm in a futile attempt to save his possessions, which were eventually all lost in the flood. Brunious lost all six of his trumpets, as well as his archived written and recorded music.

Though he was rescued from the floodwaters, his skin was badly burned during his immersion in the poison sludge, and he developed respiratory problems afterward that initially prevented him from rejoining the band. Brunious ended his days exiled in Florida and hoping to return to his native city.

Brunious and his younger brother Wendell were born to the music through both sides of their family. Their father, also named John Brunious, played trumpet and piano in the early twentieth century and transcribed the classic jazz composition "Bourbon Street Parade." The elder Brunious also wrote and arranged for jazz icons Billy Eckstine and Cab Calloway. Their mother, Nazimova, is from the Santiago family, which included her brother, Willie Santiago, a guitarist who played with Buddy Bolden.

"My grandmother and her brother were musicians, too," said Brunious's nephew Mark Braud, at the time the featured trumpet player in the Harry Connick Orchestra. "Willie Santiago played guitar and banjo. He was one of the earliest recorded jazz guitarists. It's in my blood. I can feel it when I play. I'm really proud of my family. Every time I get a chance to mention them and acknowledge the musicians in my family, I do that. Every time I play I feel like I'm giving homage to them and that I'm carrying on a very important tradition."

Braud remembered hearing his uncle John play as a normal childhood experience. "It was only when I started playing myself that I realized how much of a giant he was on the trumpet," said Braud. "The first time I played at Jazz Fest with NOCCA he gave me a lot of encouragement; he was interested in what I sounded like. We talked about music a lot. He encouraged me to learn about the traditional music. He played with a lot of musicians who played early New Orleans jazz. I tried to learn as much as I can about traditional music. It's very personal to me."

"John had great stage presence," continued Braud. "After watching John play with Preservation Hall, I learned a lot about playing lead, playing for people, about how to front the band and present the music on stage. They were really tight. I had the honor of playing them when my uncle was out of town and couldn't make the gig. I actually played with that band in my uncle's spot, and that was a great pleasure. It would be an honor for me to play with them again."

Braud not only got to play with the PHB again but also eventually took over his uncle's role as leader and front man for the group. His youthful appearance underscores the fact that this music is anything but old fashioned. "I don't feel like traditional music is something that belongs in a museum," Braud said:

> I think the music is still growing. It's called traditional music, but at the same time it can be very modern, depending on your approach. I mean "modern" in the sense of adapting to one's own style of music, not sounding like you're copying something from the 1920s. I don't think it's about that because, when Louis Armstrong was playing this music, his style was constantly evolving. He didn't play the same in the 1920s as he did in the 1950s. His style evolved, his repertoire kept expanding, he was playing all different kinds of songs, so that's what I try to do when I play. I try to have my own voice. I didn't want to sound like anyone else. I have influences, but I think the music is growing. I don't want to play the music of the 1920s or even the way John played or the way Wendell plays. There is a family sound, and I believe I have that family sound through John, through the influence of my grandfather. I can hear the influence from Wendell, and when I play I'm sure those influences can be heard.

In addition to his credentials as a traditional jazz player, Brunious was also a virtuoso performer in classical, big-band and early bop settings. "He was a very diverse stylist," said Braud:

> When I talk to my uncle Wendell, he told me that John was the greatest trumpet player that he ever heard live. He told me he used to listen to John playing Dizzy Gillespie solos and Maynard Ferguson and things like that. Then he could turn around and play traditional music but with a conception that was very modern. He was a musician's musician. Everyone who knew him knew him to be very knowledgeable and have a good understanding of the music. Also he was very interested in the music's development. He would ask me, "Have you heard this, or have you heard that? What are you listening to? What are you working on?"

Brunious's passing at sixty-seven shook the city's jazz community, where he had made many lifelong friends. "I first saw John Brunious play when I was a youngster during my Fairview Baptist Church Brass Band days circa 1970–74," recalled one of those friends, trumpeter Leroy Jones:

I remember actually meeting him for the first time back in 1976 when I was playing at the La Strada, on Bourbon Street, and John was the trumpet player with drummer June Gardner's Gentlemen of Jazz—during the early 1980s, when there were more clubs with live jazz on Bourbon Street. I had the opportunity to share the bandstand with John when he played piano for a period during his career. These were clubs like Maison Bourbon and the Famous Door. Occasionally we would also appear together within the brass-band context, usually as trumpeters with groups like the Tuxedo Brass Band, when alto saxophonist Herman Sherman was its bandleader.

The thing about John that made him stand out from others as a player was his leadership ability, and as with other bona fide jazz musicians, he possessed a very personal style and sound. The last time I saw John was before Hurricane Katrina. He was playing at the Preservation Hall. On his break we were happy to see one another. He was always telling me how great I've been sounding. But in reality I think he was the great one, a pioneer and mentor for many to follow. John's role or place in New Orleans music has been established long ago through a musical family legacy that I imagine goes back even beyond his talented father, John ("Picket") Brunious Sr., and is continued to be upheld by his younger brother Wendell and nephew Mark Braud. All is not lost with them being here.

Like Brunious, Jones was first exposed to New Orleans traditional jazz through the brass bands he saw in funeral processions on the streets as a child. Brass bands and traditional New Orleans jazz now seem to be two different genres to many people, but in the end they are the same music, an understanding that Jones shared with Brunious and is perhaps one of the key secrets of New Orleans music in general.

"I share the same experience as John in respect to being exposed to jazz through listening and performing with brass bands at funerals, as well as second-line parades," said Jones. "From my experience I've always been able to hear and see that all New Orleans music is connected, be it traditional brass band music or contemporary, rhythm and blues, funk, and soul. There is a familiar sound, a feeling, a beat, a matching blood type that flows through all of its various genres."

Clint Maedgen, the musician/conceptualist/promoter who cofounded the New Orleans Bingo! Show and became an organizer of local attractions at Voodoo Fest, joined the Preservation Hall band in 2005 as a singer and saxophonist when the group began to include songs like "Complicated Life" and "Skin and Bone," written by Ray Davies of the Kinks. Maedgen was profoundly influenced by Brunious.

"I think of him every day," said Maedgen. "John was a really special person. His death really seemed like out of the blue. I'm still trying to understand it. He was such a complete musician, so versatile. There are so many stories, like the time John got a call to play with James Brown when he came through town and his trumpeter was sick. He was New Orleans."

Maedgen pointed out that performing with Brunious was a constant learning experience, especially "the way he listened to the melodies of songs." Maedgen continued:

> We recorded "I Can't Give You Anything but Love" two years ago, but when we would go over, it he would keep exploring the melody. "Let me sing it to you one more time," he would say. You're never done with a song. It grows forever. Like the way he sang "Do You Know What It Means to Miss New Orleans?"—his signature song. That was my momma's favorite song. I've been hearing that my whole life, but he never did it the same way twice. He was always in the moment.
>
> I spent a lot of times with Mr. John before he passed. He would sit with me at the piano. I don't think a lot of people even knew he played piano, and he would say [affects a dignified, low-register voice], "Sing it again, Clint. Let's get it right. This is the melody." He was an incredible teacher. Working with him, I kept learning all these new tunes all the time. And that's just the music, man. That's not the life lessons I learned.

Ben Jaffe, Preservation Hall's director and sousaphonist/bassist in the band, had been planning to make a tribute album to Brunious's father when John passed:

"John and I were working on a brass-band project to honor the Young Tuxedo Brass Band, who were recorded at John's father's house by Atlantic records in 1958," said Jaffe:

> I brought John the idea of re-creating that record with John playing first trumpet and his brother Wendell playing second trumpet. John was touched by that idea, and we were trying to do the project at his family home in the Seventh Ward even though it was destroyed by Katrina. He was looking forward to it, and we were putting a band together to do the project and actually had a recording date scheduled for April. John had been to New Orleans recently to have some dental work done, and his chops were strong. It's even more important to do this project now that John's not here.

CHAPTER 15

If I Can Help Somebody

Though the new generation of brass bands, made up of younger performers, had a better survival rate than the old-timers (despite the fact that some of them had passed as well), many of them had been displaced to other cities and had to commute back to New Orleans just to meet their live-performance obligations. Others were still living out of suitcases in FEMA trailers or with friends. When you have to hustle to put a roof over your head every night, making your next album isn't your first priority.

By 2008 the brass bands were back in force, but they were fragile institutions after the loss of the neighborhoods that had nurtured them. Without New Orleans east, the lower Ninth Ward, Gentilly, and huge swaths of uptown and with the traditional music community of Treme overrun by gentrification, the young people who represent the future of the brass bands and of African American culture in general were diminished in number.

The entire New Orleans brass-band tradition, a central element of the cultural roots of New Orleans jazz history, was at a crossroads. For more than a hundred years the tradition was based on providing proper burial services for the members of the social clubs in the city's black neighborhoods. The repertoire consisted of a handful of compositions—dirges played on the way to the cemetery, uptempo numbers played after the burial—that amounted to a ritual in which everyone who belonged to these organizations was given a similar transition to the afterlife. A generation ago a movement of young musicians, many of whom were trained in the brass-band tradition by Tuba Fats, broke from these traditions and infused the style with an audacious sound of its own, a sound that incorporated funk, cartoon jingles, pop tunes, and eventually hip-hop into a heady mix that created a new dance music.

When this new wave of brass bands began, the traditionalists still outnumbered them, but especially in the wake of Katrina many of the older players had passed away or were incapacitated. The younger bands, unaccustomed or unwilling to handle the funeral events in the traditional manner, were no longer able to perform the ritual function of these jazz funerals to their elders' satisfaction. Moreover, these new brass bands faced another obstacle as well. Cut off from the tradition and from the ritual that supported it, how could they continue to grow and establish their own sound? The absence of a serious recording industry in New Orleans appeared to be a major impediment to their future because, without new recordings with new compositions on them, they are relegated to repeating themselves, at which point they've become another tradition. However, this time it's a tradition with no ritual or meaning to back it up, just another popular music style unable to grow past its original instincts.

The fact that so many brass bands were still working at all was a testament to the sacrifices the musicians were willing to make to ensure that they were heard. The Rebirth Brass Band was one of the first groups to return to New Orleans after Katrina. It played three gigs on October 29, 2005, opening the truncated Voodoo Music Experience, playing a daytime gig in the French Quarter, and a marathon show at Tipitina's that night. Tuba Phil Frazier was chosen to be the subject of the 2007 Congo Square poster at Jazz Fest. The beautiful poster represented the spirit of recovery and became a symbolic rallying point for the brass-band movement.

"They called me to get my permission because I had to pose for the artist," said Frazier. "I was really excited. I was so happy because it meant so much to me and all of my family and friends. To be on that poster meant that I was going to represent New Orleans. It made everybody feel proud."

Frazier downplayed the idea that Katrina stopped all the brass bands in their tracks. He pointed out that Rebirth was back in action a few weeks after the flood even though some of its members were commuting from Texas to play. Perhaps in part because the band got back on its feet so quickly, Rebirth completed its first release since Katrina, 25, in time for Jazz Fest 2008.

"It's a two-CD release to celebrate our twenty-fifth anniversary," said Frazier:

> It's got a lot of old things we did on it and some of the new things we're doing. We wanted to show where we've been but also how far we've come. All of it is new [recordings], and it all works together. None of the new songs are about Katrina. We chose to avoid writing songs about Katrina and what happened because after all everyone has been through, we didn't want to dwell on that anymore. We wanted it to be positive, like this is where we're going now. We're moving on.

Nevertheless, post-Katrina hardships were a fact of life that impacted most brass-band players. None of the new brass bands had to overcome more adversity than the Hot 8, which was in the process of putting together an album when drummer Dinerral Shavers was killed in 2006. Shavers was the third member of the Hot 8 to be shot to death since Bennie Peete had formed the band in 1994. Jacob Johnson, the group's 17-year-old trumpet player, was killed in his home in 1996, and 22-year-old trombonist Joseph ("Shotgun Joe") Williams was gunned down by police in 2004. After Katrina, trumpeter Terrell Batiste lost his legs in a traffic accident in Atlanta when he was hit on the freeway while putting up cones to alert other motorists that his car had broken down.

"We were putting an album together, a tribute album to Jacob Johnson and Shotgun Joe, when Dinerral was killed," said Peete. "We had to step back from that, but we may continue the project and include Dinerral with the others."

The Hot 8 also joined Glen David Andrews in trying to pick up the older brass-band traditions and to follow up on those roots. They turned to Dr. Michael White, a clarinetist and teacher who is a tireless advocate for traditional jazz, to help tutor the Hot 8 in the old music. Meanwhile, the members of the Hot 8 also set out to reclaim their birthright as New Orleans musicians by joining the Preservation Hall Jazz Band and other local musicians to record an outstanding album with the gospel group Blind Boys of Alabama, *Down in New Orleans.*

After sixty-nine years in the business of singing gospel, the Blind Boys of Alabama's lead singer, Jimmy Carter, still had something new to learn about his music when he came to New Orleans to make a record. "I was surprised because we've never done it before, recording with New Orleans musicians," said Carter,

Figure 26. Hot 8 Brass Band plays at the French Market stage. Photo by John Swenson. Used by permission of John Swenson.

the last remaining original member of the group. "But it sounded real good together, the gospel and the New Orleans music."

The Blind Boys of Alabama have been bringing gospel music to secular audiences for much of their career, but even though they've sung material written by popular musicians like Tom Waits and Stevie Wonder in recent years, the recordings were always gospel-style arrangements. *Down in New Orleans* was remarkable in that, like a reversible coat of many colors, it worked equally well as a gospel album backed by New Orleans musicians and as a New Orleans recording with great vocalists.

This genre-bending achievement was obviously due in large part to the extraordinary talents of the Blind Boys as vocalists and the New Orleans instrumentalists who accompanied them—the Preservation Hall Band, the Hot 8 Brass Band, pianists Allen Toussaint and David Torkanowsky, drummer Shannon Powell, and bassist Roland Guerin.

Still, something else was at work here as well. *Down in New Orleans* demonstrated the deep influence that gospel music had on the music of New Orleans, from traditional jazz to the latest incarnation of street music played by the Hot 8.

The record opened with a funk bass line and a jumping New Orleans rhythm before Carter and company joined in to sing "Free at Last," a classic piece of gospel whose rhythmic underpinnings were dislodged by the backing musicians. When Torkanowsky played the dancing piano solo, the record was pure New Orleans R&B. As soon as the Blind Boys joined in for the next verse, it was back to hard gospel. As the song moved into its coda and the voices reached an exultant call-and-response peak climaxed by eight bars of Carter's astonishing, jagged-edged scream, an amazing gospel/R&B synthesis was achieved. Carter's voice reached a place in this moment that some of the biggest stars of soul and R&B have searched for in vain.

"That's where James Brown got it from. James Brown said he got it from the Blind Boys," noted Chris Goldsmith, who produced *Down in New Orleans* and has worked on all of the Blind Boys' releases since *Spirit of the Century*, the 2001 recording that broke them through to a pop audience. "Little Richard said it, too, listening to those Specialty gospel records back in the '50s."

Even though Goldsmith helped put the pieces together on *Down in New Orleans*, he was still overwhelmed by the power of the outcome. "It went as well as it possibly could have gone," he said:

> We did exactly what we were trying to do. We wanted to go to New Orleans and make a record that incorporated the sound of the Neville Brothers and Dr. John, as well as the Mahalia Jackson influence and, of course, the Blind Boys. It all came together. It could not have gone any better. The Blind Boys and Preservation Hall are a perfect fit. There're

not many singers you could put with Preservation Hall who would be as complementary.

We were trying to contemplate how the music of New Orleans could complement what they were doing. We had a lot of discussions with the band about what the next recording would be, and the affinities with New Orleans music just seemed to work really well, songs like "Down by the Riverside" and the history of Mahalia Jackson and bands like Preservation Hall. We had played a lot in New Orleans as well, at the gospel tent and at the House of Blues. They've been around that city for a long time and always loved it.

The setting for this magic exchange was Piety Street Studio, where the Hot 8 could shoot hoops in the backyard and Shannon Powell's wife could cook gumbo, jambalaya, and cornbread for the whole crew. The whole session was finished in three whirlwind days at the Bywater studio. "We loved Piety Street," Goldsmith said. "We'd been there before. We did the Aaron Neville 'Joy to the World' track on the Blind Boys' Christmas record. We tracked that live at Piety Street in '04, and it was a great experience. The whole vibe was wonderful. There are so many memories—the food, the Hot 8 Band hanging around, the amazing moment when Toussaint came in."

Allen Toussaint played piano on two tracks, both central to the recording's success. "Down by the Riverside," which also featured the Preservation Hall band, opened with a graceful piano figure. Though this song was a regular feature of the Blind Boys' shows, Toussaint gave it a touch of Crescent City swing. His piano managed to subtly drape the familiar chorus with a new feel. The piano solo was a masterpiece of thematic translucence, a nuanced, understated translation of the melody.

"It just happened," Goldsmith marveled:

> He just walked in and did it. David Torkanowsky, who was on the session, stuck around to watch Allen, and he said, "It will be very interesting to see how he approaches this. It's a song we've heard so many times." Allen came in and took a whole different approach from what we might have expected. David said, "Wow, that wasn't at all what I was thinking he'd do. It was just perfect." It was a very exciting moment; he took the song and made it into something that hadn't been done in that way before. It was all live, one take. We did a safety take, but he nailed it first time through.

The high point of the record was the duet between Carter and Toussaint, "If I Can Help Somebody." "I can't help but crying listening to that even a month later," said Goldsmith:

Jimmy was supposed to be there already. The rest of the band was there, but Jimmy missed the entire first day because his brother had died the week before. He came off the plane right to the session from his brother's funeral, basically. Didn't even go to the hotel. Came right to the studio. Toussaint had already been there for like fifteen minutes. They were introduced to each other, and there was this most amazing, gracious exchange. Then they just went on and did it. It just floored everybody there.

"If I can help somebody in the world, my living will not be in vain," Carter sang, his ragged voice courageously forcing itself into the high register even as it imploded into its throaty rasp. The emotion was stark and inspirational, with Toussaint urging Carter on to the full power of his performance.

"We had a good camaraderie," Carter said of Toussaint. "When we played together, that was my first time meeting him. He was amazing. It's like he knew what I wanted to do without me telling him anything, and he followed everything I sang perfectly. He played along with me. He was right on top of it."

Gospel music is part of the genetic code of New Orleans music, so it's no surprise that the Hot 8 bonded so closely with the Blind Boys both musically and personally. The brass band's street enthusiasm also fit perfectly with the high-energy vocals of the Blind Boys on "Make a Better World" and "I'll Fly Away." The Blind Boys even spent a day hanging out on the streets with the Hot 8, joining in on a second line. "I got along real well with them," said Carter of the Hot 8. "They were great. We really relate to young people. Playing with the Hot 8 is a good opportunity for us to get through to young people; it was like when we recorded with Ben Harper."

Hot 8 sousaphone player Bennie Peete had been eagerly looking forward to playing with the Blind Boys. "I knew it would work out because I grew up in church singing all those gospel songs," he said. "Some of those gospel songs are already in our repertoire. We didn't have any arrangements. We just came up with the parts as we recorded. Everything was done on the spot. They were professional, and we knew what we had to do. It felt like they were a New Orleans band, like one of the local groups, because they came in and did it first time through. They did a good job of playing the New Orleans music."

CHAPTER 16

Baghdad on the Mississippi

Mardi Gras 2008 came early (February 5) and felt grimmer than it had in '06 and '07. It had been a catastrophic year for the locals, who watched the government officials' promises to renew their city fall by the wayside. Still, the New Orleanians were living their lives. The pain left by the flood was still real, and the city seemed to flinch at every piece of bad news, but where else in America do crowds of revelers walk the streets spontaneously singing "Carnival Time"?

As usual, the bullets were also singing a far less merry tune. By February 7 the city had endured twenty-one murders, including an especially bloody Mardi Gras, during which four people were murdered and twelve others were injured by gunfire over a five-day period. Three men and two women parade goers were shot as the Endymion parade, one of the most popular Mardi Gras events, rolled down Canal Street. A tourist took a stray bullet in the head while standing in a hotel lobby. Two more men were shot during the Lundi Gras celebration at the corner of Bourbon Street and Canal.

Anger at the killing of Dinerral Shavers boiled over once again on April 10, when the accused gunman, David Bonds, was acquitted of murder after a trial in which none of the eyewitnesses to the killing would testify against Bonds. One of the passengers in the car when Shavers was killed, Guy McEwen, testified in court without directly fingering Bonds. A week after the trial, the twenty-year-old McEwen was gunned down by a hail of bullets—at least a dozen of two different calibers.

Bonds was brought to trial after prosecutors interviewed an eyewitness, a teenage girl who identified Bonds as the killer. The teenage girl's mother, knowing the danger her daughter was in, counseled her not to testify at the trial. She finally agreed to appear in court but recanted her testimony. When asked whether the killer was in the courtroom, the girl said, "I don't see anybody. I must need glasses."

After reading the jury's verdict of acquittal, the presiding judge in the case, Jerome Winsberg, said to the court "This is like Baghdad."

Violence and lawlessness are long-standing problems in New Orleans, but the unabated run of shootings and murders after Katrina posed a greater problem than ever. Tourism had become the city's most important lifeline to recovery, and news of tourists' being hit by stray bullets during Mardi Gras didn't help the convention business. More important, the breakdown in efficient policing reflected a lack of city services that gave displaced New Orleanians yet another reason to think hard about returning to their beleaguered city. Without a working school system or decent medical care and with a police department in disarray, New Orleans was not an attractive place to raise children.

Nevertheless, musicians kept returning if only because New Orleans was the place that best nurtured their art, and music continued to grow in economic importance. The grim reality on the ground was offset by the relentless spirit that still resided in the music. Music in particular offered spiritual hope at the darkest moments. The French Quarter festival, the most comprehensive showcase for local music, had grown in popularity since the flood, and the 2008 version was the biggest ever. Coming as it did in early April, at the height of spring, the weather, local music, and food were a soothing balm after the difficult winter and vividly illustrated why New Orleans was very much worth saving. Hundreds of thousands of music fans basked on the banks of the Mississippi in the bright sunshine and crowded around the more intimate stages on Bourbon and Royal streets to hear local musicians play their hearts out in the twenty-fifth annual renewal of this festival. This massive free concert performed by Louisiana musicians was a joyous event that lived up to its reputation as Jazz Fest without the musical outsiders. There were plenty of visitors on hand to hear the music, though, especially from Europe and Canada, attracted by the bargain prices for travel and entertainment provided by the weak dollar.

The French Quarter Festival was always based around traditional New Orleans jazz and brass-band music, and the 2008 edition did a good job of keeping those genres in the foreground. Brass bands pumped it up at their stage all weekend, with particularly great moments coming from the Pin Stripe Brass Band and the Soul Rebels. Big Sam's Funky Nation, Trombone Shorty, and Kermit Ruffins all played memorable sets on the big stage.

The French Quarter Festival (FQF) started out in 1974 as a much smaller event that took place on the streets of the Vieux Carré, with a battle of the bands climaxing the day at the corner of Toulouse and Orleans in front of Johnny White's. Traditional bands continue to play to intimate gatherings on the streets of the Quarter during the festival, and trumpeter Leroy Jones turned in a spectacular performance on the 200 block of Bourbon Street. The festival expanded to include a Cajun/zydeco stage at the U.S. Mint, and those bands rocked hard all weekend.

The Friday show at the Pavilion stage along the river was special from start to finish. Guitarist Marc Stone opened up with an ambitious set featuring Joe Krown on keyboards (Krown later played his own set on the same stage, playing in both solo and band settings) and bassist Sam Price of Otra, which would perform at the Mint on Saturday. Stone, who had played another great set the night before at the Ogden Museum of Southern Art (an acoustic duo with Vasti Jackson), closed with a terrific jam on the folk classic "Little Liza Jane."

Susan Cowsill took things to another level with a magic set that opened with her singing Donovan's wistful ballad "Catch the Wind" and balanced Continental Drifters' material, songs from her solo album *Just Believe It*, and even a song she had performed as a child with her family band, "The Rain, the Park, and Other Things." Toward the end of her set Cowsill played a song written by her brother Barry, who died in the aftermath of Katrina, "River of Love." She brought up Paul Sanchez and John Boutté, who helped her draw the show to a dramatic close with her post-Katrina anthem, "Crescent City Sneaux."

On Saturday, Cowsill also sang with Theresa Andersson on the main stage, then joined Paul Sanchez and John Boutté at the Pavilion stage on Sunday. That set was a high point of the festival and a real tribute to Sanchez as an organizer and collaborator who is magnanimous with the stage time he offers his bandmates. Sanchez assembled an outstanding group for this performance and offered Boutté, Cowsill, and trumpeter/vocalist Shamarr Allen equal time while subtly building the set around compositions he wrote on his own or with Boutté. Sanchez handed his guitar to Cowsill for a version of "Crescent City Sneaux" that was even more powerful than the one from her own set. She conveyed a complex mixture of emotions in quick, broad strokes, contrasting the sense of alienation summoned up in the image of being "like a kite without a string" with the elation of remembered moments in New Orleans. "I'll meet you down at Jackson Square, 12 o'clock, I'll be there," she sang, just as the steamboat *Natchez* blew its deep, booming whistle in greeting to the prodigal daughter, who got herself back "to a place where I know who I am." The band backed Cowsill gracefully, with Allen turning in a beautiful trumpet solo, as she touched on Mardi Gras Indian chants and the "Saints" call and response. It was a moment of sheer transcendence.

This memorable set was all gesture and color and subtle rhythms, the two guitars playing well-crafted parts in service of each song's contours rather than leads, Russ Broussard playing drums and percussion gracefully, and gorgeous harmonies throughout. Boutté was in top form, slyly noting, "I always liked Sam Cooke" before channeling the maestro in his wonderful version of "Live in the Moment." Boutté also delivered a brilliant rendition of his first collaboration with Sanchez, "At the Foot of Canal Street," and really stirred the crowd with his flag waver, "Break Down the Door (the Treme Song)." Allen sang his own anthem, "Meet Me on Frenchmen Street," which Sanchez embellished with a chorus of "Won't you come home New Orleans" to the tune of "Bill Bailey," and the two of them performed their Wizard of Oz duet, "If I Only Had a Brain" from the *Funky Kids* album.

The work Sanchez did with what he'd started calling his Rolling Road Show at that FQF was significant because it marked a kind of public unveiling of an artist's collective supported by a group of fans who call themselves the Threadheads. The group started out as a bunch of Jazz Fest fans from different parts of the world who stayed in touch via an Internet thread. Threadheads founder Chris Joseph threw a party during the 2007 Jazz Fest and hired Sanchez, one of the favorite performers of the Threadheads, to play. After the gig Joseph and Sanchez talked, and Joseph asked Sanchez when he was going to make a record. Sanchez explained that he had the songs but lacked the funds to record them.

Joseph came up with a novel idea: The Threadheads would collect money from their members and loan Sanchez the funds to cover the expenses of making his recording, as well as a John Boutté record. Both artists would repay the loan from sales of the albums and would own the property outright thereafter. This was the kind of business arrangement that demonstrated what the music-loving culture of New Orleans could generate as a business model. The fans wanted to hear certain music and were willing to pay for it. They trusted the artists to pay back the loans, and the artists were eager to do so because they could make their records and own them outright. It was a great deal for everybody as long as the level of trust was maintained.

Sanchez recorded a definitive solo album that branded his new post–Cowboy Mouth career, *Exit to Mystery Street*. Sanchez was able to pay back the Threadhead loan within a year of making the album. Boutté also recorded a solo album on a Threadheads loan, *Good Neighbor*, the best record he'd ever made. Shamarr Allen made a strong debut record, thanks to the Threadheads, while Susan Cowsill used one loan to remaster *Just Believe It* and another to make a new album. Glen David Andrews used Threadhead funding to make a great gospel record; the innovative Nightcrawlers Brass Band made a record, *Slither Slice*, that never would have happened without Threadhead money; and Alex McMurray signed on to make his best recording, *How to Be a Cannonball*. Sanchez went on to release two more albums and a book with Threadhead backing. In the space of less than a year, Threadhead records became one of the most important record companies in New Orleans, and Sanchez was in the middle of it all.

There were many other great moments over that FQF weekend. The Radiators returned to New Orleans after a grueling run through Colorado for a Friday-night set that rippled with numinous beauty and was highlighted by an inspirational ode to the Mississippi, "Riverrun." The high water rolled majestically past and sparkled with the reflected nighttime light as the Radiators joyfully celebrated its spirit.

Fans of this extraordinary band know how special the Rads have been for thirty years. In that time no two sets have been the same inasmuch as principal songwriter Ed Volker has penned thousands of songs while he, front man Dave Malone, and the rest of the band have mined the history of New Orleans music dating back to Jelly Roll Morton and worked up arrangements of traditional folk, country, and classic rock songs that allow them to classify all their material as "Fish-Head music."

CHAPTER 17

Brown Baby Dead in the Water

In 2008, readers of the *Times-Picayune* learned something about the New Orleans Jazz and Heritage Festival before the gates even opened. A front-page story in the April 24 edition gave details of the large post-Katrina shift in the city's population: There were 100,000 fewer voters in the New Orleans area that year, and the number of African Americans was falling "sharply." From 2003 to 2007 voter turnout in the almost completely black neighborhoods of Gentilly, eastern New Orleans, and the lower Ninth Ward was down nearly 60 percent. Across the region the number of black voters had dropped 41 percent from 2003 to 2007, while the number of white voters had dropped 15 percent.

The changed demographic had an obvious effect on the traditionally interracial makeup of the Jazz Fest crowd. With the city roughly a third smaller since the storm, the impact of these visiting music revelers was even more pronounced, especially since that demographic loss was predominantly in the city's black population. New Orleans became Jazz Fest City for the ten days of the event, and the Fair Grounds crowd seemed particularly empty of locals with the notable exception of the second Sunday, when the Neville Brothers, Maze (featuring Frankie Beverley), and Santana were all on the bill.

Just as the Jazz Fest gospel tent was moved to a more prominent location on the newly configured Fair Grounds site, the African American people that had made up much of its audience over the years were in noticeably fewer numbers. The tent used to pulse with the fervor of a black, sanctified church service every day from start to finish. That year, sitting in the nearly all-white audience at the gospel tent as the MCs harangued the mildly curious and mostly uninvolved audience was a surreal event, especially when the repeated urgings to "support the troops" and renditions of "God Bless America" gave the tent the fervent but artificial feel of a political rally.

On the first weekend I overheard a woman say, "I haven't seen a single black face in the crowd all day." The statement seemed like an exaggeration at the time, but it stuck in my mind as I noticed the sea of white faces throughout the festival.

One of the nicest things about Jazz Fest was the way in which it always appeared to cross racial boundaries so effortlessly, but a tipping point had apparently occurred. With fewer blacks in the city and fewer locals able to afford the $50 ticket, Jazz Fest seemed to have edged toward becoming strictly a tourist destination, and the number of Key West and Cancun T-shirts in the crowd brought that point home. I overheard one of the security guards at the private-party Miller tent tell a local woman who was trying to find a friend, "This isn't a charity." The irony is that the city wanted and needed these tourists, but catering to them came at the price of surrendering part of the city's very identity. Moreover, that security guard should have known that the foundation that runs the festival is, if not a charity, at least a nonprofit organization.

The festival had grown into something that was quite different from what it had started out as. Corporate sponsorship had been a developing issue over the last decade, and headlining acts that had nothing to do with New Orleans gave the festival broader appeal but watered down its unique identity. However, now that Jazz Fest had become one of the key economic engines driving the city's recovery, its connection with corporate sponsorship became even more complicated. Shell Oil Company became the festival's biggest sponsor, and henceforth official descriptions of the event were required to refer to the "New Orleans Jazz and Heritage Festival Presented by Shell." However, Shell's complicity in the destruction of the wetlands protecting the city made it a prime target of the musicians and activists, who demanded that the oil companies do something about restoring the destroyed wetlands, which act as a natural barrier to the kind of storm surge that had inundated the city. The irony was profound: Shell was helping to rebuild the city's economy even as it was ensuring that New Orleans would be destroyed in the near future.

So the greatest music festival in the world took place even as some of the musicians participating in it blamed its main sponsor for threatening the future of their homes. In addition, it wasn't just the musicians taking on Shell. Walter Williams, the New Orleans artist who created the Mr. Bill character made famous on *Saturday Night Live,* used his clay puppet as a voice against the oil industry. "Shell, Hear the Music," read Mr. Bill's statement, which flew from a plane circling the Fair Grounds during the festival. "Fix the Coast That You Broke."

Despite all the hardships they'd endured, the evidence on the ground at Jazz Fest suggested that the brass bands were alive and well. The Jazz and Heritage stage featured brass bands and Mardi Gras Indians tearing it up all day, every day. The brass bands were well cared for within the confines of the festival structure, but on the streets of New Orleans, where the culture was born and was still nurtured, the future remained grim. Even as brass bands played for tourists at Jazz Fest, a short distance away police were breaking up a black second-line parade under the Claiborne Avenue overpass, part of a funeral service for a local educator. This kind of banana-republic disconnect between the tourists and the citizens of the city was more than just an embarrassment to the Jazz Fest brass. It served as a potential death sentence for the future of New Orleans culture.

When the gates to the Fair Grounds opened on Friday morning in mildly sunny, near-perfect weather, the fans encountered an expanded and reconfigured setup for the stages at the festival, passing newly erected tents for the Gospel, Jazz, and Blues stages pitched in the parking lot. The first must-see set came at 11:20, when the Susan Cowsill Band opened up the Acura Stage. Cowsill's set kicked off a full day of outstanding music performed by women on that stage—local country/rockabilly singer and roadhouse queen Kim Carson; the eclectic and imaginative Theresa Andersson; Alison Krauss with Robert Plant; and headliner Cheryl Crow. At her French Quarter Festival show Cowsill joked that she was originally going to headline but decided to switch with Crow. Crow was an interesting headliner—she'd recorded in New Orleans, an experience that she described to me as simultaneously thrilling and frightening when I interviewed her for UPI a few years back.

Cowsill, Carson, and Andersson were all New Orleans bandleaders. The three women shared the stage during each other's sets in an enthusiastic display of friendship and solidarity. "I've made it to the big-girl stage," Cowsill said happily during her set. But her voice was a fully mature instrument at Jazz Fest.

Kim Carson followed with a good-natured set of Louisiana country and roots rock, a crowd-pleasing mixture heavy on letting "the bon temps rouler," striking a Jimmy Buffet moment with the chorus, "Tequila makes my clothes fall off," and delivering lines about her favorite bar, "a shot and a beer kind of joint." Carson celebrated the fact that "the fancy crowd don't fancy me," and the unfancy Jazz Fest crowd loved it. Louisiana country music is its own tradition, and Carson is proud to be "a honky-tonk girl" who sings "we don't need no achy-breaky or Shania Twain." Carson went on to give her statement of purpose: "I like real country music, the real deal, not pop music with steel guitars. One of my favorites was Hank Williams. I was trying to channel Hank on this song." After singing the honky-tonk blues of "Hank's Song," Carson said to the audience, "It occurs to me that I write a lot of drinking songs for a Baptist girl. I didn't drink at all until I moved to New Orleans." Then she went on to perform "I Only Like You When I'm Drinking."

On the Blues stage Barbara Lynn was great, performing her hits "You'll Lose a Good Thing" and "Baby, We Got a Good Thing Goin.'" She accompanied herself on electric guitar, playing chords and note clusters to accent her vocal lines like a country blues singer, then throwing in four- and eight-bar breaks for dramatic effect. It was powerful stuff, and when she sang the gospel soul of Ray Charles's "What'd I Say," playing a guitar break in the intro that struck like lightning, I felt the first crowd-melting moment of Jazz Fest ecstasy pass through the tent.

At the Fais Do-Do stage the zydeco and Cajun acts seldom disappoint the avid dancers who congregate there. The Zydepunks, more klezmer than zydeco, really whip up a storm; as one of the most popular young bands in the city since the storm, they got things off to a raucous start that day. Dwayne Dopsie and the Zydeco Hellraisers proceeded to throw their own party, building up to Dopsie's hit "Where'd My Baby Go" and featuring the gut-busting R&B saxophone playing of Derek Huston. Huston's honking solos emphasized the connection between zydeco and classic New Orleans R&B.

The Fais Do-Do stage continued its hot run with Bruce Daigrepont, who played his diatonic accordion and sang in Cajun French with a strong, warbling voice that rolled alongside his accordion and Gina Forsyth's magnificent fiddle playing like river currents. Forsyth, who also played with the Malvinas, an all-woman group, and on her own, is a good songwriter in her own right and got a showcase spot in the set. The high point of Daigrepont's set was a new song translated as "Welcome to South Louisiana," which name-checked a series of towns with French names. Daigrepont gave a shout out to all "les habitants."

Terrance Simien closed the Fais Do-Do stage with a skillful set that consolidated a series of crowd-pleasing tunes with breakdowns that allowed him to throw beads to the audience with his toes and present the first Cajun/Zydeco Grammy ever awarded several times as if holding aloft the grail itself. As the sun peeked out from behind the luminous clouds, casting long shadows on the dancers cavorting on the clumpy grass in front of the Fais Do-Do stage, the smile on Simien's face told the story. In this moment he was in a kind of paradise, as close to heaven on earth as anyone is ever likely to get. He displayed that Grammy one more time, got a huge roar from the crowd, and finished off with a medley of "Iko Iko"/"Saints"/"Brother John"/"Jambalaya" and then the reggae tune "Pressure Drop."

At the children's tent, bands played, and little children danced on the grass, oblivious to some of the most dramatic artwork ever displayed in New Orleans. The walls of the tent were covered with children's drawings, the result of art-therapy sessions for kids who lived in New Orleans during the flood. Each of these youngsters displayed an innocent's view of this season of horror: heartbreaking scenes that were all the more powerful for their simplicity. Many of the drawings contained images of big snakes in the water surrounding the houses where they lived. One of the pictures showed a dead child in the water next to a huge black snake. There were images of houses under water and people waving from the windows. One image was of a partially submerged house with people on the roof and others peering out from windows below the water level. There was a picture of a little girl standing in front of a desolate cityscape with a question mark hanging in the sky. The girl was crying. Another picture showed a target with a house in the center. Another depicted dead birds with the inscription "Bluebirds on the ground are dead." The most disturbing image was drawn by a child artist who signed his name "Torlon." "This is the hurricane," Torlon had scrawled across the top of his portrayal of the deluge, which showed a small figure tossed on the surface. Torlon's title for the picture was "Brown baby is dead in the water."

Those images were hard to shake as I walked out of the Fair Grounds through the Gentilly gate after the day's music had ended. But the mood of the crowd was joyous, celebratory. Across the street in front of the Seahorse bar, the Free Agents Brass Band turned it up to boil, playing "Little Liza Jane" as the crowd collected around them and danced in the street. Meanwhile, the TBC Brass Band held its own street festival down the block. Day one of Jazz Fest lingered on the street outside Fair Grounds racecourse until the evening sun went down.

Jazz Fest's prime mover, Quint Davis, stood on the Acura stage early Saturday afternoon on day two and looked out over the large and boisterous crowd. Wayne Toups and Zydecajun had just finished an exhilarating set that mixed Cajun and zydeco roots with southern rock dynamics and reflected an arrangement strategy that blended electric and steel guitars artfully with Toups's accordion work. "We ain't afraid of no stinking clouds, are we?" Davis asked the crowd, which roared back its agreement. Meanwhile, Rockie Charles and the Stax of Love were playing old-school Louisiana blues and R&B at the blues tent, performing a fine version of Guitar Slim's "The Things I Used to Do."

The rain started gently, sprinkling the crowd with a soft, easygoing mist. At the Jazz and Heritage stage the Mahogany Brass Band turned up the heat with its big front line of alto and tenor saxophones, three trumpets, and two trombones, delighting the hard-dancing crowd with "Feets, Don't Fail Me Now." The brass-band sound is the kind of music that makes you want to dance in the rain. "We're gonna make everybody forget everything they shouldn't be thinking about," came the promise from the band, which then lurched into a funked-up take on "Watermelon Man."

As the strains of "Saint James Infirmary" dopplered away in the distance, I sluiced over to the Fais Do-Do stage for some Eddie Bo, who made the first reference to Jazz Fest patron saint Professor Longhair I had heard at the'08 event when he said, "My friend's up there having a conference. You know who my friend is, don't you?" He proceeded to launch into Longhair's signature, "Big Chief," and the party rolled on. Bo did his classic dance tune, "Hook and Sling," then launched a New Orleans Popeye party with "Check Mr. Popeye." When he imitated Olive Oyl's high-pitched voice, imploring "Popeye! Popeye!" the crowd went nuts. During "Check Your Bucket" Bo strutted to the front of the stage and started dancing along with the crowd. The rain kept pounding, harder and heavier, and when Bo finally knocked off, the crowd dispersed, looking for a dry spot.

There was little such relief to be found, however, and the rain inundated the Fair Grounds for the rest of the afternoon. That didn't stop the musicians from playing, though it did curtail a few sets, and it certainly didn't keep a hard-core contingent of fans from sticking it out. At the end of the day a dedicated group of those fans waited hopefully for Paul Sanchez to bring the Rolling Road Show to the Allison Miner stage in the grandstand paddock. He could have called it the Rowing Road Show that day. The fans stood in knee-deep water as Sanchez walked up to the rain-soaked platform in white rubber shrimp boots, carrying his acoustic guitar and accompanied by a makeshift band that included trombonist Craig Klein, trumpeter Shamarr Allen, and sousaphonist Matt Perrine, who walked them on the scene with an impromptu quote from "Singin' in the Rain." Sanchez apologized to the audience for not being able to perform his full show, noting that the rain made it necessary for them to do an acoustic set. Then he thrilled his followers with a sensational version of "Hurricane Party."

Standing for hours in the rain listening to music can make people giddy, and those who stuck it out had an excellent time listening to Sanchez defy the elements. He burned through a terrific set that also included the rocking "Door Poppin'," a track from his first Threadhead album. That night $1,000 Car played one of the best sets of its career at Le Bon Temps Roule. The addition of two keyboardists, John Gros on organ and Pete ("Johnny Two Hands") Gordon on piano, added another dimension to the band's great sound, and saxophonist Derek Huston was superb.

One of Sunday's highlights was a performance by the Voice of the Wetlands All-Stars. After a very funky "Ya Ya Ya Ya Ya Ya" from Anders Osborne, Johnny Sansone's post-Katrina lament, "Poor Man's Paradise," and Dr. John spitting out the line "You're saving the wetlands in Iraq/We want our goddamn money back!" Big Chief Monk Boudreaux came rolling on to the stage in full feathered regalia, chanting "Me Donkey Want Water."

What happened next was like something out of a Cecil B. DeMille epic. Monk was chanting fiercely, the band was chugging along like a steam locomotive, Monk waved his wand at the sky, and it was as if he had summoned a deluge of frogs. Unlike Saturday, when the rain started gradually and slowly built, this was a torrent of heavy drops, coming down like solid objects, exploding on impact, and drenching everyone in a baptism of Monk's creation. The band did not let up until the ritual was completed.

"I didn't care how wet we got," Dr. John chuckled afterward. "As long as it ain't a hurricane, we need da water! Dis state need water. When you need water, it don't care about no Jazz Fest. If you look at the spirit kingdom and breathing the air that it's giving you, the meat world gonna tell you something real fast."

The 2008 festival reinstated the Thursday show on the second weekend. Widespread Panic was the headliner that day. The band has a long tradition in New Orleans, where it played an annual Halloween show at the University of New Orleans arena that was always one of the most popular gigs of the year for

the Spreadheads, as the band's fans call themselves. After the death of lead guitarist Michael Houser, Widespread Panic struggled to find a replacement, but
Jimmy Herring finally completed that search. Herring, one of the finest guitarists
of his generation, was not haunted by the responsibility of sounding like Houser
and was able to blend his own musical personality into the band's sound. From
the moment they launched into "Walk on the Flood" the band soared, steaming through "Thought Sausage" and "From the Cradle," then bringing up Phish
alumnus Page McConnell for "Love Tractor" and "Fixin' to Die."

As it wound its way through "Already Fried" and "Greta," the band positively
gleamed. Herring played with a burnished metallic sheen inspired by the masters of jazz fusion from John McLaughlin to Jeff Beck. When Todd Nance and
Domingo Ortiz eased into the drum break, anybody who left the scene missed
something wonderful. Out of the wings came the Wild Magnolias, led by Big
Chief Bo Dollis, all dressed in brightly feathered Indian costumes with full head-
dresses. The Indians danced and chanted, Ortiz burned out an Afro-Cuban percussion groove, and somehow the Indians and Widespread Panic had merged
into a single unit, with Dollis chanting out "Shoo Fly" and urging the crowd to
chant along. JoJo Hermann picked up the groove on piano, playing the intro to
Professor Longhair's "Big Chief," and the Indians and the band were singing and
playing "Big Chief" together. For those moments Widespread Panic became a
real New Orleans band.

"We're the Wild Magnolias from New Orleans," said Dollis. "Where we come
from we dance in the rain!" Then Dollis chanted a tribute to the band, shouting "Widespread Panic" over and over as the music surged. It was breathtaking
to hear the humble and generally low-key Panic, a band that relies on its music
rather than any kind of hype, getting this street-music shout-out from the Indians. The band continued for another hour. There was something in the moment,
some kind of New Orleans vibe at work, the kind of experience those of us who
live in the city and know the ebb and flow of its mysticism in daily life understand. Normal events can be charged with supernatural meaning at the drop of a
hat. However, not all artists from outside the city can respond to these numinous
epiphanies, especially if they're the type of band that has a set list that doesn't
vary from show to show. Widespread Panic has the emotional scope built into its
music to respond to this, just as the band was able to survive the death of its very
heart and rejuvenate itself in a new configuration.

One of the most wonderful moments in Jazz Fest history took place that
Friday afternoon. Art Neville, the iconic patriarch of New Orleans music from
his 1954 R&B hit with the Hawkettes, "Mardi Gras Mambo," through his term at
the helm of funk pioneers the Meters/Funky Meters and his role in the Neville
Brothers family band, played his first solo Jazz Fest gig. Neville played a mixture
of R&B gems and the kind of tunes he might have played at a local bar back in

the day. The atmosphere was very loose, and Neville enjoyed himself, nailing the vocal on "Pride and Joy." As *Times-Picayune* music editor Keith Spera pointed out, Aaron Neville's return to the fest didn't take place at his gospel tent show but here, at the moment when Art said, " 'S my little brother, y'all," and Aaron joined the fray for the rest of the set. "This is the first song recorded by the Neville Brothers," said Art at the end of the show. "We weren't called the Neville Brothers at the time." Art launched into "Mardi Gras Mambo" with Aaron singing along. The crowd knew the words and sang along with them.

Neville's uplifting performance set up what was nothing short of a religious service on Stevie Wonder's part. Wonder has always been an activist who's insisted on blending his progressive views into his public performances. He was part of the radical wing of the Motown machine, opposing the Vietnam War and breaking from the company at age twenty-one to make his music on his own terms (he returned to Motown after recording his first album independently). His marvelous funk take on "Happy Birthday" was an anthem for the annual rallies that eventually led to the establishment of the national holiday for Dr. Martin Luther King Jr. With Barack Obama attempting to become the first black president of the United States, Wonder's political mindset envisioned the promised land. "Don't be afraid to win," he repeatedly said to the crowd throughout his set.

Most of all, though, Wonder came to New Orleans intending to perform a healing on the city. Before he began, he invoked a moment of silence for those lost in the flood, then started out with a song meant to be appropriate to a weary moment in our history, "Love's in Need of Love Today." He had the crowd in the palm of his hand and got them grooving hard to "Too High." He returned to his evocation of the spirit in another philosophical song, "Visions," which was fitted with a new arrangement, an Isaac Hayes–style funk vamp over which he delivered a series of preacherlike declamations organized under the refrain "I Can't Believe...":

> *Four dollars a gallon for gasoline but no health care...*
> *I can't believe...*
> *Some places are building more prisons than schools...*

He swung from the vamp into a hard chorus:

> *STOP IT!*
> *STOP IT!*
> *Stop the hate*
> *Stop the crime*
> *Stop the war*

With a dramatic flourish Wonder led the band into an early climax on "Living for the City." Just about everyone on the ground, which was crowded despite the imminent rain, was singing, and most of them were dancing, the very young and the very old. The spirit of abandon was giddy, joyous. A young girl standing next to me suddenly turned and blurted out, "I can't believe I'm listening to music my father likes!"

Wonder finished and said with a big smile, "Is this what you wanted me to do?" He followed up with "Jammin'," and Wonder was in overdrive, grooving the crowd hard. He clearly believed his music was laying a healing power on the city. Rain began falling hard, and Wonder began singing and playing "Raindrops Keep Falling on My Head," playing a full verse and chorus with new lyrics like "Don't let the rain confuse the issue" and "You brought your umbrellas" as umbrellas sprouted above the crowd. He moved aggressively into "Higher Ground." The line "soldiers keep on dying," written about Southeast Asia a generation ago but resonating with families whose children were dying in Iraq that day, sent a palpable shudder through the crowd. As he played beautiful versions of "Golden Lady" and "Ribbon in the Sky" while dark clouds occluded the afternoon sun, I thought of how often the sight-challenged Wonder had a vivid, almost supernatural understanding of the meaning of visual detail, the kind of things sighted people take for granted. Wonder played a magnificent "Overjoyed," which broke into an instrumental jam on John Coltrane's "Giant Steps," with Wonder showing off his jazz chops on grand piano. He broke into clave for "Don't You Worry 'bout a Thing" and then swept into an extended finale of a medley, beginning with "Signed, Sealed, Delivered." The crowd sang the refrain, "You Can Feel It All Over," and indeed you could. Wonder punctuated the mood with shout-out tributes to New Orleans musical legends from Louis Armstrong to the Neville Brothers. He did "Sir Duke" and "My Cherie Amour." Irma Thomas came out, and the two finished with "Superstition."

It rained hard, but nobody in the enraptured crowd seemed to care.

On the first Saturday in May the Fair Grounds' infield started out as a sea of slop, but the sun soon came out and baked the ground doughy. The Gentilly stage was a mini piano festival, with people set up on blankets and in chairs to the edge of the grass but with plenty of room to move around in the spongy mud in front of the stage. After a dazzling set from Henry Butler, Marcia Ball capped off a spectacular week of performances with a great set, augmenting her regular band with Joe Krown on organ. Ball had been at the top of her game all week. She played a set at WWOZ's Piano Night tribute to Professor Longhair, turned out the house for the Wednesday afternoon free concert at Lafayette Square, and was spectacular in Wednesday night's piano trio with Tom McDermott and Joe Krown at Snug Harbor. The songs on her just-released record, *Peace, Love, and Barbecue*, were anchoring her strong performances, and she had the crowd in the palm of her hand at Jazz Fest. Her ode to the New Orleans party ethic, "That's Enough of That Stuff," moved through a sprightly second-line rhythm and featured the updated lyric: "down in the city that Bush forgot." She played some new material and got a great response from a song she wrote with Tracy Nelson, "Where Do You Go When You Can't Go Home?"

The Gentilly stage collaboration between Allen Toussaint and Elvis Costello at the previous Jazz Fest was a happy surprise, the best work I've heard from either of these giants of popular song in recent years. I viewed it as a serendipitous one-shot built around *The River in Reverse*, but when I saw them again in 2008 playing some different material, I thought of the group as a real band that brings out the best in both artists and whose mutual respect is mirrored in the way their eccentric, imperfect voices complement each other tonally. I've been a fan of Costello's music over the years but felt that his rock could benefit from a little more roll. Toussaint's elegance as a producer, songwriter, and bandleader could translate sometimes into diffidence in live performance, but Costello's hard-hitting band kept him well engaged. The marriage of the efficient British rhythm section and the precision-perfect funk of the horns—particularly Big Sam Williams's powerful trombone work—made this one of the best-working groups on the planet. Toussaint's "A Certain Girl" and "Brickyard Blues" were miraculous remakes, and Costello's "Allison" was simply breathtaking. The show's highlight, though, was a new Toussaint composition, "It's a New Orleans Thing," which rang with the conviction of some of his most famous lines: "Anywhere I go," Toussaint sang as he played a melody with a touch of "Tipitina" around the edges, "something goes along with me. It's a New Orleans thing."

At the Economy Hall stage the venerable trumpeter Connie Jones insisted on playing traditional New Orleans jazz with his own personality, not as a credible re-creation of someone else's work. When Jones played "Do You Know What It Means to Miss New Orleans," his phrasing and his ability to work the melody to tell a story were a matter of personal expression. He made you forget that the song has been played before by countless others because for that moment on stage the song was his. Mark Braud performed "When the Saints Come Marching In" with a clever arrangement twist that allowed him to enter into the tradition on his terms.

I was thinking about how strange it was to hear Gene ("Duke of Earl") Chandler singing "Daddy's Home" at the Congo Square stage. The saccharine emotional twist of this love ballad with its deeper psychological implications—a teenager's wish for her disrupted family to be whole again—had special resonance at Congo Square, the stage dedicated to the same New Orleans African diaspora community that had been scattered one more time since Katrina.

The 2008 Jazz Fest was a particularly good moment for Glen David Andrews. Glen David had played the festival many times as a sideman, but this time he led his own band. Andrews seemed to sense that his time had arrived, and he responded with a particularly athletic and charismatic performance. The most dramatic moment came when he dedicated "I'll Fly Away" to Kerwin James, recalling the moment when he was arrested for second-lining in his home neighborhood only months before.

On the final Sunday of the 2008 Jazz Fest, a defining moment in the city's musical recovery took place when the Neville Brothers made a triumphant return to close the festival, the first time the band called "the first family of New Orleans music" had played in the city since the federal flood. The band put together a special show to mark its thirtieth anniversary, presenting a timeline of its history in music dating back to the historic sessions with the Wild Tchoupitoulas Mardi Gras Indians. The band brought back George Porter Jr. on bass for the occasion since he had played on the *Wild Tchoupitoulas* record. That 1976 album, which presented Big Chief Jolly's gang to the outside world, was the first time the Neville Brothers had appeared on a record. Jolly was the Nevilles' uncle, and the brothers were eager to back him up. Cyril Neville even wrote the opening song on the album, "Brother John."

"Every Jazz Fest used to be a family reunion for the Neville family," said Cyril:

> Cousins from all over the country would come, and people from right home in town that you hadn't seen would show up. You might not see them the rest of the year, but you'd see them at the Jazz and Heritage Festival. But that show was special because it was the 30-year anniversary of the Neville Brothers. I got to tell the crowd that for 25 of the 30 years drummer Willie Green had been up there. That was a special, special show because we went through the whole thing. The whole thing started with Big Chief Jolly and the Wild Tchoupitoulas. That record was the first record we did together in the studio. The Neville Brothers' record came along after that. What's so great about that is it's the Neville Brothers and the Wild Tchoupitoulas all together on the same record, the whole Thirteenth ward. That whole show was a tribute to the history of the Neville Brothers. It started out with the Indians on the stage. Ivan was up there the whole time. Ian was up there the whole time. The Wild Tchoupitoulas started it off. We had George Porter on bass because he was the bass player on those Mardi Gras Indian songs, and the Wild Tchoupitoulas were onstage with us.

Cyril invited a prominent Native American Indian to join the band onstage, Chief Warhorse Elwin Gillum of the Louisiana Chahta tribe, commonly referred to as the Choctaw Indians. "She was the lady standing up there with the beautiful blue outfit on," said Cyril. "That was Indian, but it wasn't Mardi Gras Indian. I was talking to her about my ancestry, and she said it was time for us to sign up because we are part Choctaw Indian."

Even though the big story at the 2008 New Orleans Jazz and Heritage Festival was the return of the Neville Brothers, the Radiators played opposite the Nevilles on the last day of the fest and filled the infield in front of the Gentilly stage. A young crowd was packed to the edge of the field for an afternoon that also featured a sharp set from the Raconteur immediately before the Radiators. Many of those fans left the Fair Grounds as newly spawned Fishheads after a white-hot performance that featured guest members Mark Mullins on trombone and Michael Skinkus on percussion.

Skinkus added a layer of voodoo cross-rhythms to Frank Bua's rolling march-step of a backbeat, giving a lurch and roll to the band's dance-oriented pulse on Dionysian excursions like "Let the Red Wine Flow." Mullins, leader of the trombone-based Bonerama, has such a strong intuition for building arrangements that he erected a new harmonic structure on a version of "Ring of Fire," a platform that enabled Camile Baudoin to launch a multichorus guitar solo that seemed to lift the stage off its moorings and had the electrified crowd raging for more. Baudoin had warmed up earlier by participating in a Mardi Gras Indians' circle dance inside the Fair Grounds grandstand as Charlie Miller played along on trumpet. Mullins also played several spectacular wah-wah trombone solos. The highlight of the set came when keyboardist Ed Volker combined "Lonely Avenue," "Serve Me Right to Suffer," and "Western Plain" in the encore. The man was stoked, pumping his fist in the air as he screamed more than sang the lyrics, turning "Suffer" inside out in the process.

CHAPTER 18

On the Fringes

Frenchmen Street was raving from dusk to dawn during the 2008 New Orleans Jazz and Heritage Festival at clubs like the Boom Boom Room, Blue Nile, and d.b.a. For this two-week stretch, New Orleans was a flashpoint for contemporary jazz. Funk and fusion's decades-old alliance was rediscovered by a whole new generation of young players who had no preconceptions as to what genre they belonged to. The music was as electric or acoustic as the players wanted it to be. It wasn't surprising to see many of the regulars on the New Orleans scene— Trombone Shorty, Big Sam Williams, Ivan Neville, Mike Dillon, members of Bonerama, Galactic, and Papa Grows Funk—but the addition of out-of-towners like Dr. Lonnie Smith, Eric Krasnow, Karl Denson, Will Bernard, and John Ellis brought in another element.

Saxophonist Ellis in particular epitomized this movement with his group, Doublewide, which included New Orleanians Matt Perrine on tuba and Jason Marsalis on drums. This band played spectacular sets at both Snug Harbor and the Blue Nile during Jazz Fest. The Blue Nile continued to lead the way in booking this new blend of funk and fusion jazz with combinations like Stanton Moore on drums, Donald Harrison on saxophone, Dr. Lonnie Smith on B3 organ, and Will Bernard on guitar. One of the most creative lineups at the Blue Nile was Papa Grows NOLA Keyboard All-Stars, a three-keyboard front line of John Gros, Rich Vogel, and Brian Coogan, with Galactic's Robert Mercurio on bass and PGF drummer Jeffrey ("Jellybean") Alexander.

The most innovative piece of programming at the Blue Nile, though, was the new music festival run by the members of Open Ears Music. The free jazz these players engage in was one of the most overlooked aspects of New Orleans music at Jazz Fest, so their Tuesday showcase is always illuminating. "The basic concept was to have a venue where you didn't have to argue with someone in order to book something really interesting," said trombonist and festival cocurator Jeff Albert:

We wanted to have a place where, if somebody had an unusual idea, they don't have to jump through hoops to do creative things. Things have happened that I don't think would have happened had the series not been available. We've had some great interactions with European musicians. We did a night when Wolter Wierbos was in town that was various interpretations of five trombonists with Big Sam Williams and Rick Trolsen and me and Mark McGrain and Wolter, and that was a blast. I'd like to feel that if there is a next Ornette Coleman and he happened to be in New Orleans, he would play in our series.

The mostly young experimental musicians in New Orleans eschewed the label of avant-garde as being out of date, but much of their music came out of that tradition without suffering from the weight of academic scrutiny or self-mythologizing. There was a real search for freedom from structure in much of the city's newest music, perhaps in reaction to the tradition-based nature of its old music. The Open Ear festival and the events that took place under the Scatterjazz umbrella were great examples of this new musical paradigm in the city, but its most extreme manifestation was presented by another of the fringe festivals, Noize Fest. There are other noise festivals around the country, but the New Orleans variation, organized in 2004 by Keith Moore, the son of New Orleans R&B legend Deacon John Moore, was a tribute to the city's eccentricities. Michael Patrick Welch, the electronic music impresario whose stage name is the White Bitch (the name his students gave him when he attempted to pursue a career as a high school teacher in New Orleans) kept the festival going after Moore was murdered in 2007. Welch held Noize Fest in his backyard at the other end of the Bywater from the Truck Farm, the site of another fringe festival, Chazfest. The festival also provided some of the most eccentric local talent for the Voodoo Festival at Halloween—local punk, noise and electronic musicians such as Ratty Scurvics, Ray Bong, I, Octopus, cellist Helen Gillet, guitarist Rob Cambre, and the only-in-New-Orleans marching band the Noisician Coalition. This group, with its distinctive red-and-black uniforms, played assorted homemade instruments assembled from vacuum cleaners, garden tools, kitchen appliances, and found objects. The resultant cacophony seemed totally appropriate on the streets of this eccentric city.

Other fringe festivals taking place around the city during Jazz Fest did a great job of showcasing music that the big festival couldn't get to. Chazfest, an alternative festival that took place between the two weekends of the New Orleans Jazz and Heritage festival, was one of the most dramatic examples of musicians' taking control of their financial destiny after the flood. When "saving" Jazz Fest became a matter of allowing its identity to be co-opted by corporate interests, neighborhood gatherings such as Chazfest took on added significance. The festival was more than just a blow against the empire; it was also a way toward self-determination.

Alex McMurray came up with the idea for Chazfest after a brainstorming session with Washboard Chaz, who played with him in the Tin Men. Chaz lived not far from McMurray's home at the Truck Farm on St. Claude Avenue, just past the railroad tracks in the Bywater section of the city. The Truck Farm, where McMurray and other musicians live, had a large but fairly typical Bywater backyard, an off-street oasis of subtropical plants and perfumed flower gardens intermingled with broken-down sheds, stables, and rusty garden furniture. It was a beautiful shipwreck of a place festooned with large-scale works of art. A chicken coop in the back corner served as a reminder of the days when people grew much of the food they ate and kept farm animals out in back of the house. The sprawling back-yard was the perfect setting for the two stages, which were set apart by subtropical plants and long-limbed live oaks.

"We moved back February 1 of 2006, and we were the only people on St. Claude Avenue," said McMurray:

> We were sitting in the backyard, me and my wife and Chaz and his wife and some friends, and the list of people who were going to play Jazz Fest had just come out. The Tin Men never got in; we played once. We played to a standing-room-only crowd but were never invited back. So we started thinking, let's play our own shows at that bar across the street from the Fair Grounds; we'll call it "Chazfest." That was kind of a joke we had for a long time before that. Then we thought, let's just do it here in our backyard. It's a whole lot nicer here. We decided that we would only have bands that were not playing at the Fair Grounds. That was the whole idea. Not to thumb our nose at Jazz Fest or anything like that, just to have a place to play during that time.

McMurray did not make a profit in this rustic setting, but he did prove that New Orleans musicians didn't have to be held hostage by Shell Oil or other corporate entities in order to work and that locals didn't have to pay tourist prices to go to a festival. There was a delicious irony at work here because Jazz Fest sponsor Miller beer has no greater hotbed of support than right there in Bywater, where Miller High Life was the drink of choice. There were no Miller signs, hospitality tents, or "brought to you by…" announcements, but everyone was drinking $2 cans of Miller High Life until there were no more left.

The icon of Washboard Chaz, slyly drawn to resemble the Professor Longhair logo hanging over the stage at Tipitina's (and, once upon a time, at the Fess stage at Jazz Fest), remained a powerful symbol, at once a reminder of how much Jazz Fest was moving away from its traditional ties to Longhair and how

Chaz Leary himself represented a tribe of New Orleans musicians clustered just across the railroad tracks in Bywater. Chaz didn't loom over this group musically the way Longhair influenced his generation, but he represented his musical peers and provided the loosest kind of conceptual continuity to this genre—if Chaz could play his washboard with whatever music it is you play, you were automatically part of the scene. And Chaz could play with anybody. "Chaz plays with everybody, not the whole time, but he'll do a song with everybody," said McMurray. "It was part of the original concept. I just think he decided he was gonna do that."

Along with his own group, Chaz played with Chazfest regulars the Tin Men and the Valparaiso Men's Chorus, both groups featuring McMurray and sousaphone virtuoso Matt Perrine. The Tin Men set pretty much defined the nature of Chazfest. As the trio tripped through Allen Toussaint's New Orleans classic "Mother Mother" and families danced with their children in the sunny garden, it was obvious that whatever future New Orleans had was being represented right there on the spot, a future about people, not institutions and corporate sponsorship.

McMurray sang a great rendition of "Take Me Out to the Ballgame," making sure to note it was the New Orleans Triple A baseball team, the Zephyrs, he was rooting for. Chaz then addressed the crowd:

Figure 27. "Washboard Chaz" Leary sings "Hard Year Blues." Photo By John Swenson. Used by permission of John Swenson.

I told my momma
Momma, one day they're gonna have a festival and name it after me!
Well, momma, I got my festival! I've made it to the big time.

Chaz proceeded to scratch a beat on his washboard and sing Fats Domino's "I'm Gonna Be a Wheel Someday." And then there was Chaz playing with the Happy Talk Band later in the day, as well as the Valparaiso Men's Chorus, fifteen voices delivering sea shanties backed by the Tin Men. Then there was Chaz joining in with headliners, Morning 40 Federation, for raucous neighborhood tributes like "A&P," which referenced the PNT Market up the block, and "Chili Cheese Fries," the story of a late night at the Clover Grill. When the Morning 40 Federation finished the last notes of its set, an enormous barking sound emanated from just over the hedges. The otherworldly cheering (or vocal disapproval) was coming from thousands of Bywater frogs who were an unintended part of the Chazfest audience.

Chazfest was only one of several alternative festivals run opposite the Jazz and Heritage Festival. The Ponderosa Stomp, which featured a roots-music lineup that dug deeper into the history of the region's music than Jazz Fest itself, had the biggest impact of the alternative festivals, so big that Jazz Fest incorporated a Stomp showcase into its 2008 lineup. Around the city, smaller festivals and parties took place, from the annual Threadhead party to special all-night showcases at the Blue Nile, Howling Wolf, and Tipitina's and the day concerts at the Louisiana Music Factory.

The New Orleans Jazz and Heritage Festival's unique identity posed an overwhelming challenge to its talent scouts. The festival began as an unabashed tribute to local musicians whose careers had not kept pace with their legends, and in its early years Jazz Fest didn't have to cast its net too far to fulfill that mission. However, as the mainstays of the classic eras of New Orleans jazz and R&B have passed away, the festival organizers have had to look elsewhere to populate its stages. Jazz Fest has aggressively replaced local talent with national acts in order to keep its tourist appeal high, a strategy that may be self-defeating in the long run. The festival organizers have been helped since the mid-1990s by the annual migrations of jam-band fans to what they call "Planet New Orleans." Their numbers have swelled the ranks of festival attendees since 1996, when Phish first appeared at the event, through subsequent years, when performances by Widespread Panic, the Allman Brothers, and former members of the Grateful Dead were featured.

Nevertheless, the subtle balance of Louisiana identity and celebrity appeal was becoming harder to reconcile each year as fewer and fewer headliners seem to have anything to do with the festival's identity. Though the festival still did a great job of promoting the New Orleans cultural heritage, the featured attractions didn't always follow through on the premise. When the New Orleans content becomes window dressing rather than the main event, people may start reconsidering the need to travel to New Orleans for their Bon Jovi or Neil Young.

Those fans found plenty of local content at the alternative festivals, however. The Ponderosa Stomp in particular had taken on a life of its own. In only its eighth year, the Stomp had eclipsed Jazz Fest as the roots-music mecca, taking over two nights at the House of Blues in the French Quarter, as well as holding a three-day conference and an exhibit at the Cabildo.[1] The Ponderosa Stomp grew out of founder Dr. Ike Podnos's desire to see some of his roots-music heroes perform at private parties and specifically at his wedding in 2000. His wife, Shmuela, was an active member of the Mardi Gras Indian community, and Dr. Ike had strong personal links to the city's traditional-music communities. Over the years he managed to find legends of Louisiana and Texas R&B, swamp pop, and Cajun and country music and convinced them to perform at his gatherings.

It was a short leap from there to the early days of the Stomp, which were free-for-all assemblages of musical greats who played until dawn at Mid-City Lanes. Those early shows took advantage of holes in the Jazz Fest lineup, but Podnos insisted he never saw himself as a rival to Jazz Fest's programming.

"Jazz Fest presented stuff that influenced me greatly," said Podnos:

> I used to go out there and see stuff I'd never seen before, people like Booba Barnes and Bongo Joe. At one point they were doing all this. As they grew over the years while they've retained some of this, they've also branched off in some other directions. I don't know why, aside from the fact that a lot of those New Orleans artists have passed on. The Stomp was never intended to turn into a festival. I would do a backyard party, then go find some people I'd wanna see play and hire 'em. For my wedding I took it to a further extreme, hired all these people who never came down here, and that was what turned into the proto-Stomp. We formed the Mystic Knights of Mau Mau and started doing shows at the Circle Bar. We were doing it on a monthly basis, and I decided to do the Stomp in one whole fell swoop. I decided to do it in the middle of Jazz Fest because the fans were there, and it would be good for the musicians' profile, but what happened is it developed its own following. So it's taken on a life of its own. It's interesting to me how it's come full circle, how you become an influence on the stuff that influenced you.

In the chaos that followed Katrina, Podnos was forced to move the 2006 renewal of the Stomp to Memphis, but upon his return to New Orleans the following year at the House of Blues, his festival exploded in popularity. Podnos boasted that most of the people who came to New Orleans for the Stomp didn't attend Jazz Fest at all. He said 70 percent of his audience wouldn't be going out to the Fair Grounds. Podnos has expanded the original vision of Jazz Fest as a tribute to Louisiana culture to embrace the entire Gulf Coast, emphasizing the interaction between western Louisiana and east Texas performers.

Perhaps the most popular alternative festival was run by the local record store Louisiana Music Factory, which hosted free daytime concerts starting on the Thursday before Jazz Fest began, continued on the days between the two weekends, and ended on the Monday after Jazz Fest. The store also supplied coupons for discount beer redeemable down the block at the Attiki Bar and Grill.

Though the Factory's shows always included some acts that didn't make the Jazz Fest cut, that's not the formula that owner Barry Smith used for bookings. "I try to put together a mix of local talent, but the main criterion is that the bands have newer product than the previous Jazz Fest," said Smith. "I'm sure some of them aren't playing the festival, but I didn't scan the list to see who's on there and who isn't when I did the booking. Being a retailer, I'm basically hoping to promote the musicians' CD sales."

CHAPTER 19

City That Care Forgot

Later in the summer of 2008 I ran into guitarist John Fohl on Decatur Street. An accomplished player and friendly, good-natured guy, Fohl was a much sought-after accompanist who played in a number of local situations, but his highest-profile gig was with the Dr. John band, the hard-hitting funk organization masterminded by the great New Orleans keyboardist and songwriter Mac Rebennack. Playing with Mac has always been serious business, but since the storm it had taken on an even intenser light, for in addition to carrying the flag for New Orleans's musical history, Mac had called on his band to help deliver a life-or-death message about the future of its hometown.

That message was delivered on *City That Care Forgot*, an uncompromising collection of songs detailing Mac's charges against a variety of villains he believed were intent on nothing less than destroying New Orleans. When he took his band to New York City to play material from *City That Care Forgot* on the *Late Show with David Letterman*, Mac gave them one specific instruction.

"He told us to look mad," said Fohl, suppressing a laugh.

That's a pretty unusual instruction from a bandleader who'd been bringing smiles to people's faces and putting quicksilver in their dancing shoes for the last fifty years as one of the key players in the New Orleans popular music scene. However, Mac Rebennack, who created the persona of Dr. John in the late 1960s after distinguishing himself as a local session star, was not smiling, and he wanted the people who listen to him to understand why he was pissed off. Like a lot of his friends and relations from New Orleans, he was fed up with the political system that had allowed the Louisiana wetlands to be destroyed over a period of decades and left no protection from the kind of storm surges that had wiped out a lot of the state after the double dose of destruction unleashed by hurricanes Katrina and Rita in 2005. If all politics is local, there's nothing more political than seeing everyone you know lose their homes after the levees failed and New Orleans was inundated.

So Dr. John put aside the gris gris, gumbo, and jive talkin' that he was known for to write a series of stark observations about the state of New Orleans. The songs on *City That Care Forgot* were by turns grimly journalistic, achingly poetic, and disturbingly emotional. Aside from "Promises, Promises," written some twenty years ago by Bobby Charles and Willie Nelson, all the songs related directly to the conditions that led up to Katrina and the political bungling that followed.

Without a doubt, Dr. John has always been a superior songwriter. A master conceptualist, he envisions lyrics and music as a continuum, part of an overall vision. He is one of the very few denizens of the fertile New Orleans R&B scene of the 1950s and early '60s to translate the miniaturist art of the three-minute hit into the long-player ethos of funk and rock. His conceptual power travels further into his interpretations of other writers' songs. Unlike most New Orleans groups that use cover material as simple fodder for jamming grooves with little regard for the original song structure, Mac Rebennack translates everything he touches, from Duke Ellington to Doc Pomus to Cousin Joe, into Dr. John material.

Aside from his apocalyptic glimpse at the chaos of late 1960s' American culture on his second album, *Babylon*, Mac had rarely ventured into political songwriting. In fact, many of his lyrics make up a kind of secret language that corresponds to the sound of his music. However, Mac had been politicized by the wholesale governmental betrayal of New Orleans before and after Katrina, from the shoddy construction of the levees that failed in the storm surge to the corruption and deceit of the recovery effort. Even before the flood he had already decided to castigate the oil companies and politicians for destroying the coast with the Voice of the Wetlands All-Stars, but after the flood he took it to another zone.

Mac worked with several writers to help get his points across, including his old songwriting partner Bobby Charles, the author of "Walking to New Orleans," the Rev. Goat Carson, and *Times-Picayune* columnist Chris Rose. The trademark Dr. John delivery, relaxed and offhanded, like a guy telling a shaggy-dog story over drinks at Markey's bar, was replaced with the unmistakable catch-in-the-throat voice of an angry man. It was a startling transition for those who'd followed Mac over the years but an effective attention-grabbing device nevertheless.

In "Time for a Change," the song he played on Letterman, Mac vented his anger and even said he was "pissed off." Mac had additional reason to be angry when he discovered that his record company, Blue Note, had no intention of releasing "another record about New Orleans." Fortunately, the situation was resolved when 429 Records stepped up to the plate and put it out. Everyone involved was vindicated when *City That Care Forgot* was greeted with rave reviews, was called the best album Dr. John had made in twenty years, and brought extensive exposure on national television and radio outlets.

The same night he appeared on the David Letterman show, Mac played to a packed house in New York's Highline Ballroom. The atmosphere was far different from a New Orleans throwdown from Mac, but he had something to say, and the New York crowd listened attentively. If there was a post-Katrina anthem in New Orleans music, a very old song that several generations before had served a similar function when the yellow-fever epidemic had ravaged New Orleans still resonated in the wake of a flood that left many people mourning members of their families. The song was "St. James Infirmary," and Dr. John chose it to open his set, playing it in an eerie, dirgelike mambo.

Though there were seven players in his band, Mac continued to call the group "the Lower 9/11," something he's been doing for at least six years now. The connection to how the world has changed since 9/11 was hard to miss, and the celebration of the neighborhood where Dr. John rambled back in the day and where many of his musician friends come from was eerily prescient now that it had been completely destroyed "like it was hit wit' an H bomb," as he told the crowd.

In addition, Dr. John's political observations didn't shy away from establishing motive and pinning specific blame on the bad guys. The motive was "Black Gold," an anti–big oil polemic from the album delivered early on in the set. When Mac spit out the words "Cheney and Halliburton," it was as if he had cursed evil spirits. A palpable shiver ran through the audience.

After the show Dr. John sat in a chair in a corner of his dressing room. The rigors of an intense touring schedule and his ancient mariner's determination to tell his story before it was too late had taken a toll on this road warrior, and he admitted to being tired. Still, he was generous with his time. He had read my review of the record in *OffBeat* and responded with an approving smile, drawling his vowels as he delivered the phrase, "Man, you really got it!" in slow motion.

It's hard not to get the gist of an epic American tragedy written in point-by-point observations, drawing on nightmarish urban-myth imagery to paint a powerful picture of systemic betrayal and even genocide, right down to the assertion that the levees were blown "with intention." He attributed motivation to that intention in "Land Grab," in which he accused the politicians and their corporate backers of trying to run the people of the lower Ninth Ward and St. Bernard off their homes in "the biggest land grab since Columbus."

Everywhere he turned, Dr. John saw evil—trigger-happy Blackwater private-security teams who used deadly force without legal restraint in the chaotic days after the storm, as well as much-needed resources wasted in Iraq, and behind it all were Bush, Cheney, and Halliburton. The resulting sorrow reached its apotheosis as a motivating factor in Rebennack's world on "Stripped Away," a loving remembrance of music in New Orleans before the storm.

Few people have done a better job of codifying the spirit of New Orleans over the years, offering tributes to its musical forefathers and participating directly in nearly a half-century of its most important music. On *City That Care Forgot* Dr. John may have fashioned its most elegant obituary.

Mac was one of my oldest New Orleans friends. We'd talked on many occasions over the last thirty-five years since I first wrote a feature story on him for *Crawdaddy* magazine; he taught me a lot of what I know about New Orleans music history, an education that included countless nights of some of the best music I've ever heard in any context. No one understood more about the relationship between spirit culture, magic, and music in New Orleans than Rebennack, who fashioned his alter ego of Dr. John out of a legendary voodoo figure and transference of voodoo rituals into song. I'd been talking with him a lot since the storm as he worked hard to get his message across.

"I was angry from the beginning," he said when I asked him about the confrontational tone of the album:

> My grief was very mixed with anger from the jump. The inclination I had was to do this record from the beginning, but when I told the record company I wanted to do it, they said "No, not another record about New Orleans." So they wouldn't release it, and they dumped me. I was just grateful somebody wanted to do this record.
>
> I had some other songs that were supposed to be for this record. Some of the songs that might have gone on the *Voice of the Wetlands* record were on this record. I had some more songs that Bobby Charles and I wrote. There were other songs that I wrote with the Rev. Goat Carson. I could have been cuttin' 'til the cows come home, but I had to finish this. I was looking at it as if all else fails, I'm going to throw all this shit to the VOW projects. You never know with the record business. I kept looking at it like we were going to do it 'cause I didn't want to give up my spirit up on it. And everybody that said that they were going to participate jumped whether it was Terence Blanchard or Ani DiFranco. I mean, Ani said she was going to do it, and we haven't even started making a record. She offered her services 100 percent.
>
> Some of the songs I got from articles Chris Rose was writing. One of the songs was based on two or three of his articles. I just took some stuff that I thought was pertinent and used it, and, of course, it was a lot of feelings that I was feeling about that stuff. The song about Treme ["Stripped Away"], the song about the city and how it used to be, any part of the city I'd go to, he wrote a beautiful article about that. Chunks of things he wrote put me in a kind of melancholy head thinking about it, about parts of town that was [*sic*] like destroyed and the families were no longer there. I just put little twists on it.

Along with the anger Mac expressed on *City That Care Forgot* came a deep wellspring of sorrow. In "We're Gettin' There" he wrote of people he knew losing the battle to rebuild their homes and simply giving up, committing suicide.

"The idea that people took their own lives since the storm," I said to Mac, "everyone knows someone who's done that." He took a long pause before answering. His heavily taped hands, worn from years of pounding keyboards for a living, moved almost involuntarily as he searched for the right words. "I think there have been so many lost friends and people," he finally replied, shaking his head, "[that] this song could have had a never-ending turn to it." He continued:

There's so many things that have happened to people. It's really bad to me, how can so many things happen, the money that was ripped off from New Orleans, the millions of billions of dollars that disappeared? It's like, how many times can New Orleans get ripped off by corruption? And it's across the board. We used to get ripped off by the mayor and the governor. But, from the federal level...it's like "holy shit" territory. That's what added to my anger to the max. It was like, okay, you want to kick somebody when they're down. I felt like we ain't the chumps you think we are. We don't want to look like mister fucking pitiful, but we're just people trying to survive shit. You talk to anybody—between the vice president taking away jobs from the locals and giving them to his people. It's just like, who do they think they're dealing with? Are New Orleans people not tax-paying citizens of the United States? I'm insulted with Mayor Nagin, I'm insulted with anybody that has anything to do with it.

The song "Promises, Promises" sounded like it was written recently even though it was an old tune. Mac explained:

We were going to cut it for the *Voice of the Wetlands* album, but we couldn't find the goddamn song. Willie Nelson wrote it with Bobby. That's one of the reasons Willie was on it. We were trying to rush to get this record out, and we left Willie's name off the credit on that. Willie and him wrote that years ago for another election. It was back in Reagan days. We were going to do a show in support of the Mississippi way back when as a result of Reagan not signing the Clean Water Act. And it was such a slap in the face that here's President Reagan, saying, "Well, we're not going to sign the Clean Water Act." Well, it added to the dilemma that led to everything—[it's] why the wetlands are disappearing.

Willie Nelson really delivered his lines in "Promises, Promises." "Yeah, I changed some of the lines for this record, and I tried that none of them threw Willie the least bit of a curvature. I just did them how I saw it, y'know?"

"Yeah, it works in context," I replied. "The line 'fought in your wars, paid with our lives,' now that applies to the people who died in the storm, too, paid with their lives."

"After we finally got ahold of this song," he said, "it was like, man, it was like an important thing coming from a lot of areas. It all connected. The dots were obvious to me on how this connects to this. I remember I was playing the demo for the band, and they got excited."

Mac saved his most intense ire for the oil companies he assailed in "Land Grab," a song that cursed the corporate sharks who hoped to benefit from the destruction of the lower Ninth Ward and Chalmette. "[A]nd they want to dig for oil," a suddenly animated Mac exclaimed, his voice rising:

> It doesn't take a rocket scientist to figure out who's going to profit. After Rita there was no more anything. Bobby Charles, where he was living is in the Gulf. It's disgusting. There's no excuse. Our wetlands could have been saved. They could have saved a chunk of Mississippi, too, and nobody cares. When you get down to it, the people care, but who cares about the people? Does FEMA care about people? No.

In the song "Stripped Away" Mac coined an apt metaphor with the image of toxic mold under fresh paint, a poetic description of the official instinct to paper over the problem. "They always do it," he said:

> You know this, and that thought is in the record a lot in different songs. "Stripped Away" has that idea in it. It's just the thought of what they've always did [sic] in New Orleans. No matter what happens in New Orleans, it's like, okay. They ripped out the projects, and all these people were living under the Claiborne Avenue bridge in tents. Well, the other day the city proudly said they don't exist anymore. That really makes me feel wonderful that they moved them out. Why didn't they leave the projects these people were living in alone? That was one of the stupidest ideas. It was some of the best housing in New Orleans that survived millions of hurricanes. This is local politics at its most bullshit. It's like elementary Dr. Watson. It couldn't be plainer than the nose on your face, some of the things that are mentioned on the record. And people say, wow, this is really clever, and I say there's nothing clever here; this is just talking about the truth. Is the truth clever? No. It's just people seem to prefer hearing the same old bullshit. What

is it that appeals to them? The lie appeals to them more. They're more used to it in this day and age. It's easier for people to go for the never-ending lies they hear on the news.

At least Mac was gratified by the positive responses his new material was getting from audiences around the country. "We've been getting damn good responses almost anywhere we've been," he said:

It's sad to be back because most people have no idea that nothing's happened and what little has happened—thank God for Brad Pitt—is not gonna get it done. And the fact that no one wants to talk about this as a flood. These are the things that bother me. When we see people out there and it's like a reunion, someone that you know from New Orleans, and they're lost souls out there wherever.

We have more songs about all this. But for the time being, with this record we picked up what we could. Let me play these songs to death. We try to carry a message, you know. Hopefully we'll make someone look at this situation and maybe make some better calls for the future of this world and this country and south Louisiana. That's my one hope.

I thought we had finished talking and thanked Mac for his time, but there was something else he felt he had to say. "Since the storm I've lost a lot of friends—recently Chuck Carbo, people who were gonna be on this record. Willie Tee passed away, Alvin Batiste passed away. There was a song of Willie's I wanted to do desperately bad about the crack in the Liberty Bell. There was a song Alvin Batiste had that I wanted to put in between songs on this record, and Alvin passed away. It was just on and on with this record—plans were just passing away. Earl Turbinton passed away. I wanted him to play on this record; he wasn't in good health, but I just wanted Earl bad. All of those people were really a part of New Orleans. That's why everybody that's on this record is people that cared. I felt really blessed that I could pull whoever we could pull on there while we were doing it, and that was that. Terence volunteered before the album, Trombone Shorty, and James Andrews.

Mac is watching the giants of a generation of New Orleans musicians he wrote history with pass away in alarming numbers since the storm. Fortunately, he was able to recruit younger players to fill the shoes of those gone by. Trombone Shorty played a spectacular solo in the song "My People Need a Second Line." "There is so many good kids that is coming up," Mac said, "and I follow all of them." He went on:

If I didn't see a future, I couldn't do this record. Then what would be the point? Trombone Shorty is the grandson of Jessie Hill. It's like everything connects in New Orleans. There's nothin' that don't connect to somethin'. That family down there raised me. Frank Lastie, Papoose Nelson. Both sides of Troy Andrews's family. All of these people are a big connection in my life. When my father passed away, Frank Lastie made me feel right at home in their house. That's New Orleans. That's what New Orleans is about. People care about people, and they're there for people. You don't see that everywhere—caring people. That's one of the ugliest things that's happened the way the government has twisted everything, having families ripped apart. People don't know where their own family is to this day. Three years after the storm—it's ridiculous…damn. The fact that we got the music helps. It's a big part of New Orleans culture. Just treasure it as a culture. I just hope it doesn't perish.

CHAPTER 20

Wild and Free

On a humid summer morning in 2008, with the sun ratcheting its way up to blister level in my neighborhood, not much had changed in nearly three years. The street signs were still twisted at crazy angles to each other. Most of the local stores remained closed. Piles of rubble, each one representing the ruins of another family's life, lingered on the sidewalks, and the acrid smell of house fires filled the air. The fires were a constant reminder of everything that had gone wrong. The cause most often given by authorities was that the fires were caused by faulty electrical wiring or gas leaks, but some of them were set by owners whose insurance companies wouldn't pay flood damage, while others were started by careless squatters or people using abandoned buildings as crack dens.

The fires seemed random, and even when the soot landed on your windowsill and you breathed a sigh of relief that at least it wasn't your house burning down this time, there was still a collective terror underlying all of this seeping destruction. The city's slow descent encompassed everyone and everything. Only the main tourist areas of the French Quarter, the business district, and the arts district had been revitalized. The massive hotel connected to the Superdome remained shuttered—its windows boarded up and broken.

Hundreds of thousands of volunteers had come to New Orleans to help by joining organizations like Common Ground, the Arabi Wrecking Krewe, and the Tipitina's Foundation. Many of these people helped individual families in the lower Ninth Ward whose houses were swept away in the flood to rebuild from scratch even as the city had all but abandoned the neighborhood. Each of those rebuilt houses was a small miracle to the people who lived in them. The volunteers helped to buoy spirits in the most deracinated neighborhoods, but their work was still just a drop in the bucket. The ongoing lack of a citywide recovery plan three years after the flood was frustrating and demoralizing. City council members had turned on each other and against the mayor, Ray Nagin, in an unseemly clash of egos while the city burned. New Orleans also suffered from the worst per-capita murder rate in the country.

In a city whose history has always been traceable in the weather-beaten façades of abandoned houses in all but the richest neighborhoods, the rapidly advancing decay was one giant Dorian Gray moment for the entire populace. Across St. Claude Avenue from where I lived was the widespread destruction of the upper Ninth Ward, desolation that continued for miles to the east through the lower Ninth and Chalmette. The city's music community had suffered crippling losses as its elders passed away, probably before their time, given the strain of the losses they had all had to endure and the lack of proper medical care in the city post-Katrina. The ever-growing list was an uncomfortable litany of the remaining essential pieces of the New Orleans heritage—Clarence ("Gatemouth") Brown, Alvin Batiste, Earl Turbinton, Wilson ("Willie Tee") Turbinton, John Brunious, Oliver ("Who Shot the La La") Morgan, Vernell ("Joe Gun") Joseph, Charlie Brent, and Snug Harbor owner George Brumat.

Many great local musicians simply left town because it was less difficult to pursue their livelihood in another location. Henry Butler was gone, as were Aaron and Cyril Neville, Mike West, Rockin' Jake, Maurice Brown, Jason Marsalis, Davell Crawford, and Peter Holsapple. A number of former residents, like Dave Malone of the Radiators and Shannon McNally, commuted to New Orleans to play their gigs from other spots in the region. Members of local brass bands who'd moved to Atlanta and Houston drove hundreds of miles to play their New Orleans dates.

Heavily armed gangs ruled the streets as murder, robbery, and cold-blooded executions became commonplace in New Orleans. It was all part of a pattern of government neglect that started at the top with the scandal-ridden careers of Nagin, U.S. Senator David Vitter, Congressman William Jefferson, and City Councilman Oliver Thomas and extended to the overworked fire department, a severe shortage of health care and hospitals, a dysfunctional school system, a demoralized and underequipped police force, and an infrastructure riddled with broken underground water pipes that bled the city's drinking water and caused sinkholes to open up in the middle of busy streets. When it rained in New Orleans, there were scattered power outages throughout the city. To top it off, the Army Corps of Engineers admitted that the levees wouldn't be strengthened enough to contain routinely projected storms until at least 2011. Until then, New Orleanians just had to keep their fingers crossed that another Katrina didn't hit. In 2008 the storm surge from Hurricane Gustav overtopped the Industrial Canal levee, which fortunately held, but it was a tense moment.

Despite all of these negatives, New Orleans continued to be a powerful lure to young adventurers and artists of all ages. Young people from around the country flocked to the city, where some took up residence in abandoned housing. Musicians who tried living elsewhere returned to revisit the inspiration that drove their work. While the small businesses that catered to the tourist trade were in denial about the perils the city faced and railed against the reports of mayhem, musicians took in the destruction, the death, and the horror and translated those emotions into the healing force of their craft.

New music venues sprouted up like mushrooms in unlikely spots around the city, and musicians emerged from the woodwork to fill them, often with unusual sounds not previously associated with the New Orleans scene. Avant-garde and experimental jazz groups were flourishing along with a variety of electronic and postrock bands. The future of traditional jazz, R&B, brass band, and Mardi Gras Indian music was still critically endangered by the destruction of the neighborhood culture that created them, but there was still enough of the culture remaining for them to be a vital force, while new music was thriving in amalgamated styles that defy categorization. Funk still reigned as the city's main rhythmic impulse, providing an essential tie to the mainstream via the jam band scene, which has accepted a number of New Orleans touring bands into its fold.

Night after night the musicians gave those of us who followed them all the reason we needed to sweat it out through that perilous summer of 2008. On one more relentlessly hot summer night that year the Radiators rolled back the clock at the House of Blues with an album-release party for *Wild & Free*, a collection of previously unreleased songs and alternate takes that mixed live and studio material covering the entire thirty years of the band's existence. The two sets were particularly eccentric, filled with quirky Radiators trademarks, like Dave Malone's decision to play one of the rare tracks from the album, "Hard Core," twice during the performance, and Ed Volker's springing a new song—"Something Fishy Going On"—on the group without warning. A crowd of sojourners who'd hopped on the Rads train at some point along the way turned out, even some who were on hand for the band's early days at Luigi's and the Dream Palace. "It was like old home week," said drummer Frank Bua after the show. "I saw faces in the crowd I haven't seen in a decade."

Many of the fans who frequented the "official" Radiators' email list greeted *Wild & Free* as the recovered Grail, filled as it was with long-requested pieces like the title track, "All Meat Off the Same Bone," and the suite "Songs from the Ancient Furnace." However, Ed Volker's liner notes wondered without sentimentality about the fans who didn't live to see this moment.

Songwriter/keyboardist/vocalist Volker began the process of curating this album when he started listening to tapes of performances dating back to the pre-Radiators days. Volker and Radiators guitarist Camile Baudoin, friends since grade school, had played in local bands since high school and first worked with Rads drummer Frank Bua in a group called the Dogs. The trio reconvened as part of the legendary Rhapsodizers, which played several songs that became associated with the Radiators. Bassist Reggie Scanlan subbed with the Rhapsodizers while playing in Dave Malone's band, Road-apple, and with Professor Longhair (the Rads would go on to back up Fess, as well as Earl King). In 1988 the five of them assembled in Volker's Waldo Avenue garage and rehearsal studio. That day three Rhapsodizers and two Roadapples became the Radiators.

The Radiators quickly built a reputation as the hottest rock band in town and recorded a couple of indie records that are still sold at gigs, and by the mid-1980s they were signed to Epic Records. The group made three albums, *Law of the Fish, Zigzagging through Ghostland,* and *Total Evaporation,* before asking for its release after Sony took over the company and drastically cut the artist-development budget. The Radiators returned to being a New Orleans institution and played at numerous local events and annual parties thrown by longtime fans in cities around the country.

The Radiators never seemed to be historically defined by any single album, but *Wild & Free* got the job done by spanning the entire era of the band's existence. Organized by Volker, with input from his bandmates, and taken from a variety of sources that covered the group's history, *Wild & Free* gave a better overall sense of what this band was about than any previous release. The title track, a studio recording from 2000, was a kind of statement of purpose for the group, Volker's celebration of the joys of playing to a crowd of New Orleans fans. The song conjured visions of the Radiators'

Figure 28. Radiators backstage at Tipitina's. Left to right: Frank Bua, Ed Volker, Reggie Scanlan, Camile Baudoin, Dave Malone. Photo by Bob Compton. Used by permission of Bob Compton.

annual performance on the final day of the New Orleans Jazz and Heritage Festival, closing out the Gentilly stage in front of a crowd of more than ten thousand people:

> *I just can't figure it out, it's a great big mystery*
> *But what the hell, I love the smell of the mighty Mississippi…*
> *You don't know what it means to me*
> *To be here with you, wild and free.*

Over the years Volker personally recorded many of the band's shows, and he drew on that collection to provide snapshotlike glimpses of some of the nights that created the legend. Many of the group's earliest shows were at Luigi's, a pizza joint near its practice space, where the band's sound was codified through risk taking and spontaneity. The gem here was "Suck the Head, Squeeze the Tip," a live 1980 recording of one of the band's signature tunes, in which Volker offered instructions on the eating of crawfish over a stark, soulful groove. The song was originally released as a two-part single, but this remastered version was definitive. The funky 1978 recordings "All Meat Off the Same Bone" and the hair-raising medley of "King Solomon Don't Mind"/"Red Dress," all within months of the band's formation, gave a sense of the vibe that surrounded those gigs. The transformation into "Red Dress" at the end of disc 2 is a Radiators trademark. Volker wrote "Red Dress" for the Rhapsodizers, but when these musicians played the song the way he wanted to hear it, the Radiators were born. Singer/guitarist Dave Malone's "Last Getaway," a song that has become a staple of the band's live shows over the years, was another gem from Luigi's, along with "Hard Core," known by Fishheads as a nasty set closer.

The other legendary Radiators venue was the Dream Palace (now the Blue Nile) on Frenchmen Street, the source of another handful of tracks from the 1980s, including Malone's great vocals on "House of Blue Lights," "Hard Time Train," "Stand by Me, Baby," and "Like Dreamers Do"; one of Volker's more eccentric cameos, "Hard Rock Kid"; the novelistic Volker set piece, "My Home Is on the Border"; and a fascinating pre-Epic version of "Doctor Doctor," centered on Baudoin's precise, hornlike slide guitar lines.

The Epic years introduced the band to the whirlwind of nonstop touring. "Have a Little Mercy," one of the best tracks on the set, came from a 1989 gig at the Ritz in New York, a venue that also yielded "Oh, Beautiful Loser" and "I Want to Go Where the Green Arrow Goes." The traveling circus also hit Saint Paul, Minnesota, where two of the most interesting live pieces were recorded in 1992, the atmospheric "Strangers" and the lessons-for-life philosophy of the suite "Songs from the Ancient Furnace." Volker's R&B vamp "Love Trouble" came from a 1978 show at Tipitina's.

Though most of the record was live, several studio tracks stood out. "Tear My Eyes Out," an astonishing vocal performance from Malone on a Volker song, turned on a theme that has fascinated artists at least as far back as Sophocles. "When Her Snake Eyes Roll," a sleek and slippery vehicle for Mr. Volker, came from the same 2000 session as the title track. The earliest studio material was from the band's first year, when they swapped recording time for session work backing up other singers at Knight Studio. The narcotic, stutter-step Caribbean pulse of "One-eyed Jack" rode on Scanlan's bass, and the tuneful "Cupid's Got a Mighty Arrow" suggested that this band could have had a hit well before Epic ever heard of them.

Early in 2008 the Radiators went into the Music Shed studio in New Orleans and recorded a couple of tracks to bring the project full circle. Volker's beautiful "The Girl with the Golden Eyes," which appeared in a different version on his solo album, *The Lost Radio Hour*, got a gorgeous treatment here, and Malone delivered a deep-dish helping of bayou humor on the cleverly arranged swamp rocker "Where Was You At?"

In a series of interviews and email exchanges with me over the course of a month in 2008, the Radiators reminisced about their long and colorful history.

"I always thought Ed was a good songwriter," said Scanlan, "and when the Rhapsodizers asked me to play with them, I was excited because it was a chance to play with Frank. He explained:

> Frank just has this really cool groove. I was on a gig with Johnny Vid-
> ocavich recently, and he just spontaneously went into talking about
> Frank's drumming and how good he thought he was. It's very subtle,
> Frank's style is kind of rock, straight in-the-pocket playing, but he also
> has a kind of funk thing going on. Frank has a kind of implied second-
> line beat. You can hear the syncopation deep in his playing.
>
> When Ed asked us to jam, Dave and I both thought it would be fun.
> When Dave came up with the cool guitar part on "Red Dress," shit, that
> was it. We're a band. I think the Rhapsodizers had one gig left. They
> were playing the Mom's Ball.

"The very first song we ever rehearsed was 'Red Dress,' " said Volker, "a song I wrote during the waning days of the Rhapsodizers and that I was excited about but thought the Rhapsodizers wouldn't be able to pull it off." He went on:

> Dave Malone came up with the repeated descending guitar figure that
> begins the song at that first rehearsal, and not only did the Rads nail the
> "tune" part that I had written, but the guitar figure set the song and the
> groove up perfectly. When we had that first rehearsal, I hadn't yet officially

bowed out of the Rhapsodizers. All of us in the Rads were delirious with how great and high our first jam together felt [about two or three days prior to this first rehearsal], but there was some question as to our chemistry lending itself to the kind of working together and studying that a good rehearsal demands, and I thought "Red Dress" would provide an excellent test and opportunity to check all that out, and, goddamn, we aced it!

"I had never met Dave before the Waldo Drive rehearsal," said Baudoin, "but there was something that happened between we three and those two. I dug the way Reggie held down the groove. Dave made me laugh, and I liked the way he played, soulful and solid. It just all fit in the beginning, and it's been like that ever since. But most of all it was a people thing, not even so much what we played as what we liked to work out on our own or listen to, like Beatles tunes."

"Everyone lived in the city," noted Malone, "and we seemed to have a lot more time to get together and just try things out." He said more:

Pre-Rads, I was already very aware of Ed's songwriting from the Palace Guards 45 and the band the Dogs and then the Rhapsodizers. I wasn't really a big Rhapsodizers fan although I loved the feel they had. I still always wondered what another set of musicians could do with Ed's songs, and then when the Rads had that first official rehearsal and we did such an amazing thing with "Red Dress," it was so damn creative and also didn't sound like anything else that I was aware of.

"We felt like the rehearsals were so good, let's try this in front of people and see what happens," said Baudoin:

Luigi's was a good launching pad. I remember the pole in the middle of the dance floor that was used by both males and females on occasion. Ray Schultz, he was one of the bartenders. He could get into some trouble, but he could dance. He was just smooth as silk. He danced wherever he damn well pleased. He'd take a couple of swings on the dance floor, then go back and do the bartending. Willie Dunkel was another character. He was Willie-burn-your-shirt. I don't know how it came about. He just got into a frenzy one night, and he burned his shirt right on the dance floor. So he became known as Willie-burn-your-shirt, and every night by the end of the night, somebody would start the chant, "Willie burn your shirt." It was like the burning of the shirt ceremony. One night he didn't get so far, and he set his polyester shirt on fire. It stunk up the place, and it started sticking to him. They had to douse him. The smoke from the polyester set off the fire alarm. The firemen came in, and that's when we got fired for a while. We could get away with most anything, but you can't have the fire marshal coming in.

The song "Hard Rock Kid" is "a title that saw at least two incarnations before becoming what fans are familiar with," according to Volker:

It was a slow Sunday morning back in 1973, and I walked from my pad on Waldo Drive out by the lakefront, along Robert E. Lee Boulevard, to Ferara's, a grocery store, where I picked up a *Times-Picayune,* and on the cover [the "lead" news!] was the picture of a wizened fellow wearing a kind of Civil War–era cap and a grin of sorts who had just been appointed King of the Hobos, and he went by the name of the Hard Rock Kid.

For Dave Malone, the song "Like Dreamers Do" conjured up images of the Dream Palace (DP), where some of the wildest moments in Radiators history took place. "The thing I most recall is how 'right' it seemed," said Malone:

It never felt like we were performing [but] rather like we were providing the musical landscape for that night's expedition. And the weirdest weird never seemed weird. Even the guy who used to just stare up at the mural of the universe on the ceiling or the girl with the bullwhip dildo and the Willie-burn-your-shirt guy. Not too long before we got there the second floor was a brothel. Before it was opened up into the big clubhouse it became, there was a center hall with 10 or 12 six foot by ten foot little "bedrooms."

"How 'bout the toga party?" added Volker. "I've still got the cassettes and talk about 'just like music but only different!!!' Every couple of years, around the second bottle of wine, I put a cassette of the occasion in my machine, and I can't make heads nor tails out of any of it. It sure is 'only different.'"

"That was where Walter Beck was outside in his toga and nothing else, dancing on top of cars as they stopped in front of the DP," said Malone:

Lady Luck must have lived there and all her cousins and aunts and uncles as well because he couldn't even manage to get arrested. In fact, none of us ever were. On top of that, one night I was loading my gear in the trunk of my car and drove all the way back to my apartment at Jefferson and Prytania and realized that I had left my 1956 Fender Telecaster by the curb where I was parked. Drove all the way back, and there it was waiting for me. Lady Luck loves a drunk.

"I loved the Dream Palace because it was always an intense gig," said Scanlan:

The audience was totally there to go down whatever road we were going to go. The wildest thing I ever saw in my life was at the Dream Palace, when we played the toga party. It was right after *Animal House* came out. Halloween was coming up, and they wanted to have a dry-run party before Halloween and decided on a toga party based on *Animal House*. Well, no matter what happened at Halloween, it was pale in comparison to what happened that night at the Dream Palace. Most of the people had on togas, which only lasted for about half an hour, so basically after half an hour, half of the people were naked running around. There were people fucking on the bar. And when you go upstairs to the dressing room of the Dream Palace, there were naked people lying all over the stairs, drunk, passed out, everybody's on acid. It started spilling out into the street, and it was so hard to get up and down the stairs that people started climbing up those poles to the balcony to get up and down so they didn't have to fight the stairs. Half of these people there didn't have any clothes on, and then it got to where somebody is in the middle of the street with no clothes on, and the traffic's jamming up because everybody's in the street. The police said they had reports as far as six blocks away, complaints of people wandering around with no clothes on, screaming and yelling. You can't imagine how insane this thing was that night. I remember we played "Morgus the Magnificent." It basically kind of encapsulated what the Dream Palace was all about.

"There was a lot of carryover from Luigi's to the Dream Palace," said Baudoin:

Frenchmen Street didn't have the number of clubs it has now. There were a whole lot of Tulane students. Barney Kilpatrick was on the Tulane radio station, and I think he was instrumental in getting us to play on the Tulane Quad. We won a lot of fans there, and through the years those fans have followed us., A lot of those people ended up in different states and cities, and when we would come there they'd phone everybody they knew. That eventually developed into the various krewes of Rads fans around the country.

"Signing with Epic put us on the road big time," said Scanlan:

They had a hard time pigeonholing us because, with something like two thousand original songs, it was hard for them to figure out an angle to put us in. We didn't really even get pigeonholed as a southern band as much as a roots rock band because, at that time, that was the thing. That was the catch word, roots rock, Springsteen, Petty. That whole genre was getting ready to make it big.

By the time of our second Epic album, *Zigzagging through Ghostland,* bands were being dropped, and tour support had dried up. We ended up begging to be cut. Most bands would have broken up even before that point, but through all of that stuff there was always this feeling of "this is the band; what are we going to do if we break up? Then what?" There's no guarantee that you'll ever be in a band this good again. How are you going to find a songwriter this good?

The Allman Brothers asked me to audition, but we all had this kind of feeling, like this is it. This is the band. And the idea of breaking up, I don't think, was even anything that was a consideration. That just wasn't even an option. The same thing happened with the Neville Brothers a year after the band got together; they asked me to audition for them.

" 'Wild and Free' I wrote not long after I had moved to Minneapolis in early '91," said Volker:

> The song, musically, was written with more harmonic twists and turns, but, like so much of what eventually becomes emblematic of the Rads ("Raindancer," "Doctor Doctor," "Seven Devils"), I simplified the tune to fit well within the repeating piano motif that intros the song, and it didn't take long, once I'd injected the tune into a gig, for it to become a likable staple. W&F says it all in the lyrics. It's a song of thanksgiving. The band sings it to the audience, and the audience sings it to the band…the graceful and grateful conviviality of community.

"It's kind of funny because sometimes you think, 'If we only had done this, or if we only would have done that,' kind of hindsight second-guessing," mused Scanlan:

> But, when you get to it, the bottom line is, here we are thirty years later, and we're still together, and we're still playing gigs. Maybe all those bad decisions ended up cumulatively being good decisions because bands that made the "right" decisions are history. You don't even remember who they are anymore. Especially at CBS, an album will come out, this guy's going to be the next Michael Jackson, he's going to be the next whatever; I can't even think of the guy's name now because you haven't

heard of him in twenty years, and there're tons of bands like that. They made all the right decisions, and say, for a year or two, they might have been flying real high, but then they all get in a fight, they break up. And, also one of the things, I think, too, that made it easy for the band to negotiate a lot of the stuff is Ed cutting the band in on his publishing. That, I think, went a long way with the band, subconsciously, at least, making a go at it because with a lot of songwriters, they're going to keep all of their royalties. Ed's attitude was, I'm writing the songs, but these guys are coming up with ideas and changing the songs—sometimes radically. So he kind of felt like everybody's contributing to the songs, everybody ought to get something, and I think, in that kind of generous spirit, everybody felt included, and nobody felt left out.

CHAPTER 21

Saving at the Bank of Soul

The American political winds raged at hurricane force during the summer and fall of 2008. The presidential campaign was taking place against the background of an economic meltdown that shook Wall Street to its foundations and sowed dissent throughout the country. Tab Benoit took the Voice of the Wetlands All-Stars on the road to both the Republican and Democratic conventions in an attempt to make the official response to the ongoing destruction of south Louisiana a real campaign issue.

Benoit tried to emphasize that his position was not ideological or partisan in a traditionally political way. "I don't consider myself an activist," he said:

> We're just trying to go around the country and educate people about what's happening and hope they want to help. What happened in New Orleans was mostly a problem of Louisiana losing its coastal wetlands. We don't want to rebuild a city that's gonna flood again. That wouldn't be smart. We've got to fix the coastal wetlands first. It's a big thing. It's not easy to do, and it's going to take some real serious leadership. Not everybody is going to benefit. When we have to fix this, not everybody is going to have a positive outlook on what needs to happen. But right now everybody is sacrificing everything. If it's not done, we have to move everything. We have to move the port of New Orleans, we have to move the refineries, we have to move all of those pipelines, we have to move all of the people. We have to move all that if we decide that we're not fixing this.

Benoit ended up getting a lot of press, and he was even able to make a trip to Washington, D.C., and present his case to lawmakers. His even-handed approach earned him an audience with Republicans, as well as Democrats. "I try to get in the middle," he reasoned, "because you've got angry citizens on one side and angry corporations on the other side." Benoit elaborated:

We walked in there and talked common sense to them and just left it on the table. One of the things that's easy about talking about the plight of coastal Louisiana is that there's a recorded history of it, so we can read it to them. We can show them pictures [and say]: "This is what it was like in the '50s. This is what it's like now. This is what it's going to be in fifty years. What are you gonna do about it?"

Though Benoit's campaign gave him a forum to talk about the problem, it still didn't produce any tangible results. George Porter Jr., one of Benoit's partners in the Voice of the Wetlands project, expressed frustration at the lack of progress the group was making.

"I'm proud of what we're doing, but we're not just a party band to make you shake your booty," said Porter:

This is a conscious effort by people to tell you what's going on. A lot of time we're just preaching to the choir. The people we're playing in front of are there for the party, so at that point we really aren't getting anything done because the people who we really need to be playing for are on the floor of the Congress. Those are the people who have written us off. The guys we elect to do nothing. They hear it, I think, but are they really hearing it? We've been preaching it since the hurricane. How much of what we've been saying has changed anything? If we get a category five tomorrow, and it's anywhere near the mouth of that river, we can kiss out butts goodbye because the new waterfront of New Orleans will be the north shore of Lake Pontchartrain. There won't be no more New Orleans. There won't be no Houma or Thibodeaux.

In late 2008 the New Orleans arts community got a huge boost from Prospect.1, the international arts festival organized by the Contemporary Art Center's (CAC) curator of visual arts, Dan Cameron. The event was designed to make New Orleans an arts destination along the lines of the Venice Bienniale. Prospect.1 presented art installations scattered across town, from Tulane University's Newcomb Art Gallery to the lower Ninth Ward, where Los Angeles–based artist Mark Bradford built a giant ark on Caffin Avenue. In addition to the numerous Prospect.1 sites, which included the CAC and the Old U.S. Mint near the *OffBeat* office, there were also numerous satellite sites, including the St. Roch neighborhood's KK Projects and the Ogden Museum of Southern Art.

My Bywater neighborhood is a traditional working-class community more recently populated by musicians and artists. Just as our paradigm of a theatrical troupe, the New Orleans Bingo! Show, rewarded the winner of each game with an onstage beating, our lives were ruled by a New Orleans variation on Russian roulette, in which the empty chambers were as full of possibilities as the winner's coup de grâce. A shot in the head was a likely way to go in a city that had become one of country's prime murder capitols. However, the fires that still leapt from roof to roof of the creole cottages of the neighborhood could be just as deadly, to say nothing of the continuing threat of killer hurricanes and the roulette of tornado activity.

Then, one day in late 2008, while the federal government was busy bailing out Wall Street, city officials shut down the Bank of Soul. The Bank of Soul was an art installation at the corner of Burgundy Street and Louisa, right in front of the Gallerie Porché, where local artist and photographer Christopher Porché West assembled elaborate works out of pieces of the rubble he had found in the ruins since 2005. Though he spent the years before Katrina photographing elements of New Orleans African American culture and learning to sew elaborate beaded vests from the Mardi Gras Indian members he befriended and documented, West stopped taking photos after the storm because he was too depressed by what he saw. Instead, he wandered through the ruins of the lower Ninth Ward and salvaged pieces of shipwrecked New Orleans history—giant mahogany bed-posts from a bedroom that no longer existed, a crumpled horn tossed on a slag heap, bits of architectural detail from gutted houses, sections of wrought-iron fence—and created shrines to the memory of a city that no longer existed.

West called these works made from found objects "reclamations," and the Bank of Soul was his signature piece, an installation meant to signify the cultural value inherent in these reclamations. The assemblage consisted of a rusty old safe guarded by a section of wrought-iron fence and crowned with a Mardi Gras Indian figure in a full suit of red feathers and elaborate, beaded embroidery. West designed it to help celebrate the first New Orleans biennial, the massive art show taking place all across the city. He painted "P.9" (for the Ninth Ward) on the front of the safe.

Somehow, though, city officials determined that, of all the art being show-cased in New Orleans at the time, the Bank of Soul was inappropriate. Perhaps the lack of corporate sponsorship spelled its ultimate doom—West had ideas about who was behind it, but the particulars are far less important than the result. Without warning, a demolition crew came around, jackhammered the piece out of the cement, and repaved the corner. West salvaged the broken pieces of his work, moved the safe up the block, and placed some of the other pieces of the installation in his front window. Meanwhile, West carefully set about realizing a clever piece of retaliation. He painted the sidewalk in front of his gallery gold, right where the Bank of Soul had been. "Let them try to do something about that!" he chuckled.

Over in Treme, another version of the Bank of Soul was being serviced. The Zion Hill Missionary Baptist Church at 1126 North Robertson Street was a modest brick structure just off of Ursuline Street. The church, right by the house on North Robertson where Glen David Andrews grew up, was established by African Americans in the first decade of the twentieth century. This is the church Glen David attended as a child, the place where he learned to sing the gospel songs that have become a staple of his live performances and where his mother, Vanna Acker, worked. When he was a child, Andrews learned that the church had been founded by his relatives. The sense that this was part of the birthright Glen David saw being challenged in his neighborhood inspired him to make an album in tribute to the church, a live recording that would capture the spirit of the gospel services of his youth.

On November 18, 2008, Andrews brought his working band to Zion Hill Missionary for a musical service accompanied by the choir and its director, keyboardist Charisse Mason. Money to fund the project came from the cooperative artist/investor venture that was changing the nature of the recording industry in New Orleans, Threadhead Records. The recording captured the emotional power of the gospel music experience by melding Glen David's dynamic performing strengths with the intensity of an African American church service. Pastor Sidney Joshua opened the proceedings by saying, "We thank you, Lord, for the benefit of another day." Glen David was introduced as the band played "Down by the Riverside," and he proceeded to preach to the audience: "Everybody stand up!" His extroverted vocal was answered and supported by the deep presence of a full-voiced gospel choir, which raised his own excitement to another level. During "Jesus on the Mainline" Andrews started improvising: "I got that number, 1-800-Jesus," and urged the listeners to send Jesus a text message.

At times the choir simply took over, as on "Just a Closer Walk with Thee," and at other times the service became more of a Glen David Andrews concert. Paul Sanchez, who cowrote the title track, "Walking through Heaven's Gate," with Andrews, joined him on that song. Andrews followed with what had become one of his signature performances on the spiritual "I'll Fly Away." John Boutté joined the proceedings to sing "Battle Hymn of the Republic," and Troy Andrews stepped up to play trumpet on "We Will Walk through the Streets of the City" and the finale, "Family," a spoken-word evocation of the consolations of domestic life, delivered by poet Chuck Perkins.

Andrews had become well known for the unvarnished emotion of his performances, but the passion in his voice during this one touched some deeper well of feeling. African American gospel services have long soothed the wounds of great suffering in the people who attend them, and Glen David Andrews was bathing himself in some much-needed salvation at Zion Hill. The last words Andrews heard at Zion Hill were this fervent message, sung by the gospel choir: "Pray for me." Two days later he flew to California and checked into a rehabilitation facility.

CHAPTER 22

It Ain't Just the Suit

On a warm, sunny winter's day in 2009 I set out to talk with one of the most important figures in the Mardi Gras Indian community, Bo Dollis Sr., big chief of the Wild Magnolias. I arrived at his home above the beauty parlor run by his wife, Rita, at the corner of Louisiana and Barrone, hoping he was in good enough shape to hold a conversation. The sixty-four-year-old big chief was in poor health and had difficulty speaking.

Dollis was born on January 14, 1944, with an extraordinary gift that eventually made him a sacred figure in New Orleans and a fabulous symbol of the city's unique culture everywhere else. Bo had a voice that set him apart. He had a native ability to sing that was apparent from early childhood. He had no formal musical training, and he didn't come from one of New Orleans's legendary musical families, but when he sang in church, people noticed. At home Bo proudly exercised his vocal talents to the delight of friends and visitors.

Dollis grew up on Jackson Avenue in Central City, where the esoteric African American society of Mardi Gras Indians offered an alluring and vaguely dangerous brotherhood. Bo became fascinated with the elaborate beaded costumes a neighbor fashioned for Mardi Gras and Saint Joseph's Day and started hanging out at a backyard Indian "practice" in the neighborhood.

Bo's parents feared the reputation for violence that had built up over the years as gangs from different sections of the city engaged in bloody turf wars. They forbade him from joining up with a gang, but Bo secretly sewed his own Indian suit out of fragments of his neighbor's old costumes and marched on Mardi Gras Day with the Golden Arrows when he was thirteen years old.

The mystical strength of the word at the heart of Mardi Gras Indian ritual resided in Dollis, whose preacher's powers made him stand out after he joined the Wild Magnolias. Though he was a relative newcomer, Dollis quickly rose from flag boy to big chief in 1964, largely because of his singing ability. As big chief of the Wild Magnolias, Bo helped refashion the nature and practices of Mardi Gras Indian culture and protocol throughout the 1960s and preserved the traditional ritual texts, but he changed the nature of the competition between tribes and brought the Indians to a wider audience. Bo Dollis was part of a new wave of Mardi Gras Indians that eschewed violence and sublimated the competition between gangs into a contest of costumes, the prettier and more elaborate the better.

Mardi Gras Indian culture made a dramatic breakthrough to the outside world in 1970, when Dollis and his childhood friend Monk Boudreaux organized a Mardi Gras Indian second line as part of the inaugural edition of the New Orleans Jazz and Heritage Festival, which took place across the street from the French Quarter in Congo Square. New Orleans had just emerged from the social restrictions of segregation. It was a truly historic moment for a city scarred by the American original sin of slavery to have an African American secret society lead an integrated public parade to a spot where their ancestors had kept alive sacred traditions brought from their West African communities. The voice of Bo Dollis called the way into the promised land.

Dollis also took a bold step toward opening Mardi Gras Indian culture to the outside world that same year when he, Boudreaux, and the Wild Magnolias made a commercial recording of their hitherto secret liturgical music, cutting a 45-rpm record produced by Jazz Fest founder Quint Davis, "Handa Wanda."

The first Magnolias recordings were fairly representative of what the gangs sounded like as they paraded down the street, playing small percussion instruments and chanting. However, in performance they began to be accompanied by keyboardist Willie Tee, who wrote arrangements for the chants and put together a funk backup for them with his band, the Gaturs. In 1974 the Magnolias released the legendary *Wild Magnolias* album, backed by a New Orleans all-star band that included Willie Tee, his brother Earl Turbinton Jr. on saxophone, Snooks Eaglin on guitar, and Alfred ("Uganda") Roberts on percussion. This band's performance at the Bottom Line in New York led to international recognition.

Eventually the Wild Magnolias developed two performance styles, traditional parade music and a funk/R&B concert band. Over the years Dollis led these bands with his commanding vocal presence and by writing some of the most important new compositions in the Mardi Gras Indian canon, including "Handa Wanda" and "Smoke My Peace Pipe." As a result, the Wild Magnolias became the most celebrated Mardi Gras Indian tribe. They built an international audience and opened up the music's conceptual borders to the point where Japanese guitarist June Yamagishi joined the band. Through it all, the keening cry of Bo Dollis's voice called the Indians to the parade.

But by 2009 Dollis could no longer rely on that magnificent instrument. Incapacitated by a stroke and weakened by heart surgery and a three-times-a-week regimen of dialysis treatments, he had difficulty speaking and suffered memory lapses. I was in luck the day I visited him. He was able to see me, and his afflictions did not dampen his still cheerful spirit. He greeted me with a warm smile and a firm handshake. The strong afternoon light illuminated scores of feathery tufts that fell from the Indian suit Bo's son Gerard had donned for a photo session. Bo's speech was halting, but Gerard sat beside him, prompting his memory at times and filling in some historical detail.

Like many other New Orleans musicians, Dollis began singing as a boy in church. "Everbody went to church. My mama and brothers went," he recalled. It was an effort for him to speak, and his hoarse, whispered words came out in short, halting phrases:

> It was just singing. I didn't think anything of it. I would sing with the choir at church. We just sang around the house. People would come to hear me sing. We would try different things. I can't say it like I wish I could anymore. Everybody liked to hear me.
>
> I sang…what's his name…Fats Domino! Yeah, that's who I liked. I wanted to be like him. He was older. Everything he would do, I'd try to sing. People would say, "He sounds just like Fats Domino."

Dollis was introduced to Indian culture by a neighbor. "He was an Indian chief," said Dollis:

> and he was right there where I lived, and I used to watch him make an Indian suit. He was with the White Eagles, and I used to watch him. He'd give me little pieces, and I tried to make one myself. So I made my first Indian suit. I went with the White Eagles, but they had a big chief, and I could only be a Red Indian with them, so I left. So I ended up with the Wild Magnolias because there I got a spot. I got with them, and I got to be a flag boy. I've been with them ever since.

Dollis must have been one hell of a flag boy because he moved up to big chief pretty quickly. "I had a good voice, and they wanted me to sing," he explained:

> With the White Eagles I couldn't sing. See, the Indians can't sing. They can answer, but they can't sing. We walk down the street, and I sing [amazingly, his voice opened up to full strength as he sang a patois that ended with "Down the Street Here I Come"].
>
> You put on a suit. You look good. I was…young. They say they want me to be chief, and some of the people in there were 35, 55. I said, "I don't wanna be no big chief," and everybody say, "Rah, you good! You gotta sang (sic), you big chief." I wanted to be the spy boy. I was young, and I could move around. I wanted to spy out on the other

tribes. I would sing, and what you hear Indians sing today is what I was singing then. You don't hear too many of the new Indians singing the older songs, but it's more of the stuff that I used to do. They don't know the words to the songs. They may know the title, like "Hey Pocky Way" or "Iko Iko," but they don't know the words to the song. Some of the older Indians—they come, they say they don't know the words. They just making it up. They don't know what they're doing. They not Mardi Gras Indians. They just talkin'... They just crazy. All that's lost. Nobody know. They don't try. There's no more Indians. We were young. One time with the Indians you could go from up here to Treme and back, marching. Now you can't go from here to up the block because the suits are too big. Heh heh heh. They got to be carried on a cart because the suits is too big for the people, too heavy. It's pretty... Everybody want to be chief, hee hee hee.

Gerard elaborated on his father's observation:

You know that flag boy might have a flag in his hand, the Wild Man might be carrying a wooden shotgun, that's how you tell who they are. The chief is supposed to have the biggest crown, that's how you tell who he is. Today you might see some flag boy with a bigger crown than the chief! When I started out, you had five, six patches.[1] Now I've been doing it a while, so I got twenty patches, but nobody starts with five, six patches now. Now I don't think nobody want to be an Indian except for the Wild Man.

In 1970, the first year of Jazz Fest, Bo Dollis and Monk Boudreaux brought the Mardi Gras Indians to the public in an entirely new way. "We led the first parade," said Dollis. "Me and Monk. I put my suit on and started singing, leading a second line, down Canal Street all through the French Quarter, singing all the way to Congo Square, and the people followed along all the way. I was singing. With all the other Indians."

Dollis recalled how the Indians replaced the violence that often occurred when rival tribes met each other on the streets with a ritual confrontation based on which group was wearing the more beautiful costumes. "We tell about the days way back they was wild wild. I mean they was cuttin', killin', and shootin'. The uptown and the downtown would fight. We didn't want that. So we stop. Tootie Montana was big on that. He wanted to get it straight. 'Cause he was beautiful. He looked so good. Then everybody wanted to be... beautiful. So we got all the Indians and all the chiefs to stop the violence."

Gerard added:

> We all just wanted to change it. It came about the suits. We fought with
> pretty suits instead of our hands and knives and guns. Y'know, back in
> the old days it was like we'd fight in the day, then at night we'd buy each
> other drinks in the bar. But when it comes to guns, there's no buying
> drinks after the fight. Once the guns come out, you're either going to
> jail, or you'll be six feet under.

Bo Dollis then made the point that the gangs behind the street violence in
contemporary New Orleans are refighting the territorial wars the Indian gangs
used to fight. "The gangs today—they kind of like looking like those old Indians
were with the way they fight and shoot," he noted.

That offered a note of hope: "Maybe they can stop the violence again like you
guys did," I suggested. "They won't until they can find somebody to lead them
there," said Dollis. "They need a chief to take care of it."

After we finished talking, I walked out into the loft space where Gerard was
working on the costumes he and other members of the Wild Magnolias would
wear on Mardi Gras day. Gerard ("Bo Junior") was busy making the suits and
helping to care for his ailing father while effectively taking over his father's role
both in live performance and on Mardi Gras day.

"I wake up on Mardi Gras morning, get dressed, and head for Second and
Dryades," said Bo Junior, referencing a traditional meeting place for Mardi Gras
Indians:

> We have men, women, and children coming out, and I have to make
> sure they're all dressed before I get dressed, especially I have to help
> my father get dressed before I get dressed. He's gonna be dressed in a
> simple suit, just shirt and pants, and he's gonna ride on a motor scooter
> to the places where we go. Then I'll suit up and do the Indian prayers,
> and then we move out. Normally we'll go over to where my dad grew
> up at on Jackson Avenue, and we'll stand in front of his old house for a
> few minutes. Then we'll move on from there. At Mardi Gras time we try
> not to book so many shows with the band because we're trying to get
> ready for Mardi Gras day.

All around the city other Black Indians were preparing their suits for Fat
Tuesday. Downtown in the Seventh Ward David Montana sat at his workspace
on a cold, sunny January afternoon meticulously sewing the costume he would
display to the world when he walked out of his front door on Mardi Gras morning. Montana sews his suits with help from friends and members of his family.

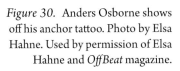

Figure 29. Alex McMurray chows down. Photo by Elsa Hahne. Used by permission of Elsa Hahne and *OffBeat* magazine.

Figure 30. Anders Osborne shows off his anchor tattoo. Photo by Elsa Hahne. Used by permission of Elsa Hahne and *OffBeat* magazine.

Figure 31. Mark Bingham at Piety Street Studio. Photo by Elsa Hahne. Used by permission of Elsa Hahne and *OffBeat* magazine.

Figure 32. Bo Dollis Sr. with Bo Dollis Jr. in background. Photo by Elsa Hahne. Used by permission of Elsa Hahne and *OffBeat* magazine.

Figure 33. Dr. Michael White. Photo by Elsa Hahne. Used by permission of Elsa Hahne and *OffBeat* magazine.

Figure 34. Russ Broussard and Susan Cowsill. Photo by Elsa Hahne. Used by permission of Elsa Hahne and *OffBeat* magazine.

Figure 35. Helen Gillet. Photo by Elsa Hahne. Used by permission of Elsa Hahne and *OffBeat* magazine.

Figure 36. Breakfast with John Boutté. Photo by Elsa Hahne. Used by permission of Elsa Hahne and *OffBeat* magazine.

Figure 37. Leroy Jones and his wife, Katja, at their home in Treme. Photo by Elsa Hahne. Used by permission of Elsa Hahne and *OffBeat* magazine.

Figure 38. New Orleans's ninety-nine-year-old trumpet eminence Lionel Ferbos. Photo by Elsa Hahne. Used by permission of Elsa Hahne and *OffBeat* magazine.

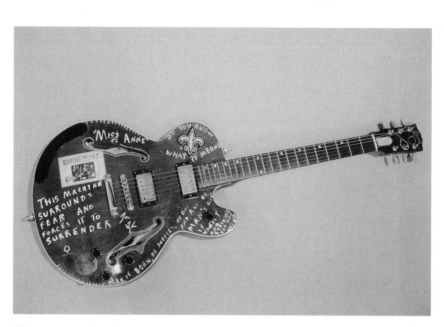

Figure 39. Portrait of Paul Sanchez's guitar. Photo by Elsa Hahne. Used by permission of Elsa Hahne and *OffBeat* magazine.

Figure 40. Paul Sanchez. Photo by Elsa Hahne. Used by permission of Elsa Hahne and *OffBeat* magazine.

Figure 41. Seguenon Kone with hand drums. Photo by Elsa Hahne. Used by permission of Elsa Hahne and *OffBeat* magazine.

Figure 42. Tab Benoit. Photo by Elsa Hahne. Used by permission of Elsa Hahne and *OffBeat* magazine.

Figure 43. Allen Toussaint. Photo by Elsa Hahne. Used by permission of Elsa Hahne and *OffBeat* magazine.

Figure 44. Left to right: Lionel Ferbos, 99; Gregg Stafford, 58; Jeremy Davenport, 40; Shamarr Allen, 29; Kermit Ruffins, 45; Jack Fine, 81; Christian Scott, 27 (current ages as of August 2010). Photo by Elsa Hahne. Used by permission of Elsa Hahne and *OffBeat* magazine.

"No one man could do this alone. I've got a lot of helpers," he said. "All of those beads, they represent many, many fingers."

David is the nephew of one of the greatest Mardi Gras Indian chiefs, Allison ("Tootie") Montana, who was with the Yellow Pocahontas Indians for fifty-two years. Tootie died in June 2005 of a heart attack, surrounded by a group of other black Indian chiefs and their families, during a dramatic confrontation with city officials over police brutality. In his role as second chief, David helps keeps the Yellow Pocahontas tradition alive by parading on Mardi Gras Day through his neighborhood.

Montana considers his suit a sacred vestment and compares it to the Holy Communion suit of his Catholic upbringing. "On Mardi Gras Day, when I walk out of my house, everybody is waiting to see me in my suit," he said:

> I think of the theme in a spiritual sense. My theme this year is wild-life. It's a scene with an eagle going into a pit of albino boa constrictors. I have a queen, dressed in a matching suit, and a special little queen, that's my grandbaby Dynasti Smith. She's a good queen. Man, she dances and sings. She knows what to do. It's in some of us, and in some of us it's not. I feel proud wearing the suit, but I feel even prouder that I can get all these people together to help me to do this.

The Indians were all trying to come to terms with a changing social landscape that no longer directly challenges the cultural heritage of distant ancestors who were brought from West Africa as slaves but now offers the more subtle challenge of merging that heritage into mainstream America in the post–civil rights era.

The Sunday practices of chants and music, the hundreds of hours of costume preparation, and the parades themselves are sacred rituals with roots in the West African tribal communities the ancestors of these men were separated from. The Mardi Gras Indians have faced myriad threats to their survival over the decades as the New Orleans political establishment passed laws to stop them from gathering and racist citizens attacked their parades. They were treated very much like Native Americans by those who believed that white, European cultures were superior, so the practice of adopting Native American appearances to preserve the tribal cultures of various West African peoples may have originally been an expression of solidarity, as well as a front for a secret society.

Ever since his mother told him that there was a Native American bloodline in his family, Cyril Neville began emphasizing the connection between the African American community he grew up in in New Orleans and the Native American community. Neville has a connection to the Mardi Gras Indians as well through his uncle, Big Chief Jolly of the Wild Tchoupitoulas. "When my uncle would be making his suits, I would be helping, threading needles and stuff like that," said Neville. "The conversations were about Native American culture and history. Being a Mardi Gras Indian is like being part of a Social Aid and Pleasure Club. It's not just something that happens on Mardi Gras Day. It's our link to our African heritage, as well as a link to our Native American heritage, because a lot of the Mardi Gras Indians have Native American blood." He went on:

> My brother Charles and I have both recorded with native people. There was a group he recorded with called Songcatchers. I just got finished recording with a Navajo group called Blackfire, the Blackfire family. The name of the record is *Common Ground*. The other thing we've been doing even before Katrina was Big Chief Tootie Montana and Orville Lookinghorse and Rev. Goat Carson put together August 27 as White Buffalo day, and it's been going on all that time. At one time people thought the Mardi Gras Indians was mockery. Reverend Goat Carson started writing letters to all the Native American people he knew, and he somehow got Tootie and Orville together. Orville Lookinghorse is a Lakota Sioux secret pipe carrier, and he's the equivalent of Tootie as far as native people are concerned. As far as we were concerned at the time, Tootie Montana was the oldest masking Indian in New Orleans and knew more about it than anybody else and came up with the idea of having something like that to further help preserve our culture and not deny the connection between Native American Indians and Mardi Gras Indians.
>
> We started bringing kids from New Orleans to the reservations in Dakota and dance with the great-grandson of Sitting Bull with the Navajo in Arizona. We went up to the Hopi, where the kids from New Orleans delivered gifts to children on the reservation. It's all documented on living folklore.com. Victor Harris can be seen on there dancing with his full regalia on. There's an amazing story that goes along with it. A chief of the Lakota had a dream about discovering this long-lost tribe, which he described as the birdmen. Their skins was black, the habili-ments looked like birds. He saw a picture of the Mardi Gras Indians and pointed at it and said, "That's what I saw in my dream." This gathering happens every year on August 27, but if you ask about it on the other side of Canal Street, they ain't gonna tell you nothing about that. So we started the White Buffalo Indian Children's Nation. We took some of the kids from our neighborhood and brought them up to Arizona. Goat Carson and Big Chief Victor Harris brought kids up to Wayne River up in South Dakota.

From the 1880s until the passage of the Voting Rights Act in 1965, New Orleans was in fact an apartheid city, but the dramatic social change that occurred during the civil rights era led to the historic moment in 1970, when New Orleans finally accepted the Mardi Gras Indians as part of its official culture at the first New Orleans Jazz and Heritage Festival.

The nature of the Mardi Gras Indian gangs has changed dramatically in recent years as women and children have begun participating more frequently in the rituals and the events have become part of the city's tourist attractions, especially at Jazz Fest, but at other festivals as well. Indians in full dress started showing up as part of New Orleans entertainment revues on the casino floor at Harrah's. However, in the first years after Katrina, the Black Indian culture was impacted by the depopulation of several of the city's poorest communities. Though the Wild Magnolias have regained a full contingent of followers, many of the lesser-known groups have declined as the Indians themselves and the communities that supported them scattered in the wake of Hurricane Katrina.

How does the new generation of Mardi Gras Indians survive? The answer seems to lie in both a consolidation of what is left of their community culture and in an outreach to those who may not understand that culture the same way but still like it. Those who claim that makes them simply entertainers miss the point. You don't spend seven thousand hours sewing a sacred costume because you want to compete on *American Idol.* The Black Indian habiliments are meant to signify nature spirits, not act as fashion statements, and the chants and dances are religious text, not mumbo jumbo.

David Montana thinks this process of opening up to the outside world was inevitable.

"It was meant to be," he said:

> When you do something for beauty, it's not meant to be locked up and not shared and showed. The time that is put into these suits give[s] them beauty. When time goes into art, then you get what you call spirit. Tootie had the spirit. My father had the spirit. Donald Harrison had the spirit. Bo Dollis had the spirit. His suits weren't as elaborate, but his words, his songs, his voice—all that goes with that. It ain't just the suit, man.

In reaching out to this new audience, the Black Indians now participate in various composite shows with other New Orleans musicians or even national touring bands like Widespread Panic. The identity and purpose of the Mardi Gras Indian organizations have been the subject of much debate and speculation over the years. Some members resist the opening up of their secret societies to outsiders. City officials still discourage their public gatherings by charging exorbitant fees for parade permits and requiring police "escorts," who often cause more trouble than they prevent. But one thing is certain. The American society that up until civil rights and the voting rights acts of the mid-1960s challenged the validity of black citizenship altogether has changed dramatically. The mixed-race band 101 Runners performed with Mardi Gras Indians in front of a nearly all-white crowd at the 2008 Voodoo Festival and had them shouting the chant "Handa Wanda Obama!" Americans elected a black president less than a week later. "I never thought I'd live to see that," said Bo Dollis.

In the wake of the federal flood, the Mardi Gras Indians represented something else along with the sacred culture they brought here from African communities. They are a very real part of American culture, period.

CHAPTER 23

Bourbon Street Blues

On Friday night, January 16, 2009 the French Quarter was bustling in anticipation of a big weekend. It wasn't too early to be thinking about the Mardi Gras festivities, which were only weeks away. Wendy Byrne, a tough, funny bartender at Aunt Tiki's bar on Decatur Street, was looking forward to "the season," which stretches from Mardi Gras through Jazz Fest, when many French Quarter service-industry people make the bulk of their yearly salary in tips. Byrne ended her shift at Aunt Tiki's and headed with a friend up Governor Nichols street toward another bar she worked at, Starlight by the Park, on North Rampart Street.

After crossing Bourbon Street Byrne and her friend were accosted by three teenage boys in a robbery attempt. Byrne, a seasoned Quarter Rat well versed in the methods of dealing with a wide range of people, just kept walking. One of the kids did what street punks all over the world learn to do. He shot her in the back. Just another stupid murder in New Orleans. But when the victim is a popular French Quarter personality and the shooting takes place a block from Bourbon Street, the foundations of New Orleans's viability as a tourist destination take another blow. Impromptu memorials sprang up in front of both bars where Byrne worked.

Bourbon Street was once a center of musical activity in New Orleans. Live music of all descriptions once flowed from just about every doorway on the strip from Iberville to Saint Ann. Since Katrina, the live-music quotient has dropped dramatically as karaoke joints, T-shirt stores, frozen daiquiri stands, and strip clubs have proliferated. Breasts are bared, and beads fly nightly as Mardi Gras has become the brand of this licentious Disneyworld, which strobes and pulses like a giant video game.

Though Bourbon Street's heyday as a live music Mecca had passed, the incredible Big Al Carson remained a true throwback to the days when the best musicians in town played Bourbon Street. Carson and his band, the Blues Masters, drew large and enthusiastic crowds at the Funky Pirate, where the lethal Hand Grenade, "the French Quarter's most powerful drink," was administered.

Figure 45. Part of Wendy Byrne memorial in front of Aunt Tiki's. Photo by John Swenson. Used by permission of John Swenson.

People often spilled out the front door into the street trying to get a good look at the 450–500-pound mountain of a man playing a persona that placed him in the pantheon of New Orleans musical deities. Though he grew up playing tuba in the city's traditional brass bands, Carson became an accomplished blues and R&B vocalist at the Pirate.

On a typical night, Carson was seated front stage, smiling at the crowd behind tinted eyeglasses, his long, curly black hair and three-quarter beard framing his jovial visage. His shirt was invariably stretched tight over his massive torso. He might have begun singing an Al Green tune like "Love and Happiness" in a sweet, rich falsetto that plummeted into baritone range whenever Carson wanted it to. When the song reached Harry Sterling's guitar solo, Carson slowly rubbed his stomach in a circular motion and smiled lasciviously at a woman seated at a table close to the stage. It was a moment of astonishing sexual power and charisma, all subtle gestures until Carson flashed his lengthy tongue, and the woman yelled her approval. Carson often resorted to onstage pillow talk with his avid lady fans, promising sexual rewards of unusual eccentricity, but his control of the range and direction of this bawdy talk as it ran from the suggestive play of "Nursery Rhyme" to the slow, nasty blues of "Dip My Dipper" was the work of a masterful entertainer.

"He's been doing that as long as I know him," said Sterling, who first met Carson in 1975 and had been playing with him at the Pirate for more than fifteen years. "He gets onstage, and he'll make a suggestion that will drive the women crazy. Then he'll take it further and further and further. When he's offstage he's a completely different person."

Carson had his own ideas about his sex appeal.

"I think it's a combination of confidence in knowing who you are and what you are," he said. "I think ladies like that when you know who you are. If you're a big man, you're a big man, y'know what I'm sayin'? Don't try to hide it. I truly believe I can be just as much to you as the man with the muscles."

Sterling has watched Carson work thousands of audiences over the years.

"People are there to have a good time, and he adopts that persona," said Sterling. "Once we talked about changing the words, and he said, 'If we do that, we'll be out of a job tomorrow. These people come here to hear me talk nasty. The men bring their wives so they can hear me talk sexy, then they bring them back to the hotels to have sex. The nastier, the better.' "

That risqué atmosphere has been a Bourbon Street staple for a hundred years or more and has made Carson a living link to the strip's heyday. "I worked Bourbon Street when I was younger as a tuba player," he said. "I played with all the old brass bands. I like the tradition. I'm definitely old school. Every once in a while, I like to take a tuba gig, although I can't walk anymore, so I can't play in the marching brass bands. But I lost my horns in the storm. I lost a couple of PA systems, all my albums, and memorabilia from when I was on the road with One Mo' Time."

Despite losing his home, Carson was back on Bourbon Street in October 2005. "We were one of the first bands back on Bourbon Street when the National Guard was running things, and there was nobody in town," he said. "It was a little creepy. There was no light at first. It was kind of dark for a while, and there was nobody in town. People who were here were just coming to town to work. Music was important then. It was important for people to know that Bourbon Street was back in action, that New Orleans hadn't lost its culture. It meant everything."

Carson was sanguine about the lack of critical credibility that comes with playing the commercial strip. "Sometimes I truly believe that I'm the best-kept secret in New Orleans," he said:

> People say "You should be in New York" or whatever, but I see a lot of people in here over and over again. Everybody has a place they go, and I guarantee that I bring people into this place, and when their friends come to town, they bring them in here because they know it's always good. I know people who schedule their vacations around seeing the

Blues Masters at Funky Pirate. They email the office to make sure they're going to see me when they get here.

Carson had no intention of leaving any time soon. "I've never thought of relocating," he said, "because New Orleans is not just my home. New Orleans is me. I always say to my wife, 'I be's Creole.' You know what I'm sayin'. That whole gumbo. It all comes out in the music."

Trumpeter Irvin Mayfield decided to do something about the decline of live music on Bourbon Street. In early 2009 Mayfield partnered with the Royal Sonesta Hotel in a new music club, Irvin Mayfield's Jazz Playhouse.

At thirty-one, Mayfield had a list of accomplishments most musicians don't amass in a lifetime—five albums by the New Orleans Latin jazz dance band he cofounded, Los Hombres Calientes, four solo albums, a duets recording with Ellis Marsalis, and two albums leading the New Orleans Jazz Orchestra (NOJO). Mayfield had won a fistful of awards and citations and built a lengthy résumé in both the civic and academic worlds.

For all that, Mayfield's biggest talent was as a businessman. He had just negotiated a new recording contract with Harmonia Mundi for the New Orleans Jazz Orchestra, one of several musical organizations he operates, and sold the Royal Sonesta hotel on a branding concept he vowed would change the nature of Bourbon Street.

"We are planting a flag together," said Mayfield as he sipped coffee while sitting on one of the plush white couches he installed in the club:

> Two businesses saying, "We are going to invest in jazz in a meaningful way." The Royal Sonesta's core values are authentic experiences. Look at the architecture of this hotel. It's 100 percent New Orleans. And that's very close to what my core values and what Irvin Mayfield's art is about. Our brands match together very well. It's not just about this room. The Royal Sonesta wants to have the effect of the brand throughout the hotel. They want jazz to be part of the experience and aesthetic of every hotel guest. It won't be just in the club. It will also be reflected in the rooms, the outside of the hotel, and even what we plan to do with Bourbon Street.

Mayfield tried to start a club before when he was a partner in Ray's Over the River in 2005, but the posh jazz club atop the World Trade Center was destroyed by hurricanes Katrina and Rita. The experience gave Mayfield some perspective on the dynamics of running a music club, but his vision for Irvin's Playhouse owed more to the success of New Orleans restaurants.

"The culinary industry is now a branded experience in the French Quarter," he pointed out:

Chef Prudhomme, Emeril, the Brennans, Susan Spicer. Where is the branded experience for Ellis Marsalis? For Aaron Neville? What the art does is give you an opportunity to provide leadership and to distill certain attributes and qualities that you think are important. You go to a club, the music might be great, but the place wasn't built for that music. Everything, from the forks and napkins on up, restaurants think this through because the culinary industry is not just about food, it's about relationships. And music in this town is the primary builder of relationships.

In the culinary industry the presentation and everything that surrounds that all is part of the artistic experience for the chef. Today the chef is the restauranteur, which wasn't the case twenty years ago. Back then, chefs were like indentured servants. With musicians, our artistic experience stops with the creation of a song or a CD. We don't create environments. I don't think we think enough about what this stuff means. Take an architect. An architect designs buildings, but it's not just an artistic sensibility at work. The architect has to think about functionality. Same with the chefs. They want to inspire the next round of chefs that are coming up. They want to inspire people to cook and eat this food when they go home. The musician only thinks about the audience, but what about the environment? The environment can inspire a lot of different things.

Mayfield's vision for the club included a remake of the furniture, the menu, and the musical lineup, which had ranged from jazz vocalists to piano trios. Mayfield booked regular appearances by vocalist Johnaye Kendrick, Leon ("Kid Chocolate") Brown, Shamarr Allen, and Glen David Andrews. He also moved his Wednesday night jam session from Snug Harbor over to the new club.

"It's not just about me," said Mayfield:

We've lined up some great young talent. Unfortunately, one of the casualties of this situation was my night at Snug's, which we really worked hard at for two years. I really enjoyed that. But I'm putting all my effort into this club, of course. Everything in this space, including the menu, will be all about the music. You want sports? There are great sports bars around here. You want to watch great jazz videos? This is the place to come.

Snug Harbor's Jason Patterson had good things to say about Mayfield's work at his club. Not only wasn't he unhappy about Mayfield leaving his Wednesday night showcase, but he also predicted that Irvin's Playhouse would do a lot to promote New Orleans jazz.

"He's driven," said Patterson:

> [H]e surrounded himself with great players here, so it was an enter-taining show, as well as being true to the art form. The gist of NOJO was having players who were all at a very high level so they would enjoy playing with each other. Irvin likes being ringmaster. I wish him all the luck with what he wants to do at the Royal Sonesta. If any-thing, it enhances what we do because it helps define New Orleans as really being a jazz capital. Irvin is a great promoter not just of his own ventures but of New Orleans. He has greater aspirations that any jazz musician I've ever known. We admire and respect the NOJO organi-zation and have no hard feelings. So we wish him well and hope he comes back to visit.

Mayfield's ultimate goal was to persuade the New Orleans business commu-nity to finance a National Jazz Center with a concert hall that would provide a home for the New Orleans Jazz Orchestra. Though the project was stalled, May-field pitched the idea with the cunning of a master salesman.

"We have to build a National Jazz Center," he argued:

> There are a lot of folks interested in making this thing happen. When they opened the Mahalia Jackson Hall, there were no dates available for the New Orleans Jazz Orchestra. We have no place to put on our 2010 dates. But that's okay because there's enough of an audience here that we should have more than one venue. I'm trying as hard as I can to bring people to the table. But we have to demonstrate what we're capable of. That's part of what this club is about.

Mayfield's main inspiration in lobbying for the National Jazz Center and becoming involved in civic and political life was Wynton Marsalis, whom he lived with in New York during the 1990s:

> Living with Wynton was probably the largest influence on my life. What really inspired me was that he was in enough of a position of leadership in New York where he could build a $185 million building. No one diminished him for being a musician. Here people say things like, "How can the chairman of the board of the public library be just a trumpeter?" What I saw Wynton do in New York was one of the reasons I became interested in policy here, interested in government, interested

in the collegiate experience. He was able to do that successfully there. He brought a fresh perspective on the role that music played in the city's culture, and he was able to convince the leaders of his arguments. I watched him tell Rudy Guiliani that no one remembers the pope who achieved economic greatness. No one remembers the pope that instituted a great sewer system or infrastructure in the city. They remember the pope that commissioned the Sistine Chapel. You want to talk about legacy. Art and culture is the stuff that really counts. Yes, we need clean streets, but use the culture as an economic engine that drives that.

Mayfield returned from his New York experience with a burning ambition to marry his musical instincts with social and political goals. In addition to his work with Los Hombres Calientes and his solo projects, in 2002 Mayfield founded the Institute of Jazz Culture at Dillard University and created the New Orleans Jazz Orchestra, a direct emulation of what Wynton Marsalis did in New York. Though the audaciousness of Mayfield's gestures raised eyebrows in some quarters, he has gone on to do some fine work with NOJO.

Mayfield also started to come to the attention of business and political leaders in New Orleans. He considers former Entergy CEO Dan Packard, who made Mayfield the first professional musician on the city's chamber of commerce, one of his mentors.

"I was chairman of the regional chamber when I met him," said Packard. "I didn't know him, but I had seem him play a couple of times. We started talking, and I realized how much he had to offer, how bright and intelligent he was. It was the whole package. I was looking for someone to get involved in the chamber from an arts perspective. He was well spoken, and he was not intimidated by being in a different setting."

Mayfield was made a cultural ambassador of the city of New Orleans, joined the Champions Group of the New Orleans Museum of Art, and served on a number of committees, including the Louisiana Rebirth Advisory Board and the cultural subcommittee of the Bring New Orleans Back Commission. Packard advised Mayor Ray Nagin to appoint Mayfield chairman of the board of the New Orleans Library Board of Directors.

Mayfield's tenure at the library was controversial. Instead of settling into a traditional role of fund-raiser, he shook up the staff, forcing out several top librarians and prompting *Library Journal* to report that the system had been showing "signs of disarray" since he took over. In December 2008 the New Orleans *Times-Picayune* published a largely unfavorable piece on Mayfield's tenure at the library.

But Mayfield took the criticism in stride. "We're surviving on the fumes of our culture now, and we've got to do better," he said:

A child will recover from a trauma, but the issue is, how will that child recover? It's the same thing with the library. The libraries are coming back, but how they're coming back is the issue. Do we make it what we want it to be, something that responds to the community's needs, or do we accept the piecemeal structure we had before? We have to integrate music into the library. We have to use it to teach the children about the history of their music, the history of jazz.

Mayfield argued that the biggest problem facing New Orleans music is how to ensure that there will be future generations of jazz musicians to continue the city's cultural heritage. "People don't understand what motivates me to get involved," he said:

I'm looking at no jazz on Bourbon Street. I'm looking at no music program in the elementary schools. The idea that some savior is going to ride in on a white horse with a bag of jewels for us is unrealistic. We have to do it ourselves. We have to nurture jazz. If you can't get the business community to rally around music, which is the number-one feature of the New Orleans lifestyle, it seems like the city is at odds with itself. It would be like Las Vegas not embracing casinos.

People call me one of the young trumpet players from New Orleans. I'm not young, I'm 31. Where are the young trumpet players? Shamarr is 27. He's not young. We've got to nurture young people to play this music. People say they want to invest in the city, but they don't want to invest in what made the city great.

Mayfield manipulated spin with the skill of a master politician. He managed to forge close political ties with both Lieutenant Governor Mitch Landrieu and Mayor Ray Nagin, who were often at odds with each other although both were Democrats. "I played Mitch Landrieu's campaign party when he was running for mayor against Marc Morial," said Mayfield:

Mitch said, "I knew we were going to lose when it was only Irvin and I at the party." I only got to know the mayor (Nagin) after the storm. I have a good relationship with them because they're music fans. I don't need a city contract. I play the trumpet. What I'm talking about is not controversial. People of differing political viewpoints agree that we need to invest in this city. The issue is, how do we make it happen?

At that point Irvin Mayfield was a lot of things—musician, bandleader, composer, teacher, cultural contractor, politician—but mostly he was a man with his eye on the deal, more Donald Trump than Louis Armstrong. His accomplishments and his ambitions were fueled by a shrewd businessman's sense of give and take and an understanding of how timing and salesmanship are essential elements in attaining your goals. He was one of the musicians who were taking the future political direction of New Orleans into their own hands, and the city's recovery depended on how successful Mayfield and his colleagues would be in setting that agenda.

CHAPTER 24

Snooks Flies Away

On an unseasonably warm February afternoon in 2009 I sat at a table across from Spanish Plaza, looking at the Mississippi River and listening to the Shufflin' Crustaceans, a band made up of Dave Easley on steel guitar, Domenic Grillo on saxophone, Sam Price on bass, and Michael Voelker on drums, playing their own unique arrangements of the season's local anthems. Mardi Gras season was heading into its sprint to the finish—seven straight days of parades, wall-to-wall music, and continual merrymaking. But this Mardi Gras was different. News was spreading quickly around town that Snooks Eaglin had died.

Snooks had been very ill for months, but the city still had not prepared for his death. He was such a part of the fabric of life in New Orleans that his loss was simply unfathomable.

Fird Eaglin Jr. was one of the greatest guitarists in the history of New Orleans music, a self-taught genius who could play fluently in any style and had an encyclopedic knowledge of songs. An operation to remove a tumor blinded him when he was a baby. Snooks began copying the songs he heard on radio and records at age six and became a session player in New Orleans during his teens, playing on Sugarboy Crawford's Mardi Gras Indian–themed hit, "Jockomo," which in turn inspired the Dixie Cups' hit "Iko Iko." In addition, Snooks led the Flamingos, a band that also included Allen Toussaint. Eaglin began his recording career under his own name in 1958 with Folkways Records, which documented him playing songs by Leadbelly and other musicians in the blues street-music tradition, which was then considered a subtext of folk music. Those sessions were reissued on the 2005 Smithsonian Folkways release *New Orleans Street Singer*, which showcases his soulful vocals and completely unique fingerpicking style. Beginning in 1960, Eaglin clicked with Imperial Records and producer Dave Bartholomew and made a series of great R&B sides that featured his distinctive voice and single-line guitar work backed by an excellent band.

Eaglin was one of the many forgotten New Orleans artists whose careers were resurrected by the New Orleans Jazz and Heritage Festival, when he was paired

Figure 46. Snooks Eaglin backed up by George Porter Jr. at Rock 'n' Bowl. Photo by John Swenson. Used by permission of John Swenson.

with Professor Longhair at the 1971 event. He reignited his legend on the Jazz Fest stages and revived his recording career on Black Top Records in the 1980s, releasing four albums with the label. In 2003 the live *Soul Train from Nawlins* came out on P-Vine Records. Eaglin continued to play at Mid-City Lanes with George Porter Jr. and offered sympathetic backup on bass until late in 2007.

So there I was at the Crazy Lobster, listening to the band playing a Snooks tune and wondering what it was about this particular passing that seemed to sum up so much of what we've lost when I got a phone call from a friend in New York. "I'm coming down for Mardi Gras," he said. "How's New Orleans holding up?"

All I could say was "Snooks just died," still shocked at the depth of sadness in my response. The futility of trying to explain it overwhelmed me. Everyone who visited New Orleans asked how the recovery was going, and at the beginning of 2009 the answer continued to be inconclusive. Downriver, the French Quarter, Marigny, and Bywater districts were thriving, and renovations were ongoing everywhere. The houses on North Rampart Street that had burned down around the corner from me in 2008 were being rebuilt. Piety Street Studio was going strong, and the coffee shops and bars were keeping us alive. Upriver, the Garden district and generally everything from Napoleon Avenue to the river was fine. Nonetheless, recovery in the rest of the city remained spotty. The *Times-Picayune* reported that half of the blighted houses in the city were still untouched. The story suggested a scandal that the Nagin administration has covered over so far but is illustrative of the corruption that has kept the recovery to a few high-profile projects, whereas funds for rebuilding New Orleans haven't produced tangible results. Millions of dollars were earmarked for the destruction of houses that were too damaged in the flood that followed Katrina to be rebuilt. Much of that work was clearly not accomplished. Contractors nevertheless submitted bills for the work and were paid by the city without verification that the work was done. It took community activists to do the research and discover that the city was paying for nonexistent work. This lack of accountability on the city's part smelled as bad as the rotting fish and dead animals in the streets of the city after the floodwaters receded. The same goes for the fight between the mayor and the city council over the outrageously expensive waste-removal contract Mayor Nagin handed out after Katrina. When the city council asked for accountability on how this money was being spent, it was rebuffed by the mayor's office.

Every now and then New Orleans offered a glimpse of what the city really can accomplish when the chips are down. The police, fire, and sanitation departments do an amazing job of organizing the action around the scores of Mardi Gras parades with a minimum of obstruction to traffic flow. Within minutes of each parade's end, the streets were clean and traffic was rolling. If this kind of effort were put into rebuilding the neglected areas of town, the recovery would be a lot further along than it was at that point.

On Thursday, February 20, 2009, I ran into Glen David Andrews outside Tipitina's. Andrews had decided to make a guest appearance at that night's show and was sitting on a bench outside the club. Glen David had gone through some trying times—he had suffered a setback in his long-standing battles with substance abuse and had just recently come out of rehab. I asked him how he was feeling, and he admitted to being depressed about his problems. "It's my own fault. I know that," he told me, then excused himself and walked down the block. I could see he was weeping.

That night, guitarist Papa Mali held his "Supernatural Ball" inside the club. It was a night of great music, and Snooks's spirit seemed to hover over the event. The Rev. Goat Carson started the ceremonies with a mystic declamation that began as a summoning of Native American spirits and somewhere along the line became a eulogy for Snooks Eaglin and a celebration of his spirit. "Death does not destroy love," Goat Carson chanted as he danced around the stage in his feathers and buckskin, shaking his staff at the sky and blowing on his "goat harp," while Alfred ("Uganda") Roberts accompanied him on congas. Big Chief Monk Boudreaux told the crowd that Snooks had been an influence on him as a young musician.

Papa Mali and John Mooney played an outstanding acoustic set, flashing slide-guitar exchanges in glorious counterpoint. Later, Mooney and Papa Mali ended the night with a lengthy electric jam that featured members of Groovesect, the Revolutionary Snake Ensemble, and bassist George Porter Jr. The Snake Ensemble, with New Orleans bassist Jimbo Walsh sitting in, had just finished marching in the Muses parade and were in rare form. The theme from the Muses parade was James Bond films, and the Snake Ensemble reprised the tune they had played as they marched, "Goldfinger."

Midway through the set Glen David Andrews came out, showing none of the remorse that had troubled him hours before. He hit the stage like a bolt of lightning, totally swamping the proceedings and immediately winning over the audience with the force of his personality. A clearly delighted Papa Mali encouraged Andrews to take the spotlight, and he turned the place upside down, singing verse after verse of "When I Die I Want a Second Line." He shifted into "Do Watcha Wanna" and had the crowd chanting "Snooks…Snooks…Snooks" before he was through. Andrews had been including a lot of gospel material in his performances, and it was clear that music was helping him overcome the troubles that were so prominent in his life.

Glen David Andrews certainly wasn't alone in his difficulties. The city was still riven by violence, and Mardi Gras 2009 was a particularly bloody season, during which twenty people were shot. That didn't stop the party, of course, which continued unabated through Fat Tuesday, when Zulu's one-hundredth-anniversary parade kicked off a day-long procession of floats, whose riders threw beads, gilded coconuts, and other favors to the revelers in the city's streets.

Only a few hours after the Zulu parade rolled down St. Charles Avenue, two men began shooting into the enormous crowd watching a truck parade at the corner of St. Charles and Second Street. Seven people were injured in the melee, including a twenty-month-old boy, a seventeen-year-old girl, and a fifty-year-old woman. As the victims were treated in the street, the parade rolled on, and people dived into the street for beads right next to the ambulances where the shooting victims were being treated. It's hard to comprehend the contrast between people being shot and people being transported by unseen spirits to remarkable heights of celebration, but that's what was happening.

Mardi Gras day marked the debut performance of the Mardi Gras Indian Orchestra at the Hi-Ho Lounge, an extraordinary event. Kevin O'Day set a powerful pulse on drums, and Reggie Scanlan rolled bass lines over three sets as guitarists Papa Mali and Camile Baudoin churned away, Evan Christopher played masterfully on clarinet and soprano saxophone, and Helen Gillet added deep, resonant cello lines to the rhythmic mix. Sunpie Barnes sang the Mardi Gras Indian chants, and the crowd sang along lustily to "Handa Wanda," "Meet

Figure 47. Deacon John leads jam at Ernie K-Doe's Mother-in-Law Lounge. Photo by John Swenson. Used by permission of John Swenson.

the Boys on the Battlefront," "Big Chief," "Mardi Gras in New Orleans," "Indian Red," and other classics.

Through the haze of Mardi Gras activity we learned about the loss of another local institution. Antoinette Fox K-Doe, the wife of Ernie K-Doe, died that Mardi Gras day. Antoinette was a New Orleans icon. She took such good care of Ernie K-Doe that he was able to enjoy a last hurrah before his death in 2001, holding court at his headquarters, the Mother-in-Law Lounge on Claiborne Avenue. Ernie hosted parties at his club and even made a new recording before his death, "White Boy/Black Boy," a soul ballad that promoted his own brand of racial equality (he pressed it on a CD with another new song, "Children of the World"). On Sunday nights at the Mother-in-Law Lounge, K-Doe would sing, accompanied on the keyboards by Rico Watts. When it came time for him to sing "White Boy/Black Boy," K-Doe would walk around the bar and make everyone sing along with him. It was silly and it was wonderful. Antoinette kept the place going after K-Doe passed, and the Mother-in-Law Lounge became the one place in town where the musicians that made up the New Orleans neighborhood R&B underground and the young, white rock and avant-garde musicians all hung out together. The Mother-in-Law Lounge became a kind of headquarters for the electronic musician Quintron and his wife, puppet show impresario

Miss Kitty. At the same time, it was also a hangout for Mardi Gras Indians, brass bands, and expatriate poet John Sinclair.

As it turned out, the funeral service and second line for Snooks Eaglin at the Howlin' Wolf took place on the same day that Antoinette K-Doe was waked at the Mother-in-Law Lounge, Friday, February 27, 2009. It was a full day of mourning and celebration in New Orleans as both events took place in ideal spring weather.

CHAPTER 25

Ghosts of Traditional Jazz

Doctor Michael White is haunted. Everywhere he goes, he encounters spirits. White isn't particularly superstitious, nor is he charismatic in either the born-again or the voodoo sense. Nevertheless, he is a haunted man. That's life for a fifty-three-year-old, traditional New Orleans jazz musician whose best friends were first-generation jazz players mostly born before 1910.

I ran into White outside of the Howlin' Wolf just after the funeral parade for Snooks Eaglin. He was packing up his clarinet into his car on South Peters Street after the ceremony. As usual, the professorial White exuded an aura of dignity and thoughtfulness, but behind his wire-frame glasses his eyes revealed a deep sadness. Even the shining sun and blue sky afternoon could not mask White's somber mood.

"I'm troubled," White admitted, giving in to the blues on a perfect day. "I'm having a difficult time." Despite his ongoing efforts to cure those blues, White was still suffering from the aftereffects of the flood. Like many other New Orleans musicians, he lost everything during the deluge, lost family members after it, and still struggled to regain his emotional equilibrium while shouldering an immense cultural burden.

White was a primary force in keeping traditional New Orleans jazz alive. His album *Blue Crescent* was a dramatic example of the way traditional New Orleans jazz could stay true to its century-old roots and still make a resonant, contemporary musical statement. As such, it was one of the most important New Orleans recordings since the federal flood.

In 2004, after a career spent perfecting his ability to play the traditional New Orleans jazz canon, White had a creative breakthrough during a stay at A Studio in the Woods in Algiers, a New Orleans neighborhood, where he discovered that he could write compelling original material in the traditional style. After losing everything in the flood and falling into a deep depression, White returned to A Studio in the Woods, where he was revisited by his muse, and emerged with an album that will take its place in history alongside the city's most memorable musical creations.

204

Figure 48. Dr. Michael White plays clarinet at second-line funeral for Snooks Eaglin. Photo by John Swenson. Used by permission of John Swenson.

White traced his interest in music to the Carnival parades his mother took him to as a child. He remembered being impressed with the big sound and colorful uniforms of the St. Augustine High School marching band. White later enrolled in St. Augustine and began his musical career playing clarinet in the Marching 100 and the school concert band. He took private lessons from band director Edward Hampton and practiced at home along with the radio, playing the melodies to popular songs. Still, he knew he was looking for something else, something he couldn't put his finger on. He began to find his direction by accident when a friend brought over a copy of *Jazz Begins*, by the Young Tuxedo Jazz Band, and he learned several of the songs.

What White didn't realize is that he was born to play this music. It wasn't until he'd already started to play traditional music that his mother told White about his blood lineage, which dates back to early jazz. Among White's immediate ancestors were two brothers, Papa John and Willie Joseph, who played in some of the first jazz bands. Papa John was a friend and bandmate of trumpeter Buddy Bolden, who ran a barber shop down the block from Bolden's house. Though they were related, White never knew the Joseph brothers. Willie died in a car accident three weeks before White was born. White thinks he saw Papa John once at a family gathering. Papa John died onstage at Preservation Hall after performing a spirited rendition of "When the Saints Go Marching In."

"A lot of things that have happened to me have been strange coincidences, often involving my family," said White. One of those strange coincidences involved another of White's mentors, Danny Barker. Barker, a musician and historian who did extensive research into Bolden's life, certainly knew of Bolden's relationship with Papa John Joseph, but he didn't know White was a relative when the young student showed up for his class at Xavier University.

"Danny Barker used to teach African American music, which is actually the same class that I teach now," White explained:

> It was kind of strange the way I met him. I was in the library one day—in the room that collected all the books about black history. I looked up, and there was Danny Barker, standing in the door frame, holding his guitar. I looked down, and I looked back up, and he was gone. I thought it was a ghost or something. So I searched all over the library for him. Finally, at the top of the last floor in the last room I looked in, that's where he was. I walked right in, and that was the first day of his class.

White began playing in Barker's Fairview Baptist Church marching band, where he got a close look at some of the last old-school jazz funerals and social club parades. "Every job was different," he said:

> The first funeral I played was just a pure ceremony with an organization. This was 1975. I remember as clear as day the looks on the faces of the members of the organization. Even though I'm black and from New Orleans, I'd never seen people who looked like that. They marched with a certain kind of solemn dignity. They looked like terra cotta soldiers. The men had military uniforms in Napoleonic style, with an admiral's hat and gold buttons, shoulder epaulettes, and shiny swords. These were the old benevolent organizations, a tradition that was dying out. What I didn't realize is the very first funeral I saw was really one of the last of those kinds of funerals for that generation of people. I've never seen anything like that since. The onlookers took on the solemnity of the ceremony. It wasn't like nowadays, where it's an extension of Jazz Fest or something.

Meanwhile, White was unsuccessfully trying to play in the university's jazz program:

> I used to hang around the jazz band at school, but the band director at the time was not too crazy about clarinets or traditional jazz. At

the time it was kind of devastating because that's what I was trying to get into, but actually it was good training for me because it foreshadowed an attitude I've had to deal with all my life, people who don't like traditional jazz and don't consider it a valid form of jazz as opposed to bop or big band. The band director didn't like clarinets because he was interested in big bands, and his vision of a big band had saxophones.

White finally got a chance to play traditional jazz with Doc Paulin, whom he met through tuba and sousaphone player Big Al Carson, who went on to fame as a blues and R&B singer on Bourbon Street:

Doc called me for a job. It was a Baptist church parade in Marrero, an anniversary parade. I was scared to death and kind of lost. I knew several of the songs that Doc played because they were on the Young Tuxedo record. Doc would play a few bars of a song, which was usually not that recognizable, and, the next thing you know, the drum kicked off the song. I didn't know the title, the key, or the harmony. The songs that I knew I tried to play along with and the songs that I didn't know I tried to find some high notes that I could sustain at the end of choruses.

It was while he was with Doc Paulin that White began to meet some of the older players, who would greatly influence his career. One of them was Eddie Richardson, who was born in 1902 and played with the Eureka Brass Band.

"Doc also had guys who were rhythm and blues saxophonists who ended up playing in brass bands," White recalled:

Some of those guys, like tenor saxophonist Joe Tillman, cut famous local records. The first thing I learned about this music is that it was nothing like what I'd heard before on Bourbon Street. It seemed to be dealing with a way of life that was both familiar and strange to me at the same time. Doc also lived uptown in the general vicinity of the Bolden neighborhood, and a lot of his work came around LaSalle and Washington, what was Shakespeare Park at the time. A lot of the social aid and pleasure clubs started around there. Also, there were a lot of funerals there because there was a cemetery there. A lot of the parades I played early in my career started or ended in the Bolden neighborhood. When I was parading, I could see Bolden's house. It was on First between Liberty and LaSalle. Papa John's barber shop was there a long time, and then one day it was just gone.

While playing in Paulin's band, White had what he called a "defining moment" when he discovered New Orleans jazz pioneer George Lewis. "It was another one of those strange things that seem to happen," he says:

We played an anniversary parade at Mount Mariah Baptist church. It used to be Mahalia Jackson's church when she was in New Orleans. After the parade I went to a record store, and almost by accident I bought my first George Lewis record. A guy had picked up this record and said to me, "You ever heard about this guy, George Lewis?" I picked up the record and something about it said, "You have to buy me," and I spent most of the money I made at the parade on this record. I bought that record, came home, put it on, and it was as if my life had been in darkness, and all of a sudden a light came on. That record changed my life forever. It was like a spiritual experience that defined for me everything that I felt inside about being from New Orleans—the food, the music, the spirit of the people, the climate—all of it was in the music. The music was so passionate and so soulful and so alive and beautiful. I remember listening to that record over and over and over again, trying to play along with some of the songs. That was really the beginning for me of seriously getting into New Orleans jazz in the authentic side of the clarinet style beyond the brass band. I wanted to know more about the music. I wanted to know more about the people who made the music. That's when I started reading and collecting records and books and memorabilia, and then eventually going out and meeting musicians. In the early '80s I started a lot of these associations with more than three dozen musicians born between the 1890s and 1910. A lot of those musicians became my friends and mentors and eventually bandmates. I toured with some of them. We became friends, and I went on tours with them and went to parties, then hospital visits and funerals.

In a strange way everything seems connected spiritually. When I heard that first George Lewis record, among everything I loved there was one song that was particularly special for me. I remember that first night listening to it for hours, going over the song until I learned to copy it note for note. I didn't know the song was famous, but it was "Burgundy Street Blues." I was connected to this music in a strange sort of way. First of all I didn't even know that Papa John Joseph was on that record, so I had a relative who played on the record, which made it even more powerful for me when I found that out later.

That record became an inroad for me to the older musicians in a strange sort of way. I had a job in Jackson Square. I used to play in a lot of different bands, and there was one guy who used to hire a lot of older musicians. On this one job he hired musicians like Kid Thomas Valentine, Louis Nelson, and Emanuel Sayers on banjo, all guys who had recorded with George Lewis. The band leader asked me if I knew "Burgundy Street Blues," and I started playing it. I closed my eyes. I was scared to death, but it was a spiritual thing again. After a few choruses it started raining. Somebody said, "Oh, you made the sky cry." We had to stop playing. Emanuel Sayers came over, and he shook my hand.

I didn't realize what that meant because there were no younger black traditional players that were seriously getting into what the older guys were doing. Of course, there were a lot of great younger musicians, but they weren't getting into the traditional style. The trumpet player Kid Sheik, who was also a popular traditional jazz figure, he said he was three blocks away, walking down the street, and he heard "Burgundy Street Blues," and he came running to see who that was.

Kid Sheik invited me to a jazz party. There were a lot of older musicians there, and they asked me to play "Burgundy Street Blues." When I finished, they made me play it again. That was my introduction to all these older musicians, and eventually they found out I was related to Papa John, and they all knew him, so that was more of a link to that extended family of jazz.

White went on to play with the Preservation Hall Band and organize his own groups, the Michael White Quartet and the Original Liberty Jazz Band, through the 1980s, but his most important association during that decade was with Wynton Marsalis. White somehow convinced the iconoclastic Marsalis to refocus his musical attention on his New Orleans roots, an interest that led to Marsalis's breakthrough album, *The Majesty of the Blues*. White met Marsalis in 1985, just as Wynton's band broke up after his brother Branford left to play with Sting. White had a premonition that he would meet Marsalis and convince him to play traditional jazz.

"I had a dream before we met. It was kind of prophetic that Wynton was going to play New Orleans jazz, and I was going to have something to do with it," White recalled:

In my conscious mind I thought that was crazy because he was living in New York, and he was playing bop, and in interviews he said some very un-nice things about New Orleans jazz. So consciously I knew that my dream was never going to happen. But after that first meeting, I kept crossing paths with Wynton. We'd meet in strange places—airports, jazz festivals in places all around the world, and I would tell him stories about King Oliver and Jelly Roll Morton, Sidney Bechet. He'd look at me like I was nuts. Then there was a party in New Orleans for *Essence* magazine, and there were a lot of celebrities there. He came, and he sat in with us, and he really didn't know that music and didn't know what to do. So I gave him my card and told him, "Give me a call. I have a lot of records you can listen to, and I can tell you a lot about the music."

He called a year later and said he had this idea, and he wanted to listen to some New Orleans brass-band music. I sent him a cross-section of brass band music from the earliest recordings all the way into the Dirty Dozen and Rebirth stuff. He called me back a while later and said he had an idea for a recording that would use some of those New Orleans jazz influences, and he wondered if he could pull it off. He played a little bit of it on the piano for me, and I said, "Yes, of course," but meanwhile I'm thinking, "What the hell is that?" So he says, "Do you think we could get some of the guys from New Orleans to do this?" He asked for Teddy Riley on trumpet, Danny Barker, Fred Lonzon, and myself. The four of us went up to New York. We went in the studio, and he showed us his idea for *The Majesty of the Blues.* There were five songs on the CD, and we recorded three of them, a dirgelike ballad called "The Death of Jazz," the part that had the sermon by Rev. Jeremiah Wright [he laughs], so I had my Jeremiah Wright experience back then because it was controversial when it came out, and then "Happy Feet Blues," a takeoff on the brass-band style. That record changed some of the thinking on Wynton because it was the first time he tried to do traditional stuff and also the first time he employed that folklike feeling, using growls and smears and the way he played the mute in his own playing. It put his career on another plateau. It was great for me, too, because I didn't realize it at the time, but my parts in there kind of stand out. It was like my dream had come true. I can't believe it: I had this dream and here it is. It happened.

White became a regular at Wynton's concerts and on special projects for Lincoln Center, working as musical director on programs based around Jelly Roll Morton, King Oliver, Louis Armstrong, Sidney Bechet, and one called Jazz in the '20s.

"People called it a repertory style, but the notes were not copied. The clarinet parts were always improvised over chord changes," he said. "I didn't even have the notes that people were playing written down. Later on, when they did the complete transcriptions, I still played my solos from chord changes. I didn't copy any solos. I wanted to capture the spirit of the music. I knew it could be done if it was played like they did it as opposed to exactly how they did it. Where they improvised, we improvised."

White noted that Wynton's desire to use the older sounds to compose new compositions influenced him to move in a similar direction, but it took his first residence at Studio in the Woods for White to figure out how to accomplish that task. The result was *Dancing in the Sky*.

"In my first residence I realized it was a place where I could be removed from all of the distractions of everyday life," he recalled:

> No people, no radio, no cell phone, no TV, no computer, no noise. You could hear quiet, and you could hear nature. Nature for me was an unexpected benefit. I learned that we're designed to be in nature. From a musical perspective or a creative perspective, part of what it's all about is nature. To be out in the trees, breathing fresh air, to be in touch with animals and water. There's a harmony in nature you don't normally get. In the evenings I would get all kinds of music from the crickets, from different birds, owls. Sometimes I could hear a balance, like a call and response going back and forth. It even got to the point where once I started playing, I would do that with some of the birds. We would kind of chirp back and forth. I would play my instrument, and they would answer it, and I would try to get as close as I could to play the notes that they were singing. This happened several times, and when I would play, certain animals would come, and they would stop, and they would look and listen. They were part of the process, and that was being in touch with nature. Studio in the Woods is right on the river. You grow up in New Orleans, and you know the river. You see it a million times, but there you can be on the river and never see another soul, no buildings. You can look at the river and see the way it was two hundred years ago. The river took on a different meaning for me, a way to travel to my inner spirit. At night, if you just sit there, you start to feel a certain kind of power. It's humbling. You feel insignificant. The rippling of the water was, like, rocking you to sleep. It put you into a meditative state. I discovered the right combination of elements for writing songs. I practiced like hell, ended up with a new corn on my thumb. Listening to different kinds of music, praying, meditating, walking along the river, and just letting go. I stopped trying to think about it, and it came.

When the 17th Street Canal levee failed, White's Gentilly home was destroyed, and along with it went one of the most important collections of early jazz memorabilia in the world: documents, books, records, and instruments personally obtained from the original players themselves. White lost all of his music and felt like he was losing his mind.

"My Katrina experience has been really rough," he said:

People talk about "I lost all this stuff." I'm not over that yet. I've moved on, but I'm not over with it yet. As time went on it became worse, with displacement and illness in my family. My mother went from being independent to having an advanced case of dementia. I had to put her in a nursing home. She's been in a bed for two years. Until December I was driving back and forth to Houston to see her.

White, who was under contract to the New Orleans label Basin Street Records, was overdue to deliver his next record. He decided to apply for another residence at Studio in the Woods to see whether he could recapture the spirit of *Dancing in the Sky.*

"By the time I got to Studio in the Woods, I had not had a break since Katrina. I was depressed, and I was going through a lot of bad stuff," he said:

I didn't think I would be able to create anything at first. I was even more depressed because I thought I wouldn't be able to do anything. I'd been putting Basin Street off for a few years. I thought maybe I'd re-record some of the stuff I'd done before. That's how it was for the first couple of days. I would walk on the river an hour a day. I stopped thinking about the pressure, and I played a lot.

White tried to find inspiration by listening to a variety of music, from African and Caribbean records to Bob Dylan to Mahalia Jackson. He contemplated images of New Orleans after Katrina in books and magazines. He looked for a way past his writer's block in the writings of Julia Cameron, an artist's consultant whose self-help volumes include the popular creativity handbook *The Artist's Way.*

White noted:

One of her suggestions is that you should get up every day and write what she calls "morning pages." You get up and write the first thing that comes to your mind. I tried to do it, but it didn't work because when I got up in the morning my brain was not working, and I didn't feel like writing. So I converted the idea into something that worked for me. When I would get up, instead of writing the first thing that came to my mind, I would play the first thing that came to my mind. Even if it didn't make sense, I would just play whatever I was feeling on my horn. And that led to songs. The ideas would come, and every time I had to stop to eat or something, a lot of times I passed up on meals. I would start writing, and I would have an unrealistic perception of time. I would get up and start writing at seven in the morning, and before I knew it, it was two o'clock, and then it was dark. But if I was writing a song idea and I'd stop, when I came back, what I'd been writing would be gone. I would have incomplete parts of songs. But then other ideas would come based on sitting alongside the river or something else I looked at. I would write these ideas, and then I would go back later and try to finish. So after I finished, I had a wide range of stuff, thirty-six songs in all.

What came first was a series of songs that were in a minor mode and that were very, very sad. I had been listening to a lot of things in a minor key, a lot of early gospel music, old spirituals, and I really like Mahalia Jackson a lot. I like the passion of her voice. I had mostly records just with her and a piano, where you can hear the purity of the spirit of her work. The song "Soon Will Be Gone the Troubles of the World"—that song is so sad, I started playing that, and it seemed that a lot of the stuff that I wrote was kind of in that mode, just sad and melancholy feelings.

Several of these compositions were combined in the centerpiece of *Blue Crescent,* "Katrina," which begins with the sounds of the storm's howling winds and proceeds through a solemn funeral march. "I had songs that were even more melancholy than 'Katrina,' " said White. "I had a march, a rag, some blues songs. A lot of stuff came out."

Somehow White's music encompassed a lot of joy along with the sorrow, from the carefree attitude of "Comme Ci, Comme Ça" to the sheer abandon of his tribute to Doc Paulin, "King of the Second Line." "I don't know where all the joy came from," White admitted:

At some point I started to see how the range of emotions tells the story of the city from the early days to Katrina and beyond. So really it answers for me the question, how do you play traditional New Orleans jazz today? How do you play traditional and contemporary music at the same time? There are a lot of answers to that. I don't claim to have the only answer. Some people look at the young brass bands as a way of doing that. I wanted the dominant style to be traditional because I think it can take on other influences and also reflect contemporary life, emotions, and events.

For many years White was the youngest member of all of the bands he played in. Now he is the keeper of the flame, and he finally understood what his old friends were trying to tell him all along. "I really feel that through Papa John and Buddy Bolden and the rest of them there's a connectedness," he said:

A lot of older musicians feel that way. When they were dying, they would say stuff to me like, "It's up to y'all now." And I'm thinking, "You're dying. What are you thinking about music for?" But I came to understand exactly what they meant because they realized this is a very important gift that needs to continue.

It's like the music regenerates itself. I didn't understand it then, but I very much understand it now. I felt like I channeled the music on *Blue Crescent* more than composed it. It's almost like this stuff came from somewhere else through me. It's all of those people I saw and played with before. It's all of those experiences I've had in life, through Katrina and into now. It's like all of that converted into music. Even though the music is contemporary because it reflects what's happening today, those people who I knew, they're still alive in it somehow. Their spirit informs it.

Accordingly, White reached out to the younger brass bands to teach them the tradition, working closely with the Hot 8 Brass Band and performing at special events with them. "It's a simple process," he explained:

I show them some different ways to play the music. We play it together, and I explain how it relates to our cultural history.

A lot of people I know over the years—musicians and teachers alike—think of this music as comic, simple, not really jazz, something just for tourists, something that had no meaning or feeling as a liturgy. But I came to see it from the parades and my work in the community as a source of tremendous pride and spirituality, an expression of a way of life that is on one plane black, on one plane New Orleans, on one plane American, and all very much universal.

That music sustained White even in his most troubled moments, haunting him and reassuring him at the same time. He repaid the spirits who created that music by keeping it alive, playing, and passing on to others the music of the friends and ancestors who live forever in his mind's eye.

CHAPTER 26

New Blood

On March 18 an old friend and I were sitting at an outdoor patio in Austin, Texas, during the South by Southwest music conference. We started talking about New Orleans, and he asked me who was left among the great New Orleans musicians. Eddie Bo, the R&B legend who was responsible for so many classic New Orleans recordings from "Pass the Hatchet" to "Check Your Bucket," was the first name off my lips. I didn't realize he had passed away that very day. Bo's death came hard on the heels of his contemporary Snooks Eaglin. I had known Snooks was ill but had no idea that Edwin Joseph Bocage, whom I'd seen dancing with the crowd at Jazz Fest the year before, was gone forever.

However, every time New Orleans loses another music icon, young people emerge out of sometimes unlikely situations. The music never stops reaching out for new converts. Those who play it have a burning desire to pass the message down the line.

Davis Rogan's six foot four inch frame stood out in dramatic contrast to the scores of grade-school children he had assembled along the Mississippi River on a sun-bathed April day in 2009. Davis and his students from the International School were set to perform on the children's stage at the French Quarter Festival. He set the tone for the show by playing "The Coolest Party in the World" with his trio, all the while glancing repeatedly at the restless children assembled just off of stage right. "I don't know why performing with kids makes me so nervous," he remarked. Most likely it was the presence of so many of those kids' parents in the audience.

Davis often plays the witty wise guy in concert, but he had his hands full wrangling sixty kindergarten and first-grade children into their places on stage. The kids, a mixed-race group looking nervous and fidgety but all paying close attention to Davis, watched intently for their cues. "What three animals are at the Audubon Zoo?" Davis asked the children rhetorically, giving them a mental cue to remember the words of "They All Asked for You." Their charming voices massed beautifully—Davis worked magic with these kids, who shifted their weight from side to side and waved at family members in the audience but sang together in perfect harmony, working through "What a Wonderful World" and "Mardi Gras Mambo." Some of the city's best-known names could learn a lesson in sincerity from the emotional commitment the kids brought to those songs. They sang "This Land Is Your Land," and one of the children in the middle pointed out to the crowd with a relaxed gesture that suggested he would be doing this for a long time. Though the massed voices sometimes wavered on the words in the verses, they really nailed the choruses.

"These are New Orleans kids," he later told me. "I'm so proud they know the second verse to 'Mardi Gras Mambo.'" The kids went on to sing "When You're Smiling" and "Iko Iko," then filed dutifully offstage, to be replaced by a similar number of second- and third-graders who sang some of the same songs.

Downriver, the Tin Men, driven by the amazing percussion work of Washboard Chaz, Matt Perrine's virtuoso sousaphone playing, and the great songwriting and guitar playing of Alex McMurray, turned in a jolly performance. Perrine had a great time answering the bellowing blasts from the steamboat *Natchez* as it left the dock. The interaction of the river and the music has become one of the most endearing things about French Quarter fest. Smaller stages dotted the streets of the French Quarter, and hidden spots like the back garden of the Mississippi River Bottom tavern on St. Philip Street offered more intimate music scenes, where international traditional jazz bands were able to realize their dream of playing New Orleans jazz in the Crescent City.

Pity the poor musicians who had to play opposite the Lost Bayou Ramblers on Saturday at the U.S. Mint. Not only did the Ramblers draw everyone to their stage, but they also had a huge crowd backed up on Barracks Street. The band is the latest example of a new generation of Louisiana roots music, a hybrid of Cajun, zydeco, and rock sensibilities. The fiddler sawed away in the great bayou tradition, but the way the bassist slapped his upright went right past punk back to rock's ancient roots in rockabilly.

The Fatien Ensemble offered a great example of how the historical hybridization of music in New Orleans keeps evolving. The group, led by drummer and dancer Seguenon Kone from the Ivory Coast, included local musicians Dr. Michael White on clarinet, Jason Marsalis on vibraphone, Michael Skinkus on drums, and Marc Stone on steel guitar. Kone moved to New Orleans after the storm and found himself at home. He delighted in bringing his drums down to Frenchmen Street and playing for hours to the local crowds and was fascinated by the different styles of music coming out of the different Frenchmen Street clubs. The eclecticism of his ensemble's sound came from his decision to ask musicians to join him based on their individual sound rather than on any format he wanted them to play in.

The members of the original Hurricane Brass Band sounded like they were making commercials for the chamber of commerce. "We want you to go back to the rest of the United States," they told the crowd, "and tell them New Orleans is back." As if to put an exclamation point on the message, the band proceeded to play "Back Home in Indiana."

Bo Dollis Jr. showed how totally he'd inhabited his father's role as big chief of the Wild Magnolias. Dollis Jr. showed up during guitarist Billy Iuso's set at French Quarter fest and electrified the crowd with a star turn.

The presentation of *Gambit*'s Big Easy Music Awards started as French Quarter fest was wrapping up. The awards reflected some of the realities that had settled in as New Orleans attempted to rebuild its cultural traditions. Two unorthodox winners showed how much the city's music had changed in a few years. Rotary Downs, the eccentric indie rock band that eschewed any direct relationship to New Orleans musical traditions, won the award for Best Rock Band for the second year running, and MyNameIsJohnMichael, a young group who'd released a downloadable single each week on the Internet the previous year, got the nod for Best New Rock Band. In a city whose music has nearly always been instantly recognizable, the success of young musicians trying *not* to sound like the locals was significant since it reflected the changing tastes of a new generation of listeners whose cultural touchstones were the eccentricities of indie rock and the global village of the Internet and social networking. At the same time, music remained so close to the heart of New Orleans life that Rotary Downs had become a local cultural nexus anyway and had hosted its own Mardi Gras costume party, the "Not-So-Super, Super Hero Party," with revelers dressed as unlikely or underachieving superheroes.

Gambit publisher Clancy DuBos gave a stirring speech at the awards ceremony, in which he denounced Gov. Bobby Jindal's decision to slash public-arts funding. Clint Maedgen was really entertaining as the show's main host and scene stealer. Art Neville cracked the audience up with his ad libs and lack of interest in the teleprompter script. "I can't even see that thing," Art said.

The most spectacular moment of the night was Theresa Andersson's solo performance, a stunningly cutting-edge and creative showcase of her vocal, instrumental, and electronic skills. Andersson is one of the city's truly original artists.

In addition, Dr. John won a couple of awards and got a chance to answer those who'd been lambasting him for saying that Jazz Fest sponsor Shell Oil should bear some of the blame for the destruction of the Louisiana coastline, which had led to the inundation of New Orleans. Mac explained his support for the organizations that were protesting the oil companies over and over.

"Anybody that's speaking up against a lot of these things, I'm for it," he said:

> There's a lot of issues here. One of my issues is with the Corps of Engineers. Dat was one of the things my father and the people of south Louisiana used to talk about, was once they diverted the Mississippi River,

things started falling apart. Wetlands started becoming destroyed from dat. Then it became a bigger issue with oil companies. I'm sure dat it was an issue back then, but I was too young to know it. But as you grow a little older and a little wiser, you love your land enough to say enough is enough, and it's time to tell the truth. I was so tired of hearing lies for so long, it wasn't so much that I took a political stance. I just wanted somebody, anybody to tell the truth.

However, Mac's statements led Jazz Fest sponsor Shell to insist on a retraction. As a result, Dr. John was forced to offer a detailed apology to the Jazz Fest and Shell Oil in the *New Orleans Times-Picayune* in the Sunday edition, which came out the same day as the *Gambit* awards. In the apology he drew a distinction between opposing Shell for its complicity in the destruction of the wetlands and lauding the company for supporting Jazz Fest.

"Whatever other issues I may have with the oil companies," his statement read, "we can all agree that Shell's rescue of Jazz Fest after Katrina and their continued support of the festival is a good thing for the community, our music, and our culture."

Nonetheless, while accepting his prizes at the *Gambit* Big Easy Music awards show that night, Dr. John had the last word: "If you don't stand for something, you've got nowhere to stand."

Mac was set for a showdown at Jazz Fest, but in a way his contretemps with festival sponsor Shell showed the strength of a New Orleans musical community that was not afraid to bite the hand that fed it.

CHAPTER 27

Jazz Fest Turns Forty

The Jazz Fest producers put together a powerful lineup for the event's fortieth anniversary, which they took pains to make connections with the Woodstock festival's upcoming fortieth anniversary, and went so far as to market a Jazz Fest T-shirt with a peace symbol. Each stage established subtle connections among the acts that appeared. The paddock stage was a particularly good place to listen. The stage was fronted by a beautiful garden planted by Alice Stevenson, the racetrack's supervisor of flora. Alice was able to watch her flowers closely from the beer stand at the back of paddock, where she spent her afternoons during Jazz Fest pouring suds and talking about her pet goat, Evangeline. During his set at the paddock stage, Greg ("Schatzy") Schatz sang the line "like a shooting star," and a sparrow flew up from the horseshoe-shaped garden in front of the stage to punctuate the line. Backing Schatz were Alex McMurray on guitar and Helen Gillett on cello, who were both outstanding, particularly on "Crazy about You," the waltz "I Can't Stand Up," the gypsy ska "How Is the Housecat," the beautiful "Give Up," and the ridiculously great "Something Important to Say."

The incomparable Rosie Ledet blew the lid off the Fais Do-Do stage. Rosie used to be shy, and it would take her a while to get rolling, but she'd become a powerhouse from the first note of the set and was completely in control of the stage, her band, and the crowd. Little Malcolm also turned in a great zydeco set on his piano accordion. It was interesting that Malcolm announced "We're going way back" during his introduction to Ray Charles's "I Got a Woman," interesting because a lot of the traditional zydeco tunes he played or embellished on were a lot older. But for a young guy, "way back" is relative. He also certainly understood something about Ray Charles: "Ray Charles, yeah, it's all about a good time." And so it was: ecstatic dancing on the straw field under the bright afternoon sun, with Malcolm playing the accents more like an organ than a traditional accordion. Chubby Carrier hit the same stage later with a sound that featured his beautiful voice on a lighter, sweeter R&B version of zydeco. "This is my twentieth anniversary at Jazz Fest," he proudly announced.

"Four years ago people said there would be no fortieth anniversary of Jazz Fest," the preacher MC testified in a stentorian cadence to the gospel tent crowd on the festival's first weekend. "But they don't know that *Jesus* lives in New Orleans!" It was certainly clear that global spirits of all denominations were pumping their blessings into New Orleans during this remarkable time. Much of the city was still in ruins, but its culture endured, bolstered by an astonishing array of fellow travelers from around the country and the world. Bands from Africa, France, and Brazil were among the highlights, and a new generation of local musicians has clearly assumed the role of carriers of the flame for New Orleans music and the imperiled future of southern Louisiana overall.

The deaths of Snooks Eaglin and Eddie Bo, two of the most iconic Jazz Fest performers, expanded the giant loss of the old-school New Orleans legends, which has accelerated in the aftermath of the federal flood of 2005, leading *OffBeat* editor Alex Rawls to raise the once-heretical question: "Is New Orleans R&B dead?" Though most of the practitioners of this cherished tradition are indeed gone, their music lives on in younger players who are carrying the spirit of their music forward.

Though he no longer resided in New Orleans, Wynton Marsalis had assumed an elder statesman's role in New Orleans music. His masterpiece, *Congo Square*, was one of 2009's highlights, and he also performed a Duke Ellington tribute with his Lincoln Center Jazz Orchestra, an organization that continued to spotlight talented young jazz musicians from New Orleans.

Other young players stepped up their game at Jazz Fest to fill the giant shoes of their musical forebears: Trombone Shorty, Shamarr Allen, Amanda Shaw, Marc Broussard, Benjy Davis, and the Pine Leaf Boys all turned in outstanding sets.

One of the artists that had shown the most growth since Katrina was Tab Benoit, the Cajun vocalist and guitarist who had become the leading voice for saving the wetlands, which were literally all that was left of southern Louisiana, a landscape that was rapidly being sucked into the Gulf of Mexico by massive erosion. Benoit knew exactly what to tell the audience during the Voice of the Wetlands show.

"We're losing an acre of wetlands every hour, which is why there's nothing left to prevent the Gulf of Mexico from rolling right over us," said Benoit. "This could be the last Jazz Fest if we don't start doing something about it today!"

The organizers of the New Orleans Jazz and Heritage Festival have done an outstanding job of linking the city's indigenous music to related sounds from around the world. Festival goers witnessed a great performance from South Africa's Hugh Masakela, who played the flugelhorn with a gleaming intensity over a bed of African rhythms that are cousin to the pulses heard in New Orleans R&B. As anyone who took in his wonderful set at the festival can attest, Masakela, with his strong singing voice and powerful technique, is still a creative giant at age seventy. An icon of South African music for more than forty years, Masakela was still fresh without abandoning the characteristic signature of his bright, melodic sound. His ability to surround himself with creative African musicians keeps his approach contemporary and easy to digest without ever descending into the clichés of smooth jazz.

France contributed two of the more unusual acts at the 2009 Jazz Fest. Tarace Boulba, a combination brass band and vocal orchestra, created a sound totally suited to the streets of New Orleans. Though the charts were more intricate than New Orleans brass-band arrangements and left less room for improvisation, the overall effect approximated the excitement of a hot night at the Blue Nile (the band did in fact play a late-night gig at that club).

Bombes 2 Bal, a stripped-down, rhythm-and-voice ensemble from Toulouse, used call-and-response chants, an archaic three-stringed instrument called a *violon-sabot esclop,* a diatonic accordion (*esquilons*), and a Brazilian zabumba drummer and percussion to fashion a hypnotic dance music. They played at the children's tent at Jazz Fest and induced nearly the entire crowd to form a giant ring dance in front of the stage. The group also played a spirited outdoor set during French Quarter Festival. The album *Bal Indigene* does a great job of capturing the trance-music aspect of the Bombes 2 Bal sound.

Rarely has the weather at Jazz Fest been better than in 2009, and the crowds responded to the music on a mass, folk-scene level. Toward the end of his set John Gros kicked it into high gear for "Rat a Tang Tang," and June Yamagishi played a great guitar solo, referencing the iconic "seesaw" nursery-rhyme riff from Miles Davis. Gros' tribute to the great New Orleans legend Champion Jack Dupree, "Junker," followed, and there was a hell of a lot of energy in that Gentilly stage crowd. "Lemme hear you scream!" yelled Gros, and scream they did as the band played a funk strut with June really smoking and Jason Mingledorff playing a soulful tenor break in his own style, mixing lots of elements. Marc Pero's bass was popping along, and Jeffrey ("Jellybean") Alexander was slinging the drum groove. Pero drove into a bass solo, and the crowd was all over it. "Jazz Fest, can you feel the funky soul music?" Gros asked. The resultant roar proved that he had the temperature of this crowd perfectly measured. Everyone was singing the simple, follow-the-bouncing-ball chorus, Gros soloed on B3 organ, and then as Pero played another bass solo, Gros carried Pero's baby daughter out on stage to kiss her papa as he played. "Hey, everybody," Gros concluded, "we're Papa Grows Funk from New Orleans, Louisiana!"

Mardi Gras Indians may be an endangered species, but they made the most of their presence at Jazz Fest. Two exciting hybrid groups, 101 Runners and the Mardi Gras Indian Orchestra, turned in historic sets. Monk Boudreaux was everywhere, reuniting with the ailing but still gamely hanging-in-there Bo Dollis;

Figure 49. John Gros goes goggle-eyed at the Maple Leaf. Photo by John Swenson. Used by permission of John Swenson.

showing up for the Snooks Eaglin tribute at Rock & Bowl, where he kicked the band into gear from a standing start by just humming a chant; with the high-octane backing of Papa Grows Funk at d.b.a.; and in spectacular fashion at the Heritage stage, where he showed up with eight Indians in white, green, and red suits, including a couple of minisuited toddlers. All of them were percussionists, of course. The Rev. Goat Carson was up there along with bass, drums, two guitars, and congas. The band shuddered through massive folk-music jams, diddley bow shuffles, single guitar notes held for an entire chorus, Monk chanting on his "Golden Crown," Monk delivering the promise "We're the Wild Magnolias and nobody dies," Monk chanting "Two-Way Pocky Way," mellowing on "Rasta Is the Rising Sun," then steaming in a funk groove for the climax:

> *You got to be ready,*
> *I got to be ready now*
> *Tell my father*
> *Tell my mother*
> *I'll be gone in the morning*
> *Goin' downtown*
> *Won't turn around*

Monk told his story of Indians' marching on Mardi Gras morning and turned it into an epic poem. The crowd danced in ecstasy to his chants.

Doctor John, Monk's partner in the Voice of the Wetlands All-Stars, marveled at the chief's accomplishments. "Monk Boudreaux, he's got a history here with the Mardi Gras Indians that goes so deep," said Mac:

> If you look at it from this end of it, from this point, being with the Wild Squatoolas, all the way to him being with the Golden Eagles, all that he represents in the thing is a specialty all up to hisself. Monk is one of those guys who still breathes the old-school thing into the thing and still knows a lot of that old Injun stuff. I think one of the reasons when him and Bo did that first Wild Magnolias record showed up so good, not only that Willie Tee's writing was great, but the fact that I think that a lot of the stuff that wasn't Willie Tee originals was stuff that Monk kept going into a zone of traditional Mardi Gras Indian thing in a weird way. And I'm not takin' nothin' away from Bo Dollis. I'm just sayin' that Monk had that talent. That's his thing. and it's special. No matter what he's gonna do. Monk Boudreaux is my partner. and I feel good about it. He's a great Big Chief. and he got a heart of steel.

The brass-band scene continued its recovery after the storm. Philip Frazier, the tuba and sousaphone player for the Rebirth Brass Band, had been hospitalized with a stroke in December 2008 but recovered quickly and was in great form at Jazz Fest. The New Orleans Nightcrawlers Brass Band, made up of musicians from other groups, showcased material from an outstanding new album, *Slither Slice,* which featured compelling new compositions in the brass-band format.

Matt Perrine, the sousaphone player with Bonerama, the Tin Men, the Danza Quartet, and the Royal Fingerbowl, provided the fulcrum of this band's sound by blowing full-throated ostinato bass lines that formed a rhythmic counterpoint to Terence ("T-Bell") Andrews's bass drum and Derrick Tabb's snare. Perrine also contributed two vital compositions to the set: the title track—a dense, funk breakdown with support from Galactic's Stanton Moore on drums and Rich Vogel on keyboards—and the old-timey "Pontchartrain Beach," with Alex McMurray sitting in on banjo.

The front line's interlace was astonishing on a pure jazz level with the paragon jamming brass band, the Dirty Dozen Brass Band. Perrine's Bonerama bandmate Craig Klein brought his bold trombone figures to the arrangements, while saxophonists Jason Mingledorff and Brent Rose and trumpeters Barney Floyd and Satoru Ohashi engaged in a furious choreography of funk soloing, at once groove oriented and full of melodic variety. Mingledorff, the regular reedman with Papa Grows Funk, played some of the filthiest lines on his three songs for the set, "Krewe Cut," "Come Back with It" and "Clean Up." Ohashi also wrote two tunes on the album, the good-time chant "8th Ward Strut" and the album-closing spectacular "Okinawa."

"Hold 'Em, Joe," a traditional brass-band/Mardi Gras Indian chant, got enough of a novel arrangement here to merit the Nightcrawlers' taking writers' credit for it. But that's about as close to traditional as this extraordinarily creative band got.

Brass bands, especially the younger ones, are known for their ability to work unusual material into their repertoire, but none of them have come up with as novel an idea as using the fanfare from Giuseppe Verdi's *Aida,* which is tailor made for this treatment. The band segued from this glorious theme into a feel-good anthem for New Orleans's recovery, "Alright Alright." If more groups show this kind of creativity with traditional forms, the future of New Orleans music will be in good hands. Unfortunately, the school system was no longer providing the musical education that had been available to students before Katrina. Most New Orleans middle schools fielded marching bands before the flood, organizations that marched in Mardi Gras parades and often put instruments in the hands of students for the first time. However, in the scramble to refurbish a collapsed educational system, many schools discontinued the programs. It took grassroots efforts by working musicians in the city to educate the kids. Derek Tabb, who played with both Rebirth and the Nightcrawlers at Jazz Fest, started one of the most successful of these pedagogic enterprises, the Roots of Music. After starting the program in 2008, Tabb was able to field a full marching band by early 2009.

Roots of Music also provides music education in history, theory, instrumental instruction, and ensemble performance, as well as tutoring the students to ensure that they maintain at least a 2.5 GPA in school. The program is free for the students, but attendance is mandatory. Tabb knew from personal experience how difficult it was for inner-city teenagers to avoid getting into trouble, and he pointed to his program as a way to counteract the gang violence that had plagued the city. "I tell everyone I'm competing with the drug dealers," said Tabb.

Tabb's brother Glen David Andrews made a transformational appearance at the 2009 Jazz Fest, a performance that was widely acknowledged as the festival's high point. Andrews reprised material from his album *Walking through Heaven's Gate* at the gospel tent on the second Friday of Jazz Fest. He fronted an outstanding gospel band that included his cousin Troy Andrews on trumpet and Paul Sanchez on acoustic guitar. Glen David appeared in a white suit and immediately took emotional control of the tent, which was packed with almost all-white fest goers, who were definitely not regular, sanctified worshipers. Nevertheless, in a truly amazing process, Andrews had them fervently chanting "Help Me, Jesus" and screaming as he doffed the white coat in a Prince-like gesture, jumped into the crowd, and created frenzy on the floor. People were clamoring to touch him, to take a spark from this burning light of a spiritual force in their midst.

"Anybody out there want a blessing?" He asked, and they shouted affirmation, and it was Andrews doing his regular routine, except he was preaching, and everyone was with him on the call-and-response: "Thank you, Jesus/Thank you, Lord," over and over again, ecstatic in what would be an intensely sexual way in any other setting, but here it was pure spirit. "Somebody scream" didn't sound at all rote when he pulled it right at that moment. At the close of his set Andrews got the whole tent singing "The Battle Hymn of the Republic" and jumped into the crowd again. Suddenly Quint Davis was center stage like he was going to talk Andrews to the end of the set: "This is New Orleans sanctified music," Davis announced, "one of the great talents of New Orleans music, Glen David Andrews!" Meanwhile, Andrews had put his white coat back on as the band vamped. It looked like the show was over, but instead Glen David took a cue from James Brown, slipped the white coat off his shoulder, and removed it in one powerful, sexually charged gesture. He got the crowd chanting again. He and cousin Troy were grinning like school kids, wrapped in each other's arms, and finally the MC took control of the stage.

This would not have gone down the same way in the old gospel tent, which was always filled with real African American sanctified churchgoers. They are, for whatever reason, no longer at the gospel tent in the numbers they used to be. The white gospel fans in the tent are watching something they are not part of. They are being entertained. They dance and wave their arms around and drink beer just like at the other stages. However, for this one show, Glen David Andrews brought them all to church, and the tongues of fire burned brightly. I doubt that any recording could really capture what went down in those moments, but I know it was as exciting as anything I've ever seen at Jazz Fest in all the years I've been there.

Though Snooks Eaglin and Eddie Bo died in 2009, there are still a handful of old-timers left to represent the glory days of New Orleans R&B. Deacon John welcomed "that icon of Mardi Gras, he's got his new house in the Ninth Ward," and Al ("Carnival Time") Johnson came out in a brown suit and a wide brim straw hat. Johnson sang two songs, but everybody was waiting for "the Anthem." "What time is it?" asked Johnson. The crowd had been waiting to shout "Carnival Time," and mayhem ensued. Deacon blew his whistle, Wanda Rouzon twirled her parasol, and all was right with the world.

The nighttime revelry continued without a break. Frenchmen Street had been hit hard by the recession. Clubs that had recently closed included the Hookah Café and Ray's Boom Boom Room, while the Spotted Cat was in legal no-man's land regarding its liquor license. Still, the Frenchmen Street scene continued to showcase some of the city's most interesting sounds, including a great Dr. Lonnie Smith and Donald Harrison show at the Blue Nile, an apocalyptic performance from DJ Davis at Café Negril, and excellent Apple Barrel showcases from the Fens and guitarist Michael Sklar, with Dave Easley on steel guitar. Sklar demonstrated how John Fogerty built a career out of a purloined New Orleans rhythm by playing "Holy Cow" with a "Born on the Bayou" riff. Uncle Lionel Batiste and Chief Alfred Doucette sat in on numerous Frenchmen Street gigs.

Irvin Mayfield delivered on his promise to bring music back to Bourbon Street. During the 2009 Jazz Fest Irvin Mayfield's Jazz Playhouse in the Royal Sonesta was one of the hottest new clubs in town, along with the refurbished Rock & Bowl on Carrolton Avenue, next to Ye Old College Inn and Chickie Wah-Wah at 2828 Canal Street. The latter has been around for a while, but this was the first time the club had tried an extended sequence of bookings. Wynton Marsalis showed up at Irvin's for a trumpet-cutting session with Irvin. Shamarr Allen and others joined in the mix. Chickie Wah-Wah, an intimate club with great sound, featured some of the best music of the Fest season, including multiple performances from regulars Jolly House, John Mooney, and Johnny Sansone, a spectacular night from Roy Rogers after his barn-burning set at Jazz Fest, with Marcia Ball sitting in, an acoustic set from the Radiators, and the second lifetime performance by the Mardi Gras Indian Orchestra.

Even on days when the festival was dark, the music drove relentlessly on. Monday night the new Rock & Bowl hosted a tribute to Snooks Eaglin, who had played there regularly, curated by one of the city's greatest musical resources, guitarist Brint Anderson. Anderson skillfully led his own group through several sets of Snooks's favorites before bringing up Tab Benoit, Anders Osborne, George Porter Jr., and finally Big Chief Monk Boudreaux to pay tribute to Snooks.

CHAPTER 28

New Atlantis

What we're looking at here is the new Atlantis. —Tab Benoit

One of the most remarkable things about the New Orleans Jazz and Heritage Festival is the spell it casts on musicians from other parts of the world. Few musicians who play the festival are not somehow transformed by the experience; some seem to realize new insight into their craft through their participation in it. A very few become part of the proceedings, sort of honorary members of an extended Jazz Fest family. Roy Rogers, an extraordinarily gifted slide guitarist from northern California, falls into that category.

Rogers, a long-time member of John Lee Hooker's band who produced and played on the blues giant's last few albums, has delivered memorable performances at Jazz Fest, fronting his own band, trading slide solos with Bonnie Raitt, and supercharging a great blues-oriented set from Steve Miller. At the 2009 festival Rogers delivered one of the best shows of the first weekend at the blues tent, then later that night played a great set at Chickie Wah-Wah. Rogers performed a well-received new song about the flood, "Walkin' the Levee." The resultant buzz made his latest album, *Split Decision*, a sought-after commodity. The Louisiana Music Factory reported it was the surprise hit of the weekend as the store sold every copy in its inventory.

Rogers had one more performance left in the area, though. On the Monday after the first weekend of Jazz Fest, he and his wife, Gaynell, traveled down to Houma to play with Tab Benoit and Chubby Carrier at a Voice of the Wetlands event. The couple, who were celebrating their twenty-fifth wedding anniversary, brought a busload of Jazz Fest attendees, potential donors, journalists, musicians, and friends down to the event with them.

The bus pulled up to an airplane hangar at the Houma-Terrebonne airstrip, where Benoit greeted the guests and introduced members of the VOW organization. It was a sunny, windy day, and Benoit looked out from under his brown,

wind-tousled hair as he stood up before the crowd and gave the best presentation of the destruction of the Louisiana wetlands I've ever heard.

"What we're looking at here," said Benoit, gesturing at the flat grassland
stretching off into the horizon beyond the runway, "is the new Atlantis. Out
there are the places where people lived that don't exist anymore. Indian burial
grounds that don't exist anymore. I've watched the land I grew up on here in
Houma literally disappear. Places where I used to go to camp out don't exist
anymore. The house where my grandma and grandpa lived in is under water. You
have to take a boat to see where it was."

The most impressive part of the presentation was when Benoit, a pilot himself,
and veteran aviator Charlie Hammonds took the guests up in four-seat Cessnas
for an aerial view of what was happening to south Louisiana. The planes took
off and headed over the Mississippi delta. The land stretching along the course
of the river south of New Orleans was brown, the color of death, empty of any
signs of life. Not a bird flew in the sky over this wasteland. The planes then flew
west, toward the area around the Atchafalaya delta, where the ground cover was
a deep, vibrant green, trees grew bountifully in the cypress swamps, and flocks
of birds populated the air.

Rogers joked with Hammonds about his singing cowboy namesake, and the
grizzled pilot proceeded to give the guitarist a history lesson. "We took the pipe-
lines and the oil rigs," he said. "We invited the offshore drilling. Now we're paying the price."

Rogers sat in the front seat next to Hammonds and came back with a renewed
sense of the problem staring New Orleans right in the face. "It was educational
for us," he said:

> Charlie had been doing this since he was a teenager, and he knew the
> country backwards and forwards and inside out. You believe this guy.
> This was his home. He wasn't on a soap box. He was just pointing things
> out that had changed since he was a kid. He was explaining what was
> happening to his home in a very plain way, a commonsense way. He
> wasn't making accusations. He just wanted to get the message out. That
> was more impressive than somebody giving a speech.

Hammonds gave Rogers a close-up view of the landscape. "He was pulling
the throttle the whole way," said Rogers:

> It was great to be up there in that little plane. He showed us where the
> gulf [had once been] twenty miles away, and now it's five miles away.
> You could almost see it happening. It was stunning. When you see
> something up close like that, it's always more dramatic. He showed us

what healthy wetlands looked like as opposed to what we were losing. On one side you saw the dying marsh encroaching on Houma. On the other side you could see what a healthy delta would look like.

The difference between the dying and healthy wetlands on the Gulf Coast is not a natural disaster. The Mississippi levee system has been keeping the river silt from feeding the delta for decades because of a decision made last century by the U.S. Army Corps of Engineers to narrow the gulf outlet of the river for shipping purposes. The canals crisscrossing the wetlands en route to the Gulf of Mexico, built by oil companies to service their rigs, have allowed salt water to flow in and kill everything in its path.

"It's very simple," said Benoit. "I live not far from the Atchafalaya River, and the Atchafalaya is allowed to do its thing. It's building land like crazy. It's filling the oil company canal, and it's rebuilding the marshland like it's supposed to in nature, and the Mississippi is not. It's choked off all the way to the gulf."

Benoit pointed out that seventeen years ago the two sections of this eco-system were suffering from the same problem. "It's only been since Hurricane Andrew [in 1992], when they busted through the Atchafalaya levees and let the river flow," he explained:

> I've seen a tremendous difference since then. You can see it from the air. Over here it's brown, and there it's green again. Where you see the brown, it's dying. What else do you need to know? When the grass dies, it turns into open water. When it turns into open water, you're seeing the land eroding. You're losing your protection. You're losing your land. Forget about rebuilding land for a minute. We've got to stop the erosion first. If we can get fresh water back in there, it's going to at least stop erosion, and we know that works because we know that's the way Mother Nature works. The delta was built by Mother Nature. It was built a long time ago, and it was working fine before we messed with it.

Benoit insisted there was only one way to address the problem. "We have to open the Mississippi River up back to the areas that it used to flow through," he argued, "like down here at Bayou Lafourche. A bayou is a small river that comes off the Mississippi, and that's where they closed it off. Open up Bayou Lafourche, open up Bayou Terrebonne—it's a natural pipeline of river water to the wetlands, and that land needs the river water to keep building."

The solution may have been simple to demonstrate, but it was difficult to iso-late from the sense of inevitability that accompanies the grim fact that the oil companies exploiting the area are not interested in restoring the wetlands. All aspects of government had either turned a deaf ear to the problem or exacerbated it.

"Basically we sacrificed the coastline of Louisiana for oil," said Benoit, who quickly added,

> and I made a living off of it. Everybody around here worked for the oil companies at some point. But we have to make a decision. Everything from the North Shore and the Atchafalaya down—you scoop that whole piece out, and look at what you're missing. Look at what you're gonna lose. Baton Rouge will be the coast. Mandeville will be the coast. Everything south of that was built by the Mississippi River.

Benoit was flying pipeline patrol when he first started seeing the results of wetlands erosion. "You can see things better from the air," he said:

> That's why we take people flying. I started noticing while I was flying on the coast, looking at all those coastal pipelines running through the marshes around the edge of the gulf. You'd see little islands disappear in a matter of months. Then I got a chance to see it speed up, things that would change monthly were starting to change weekly. When I started talking about it, people would say, "Ah, that's never gonna happen in our lifetime." I would have to say it looks like it's happening faster than anybody could imagine. From the air you can see the whole thing. Go talk to the people who fish in the bayous. Go talk to the people who fly over the river to the rigs all the time to go to work. They're gonna tell you exactly what I'm telling you. That's why I want people to see it. I want them to form their own opinion and not listen to somebody else's opinion about what needs to happen on the coast of Louisiana.

Benoit had always played music on the side, and one day while he was flying he came to the decision that music was his real calling. "I realized that music was a better way to help more than just myself," he said. "I wanted to do something that would give me a chance to make my mark, to leave the world a little bit better place than it was the day I found it. It seemed the right road to take. I didn't know at the time what role music was gonna take in the wetlands struggle, but it became clearer as time went on."

Benoit would go into the swamps to write his songs, and he saw those swamps dying around him. "I was writing about this stuff before we formed Voice of the Wetlands," he said. "I spent a lot of time writing in the swamps, and they were dying as I was writing the songs. I was feeling that out there—I was feeling the land talking to me, telling me it's in trouble."

Benoit decided to join a wetlands preservation organization:

> I went to different meetings, and every time I'd go to one, I'd find out
> that these people are making a living at this. Where's the incentive to
> really get it fixed? Look, I live there, and none of these organizations
> were formed by people that live there. So these people are talking about
> they're gonna fix my home, and they don't even live here. You get this
> backed-into-a-corner feeling, and you realize we're going to have to
> start our own organization.

The VOW All-Stars went on to be a powerful performance unit. Live shows,
especially at the VOW festival and Jazz Fest, have become rallying points. Doctor John has taken the cause a step further, taking on Jazz Fest sponsor Shell Oil
directly. When news came out that a plane would circle the Fair Grounds during
Mac's Jazz Fest set, calling on Shell to acknowledge its role in the destruction of
the wetlands and do something about it, he was forced to issue a formal apology
to Shell and the festival. But when he spoke for himself, Mac didn't bow down.

"Mac is old enough where he doesn't have to care about who he pisses off,"
said Benoit. "But somebody has to get aggressive. When you see what's happened and what's still happening, it's hard not to get angry. I think Shell takes a
lot of the heat because they claim to be doing something about it, but so far we
haven't seen any results."

The VOW band may have had a great future, but time was running out for
the cause it was fighting for. Benoit realized that his efforts to lobby congres-
sional leaders and even the oil companies were getting nowhere. "I've been to
Congress," he said:

> I got nowhere in Congress. All of them said the same thing. We walked
> in there and talked common sense to them and just left it on the table.
> They look at me and go, "Man, it's not our decision. All we can do is
> fund it. All we can do is vote on the funding." It has to be a decision by
> the president, who controls the Army Corps of Engineers; the com-
> mander in chief is the head of that. So all we can do is get a bunch of
> people and make a bunch of noise and hope the president hears it.
>
> They got one shot to make it right. We've got one shot to ask for help
> one more time. And even that's pushing it. A lot of money has been
> spent on the coast of Louisiana, and a lot of money has been wasted.
> We've got to make sure that we have a voice the next time the federal
> government spends money on the coast of Louisiana. I want to make
> sure that the local people here have a voice, that the area has a voice, and
> not just the people, the land itself. That's what Voice of the Wetlands is

all about. It's making sure that the right things are brought up and the real problems are brought up and the real solutions are brought up.

Benoit was issuing an ultimatum. "Just tell us whether you plan to fix it or not," he said. "It's a 50/50 proposition. Either you fix it, or you're gonna have to move the port of New Orleans, you're gonna have to move the refineries, you're gonna have to move the people. I'm going to fight this with everything I have because I'm fighting for my home. If you see me leaving, you better move fast because the only way I'm going is if it's all over."

CHAPTER 29

McDermott's Duets

When the 2009 festival season ended in early May, the town emptied of tourists, and the languid New Orleans summer commenced. You could feel the pace of activities slow perceptibly as sultry Sunday afternoons became the time for a slow, desultory walk and a seat on the grass to hear the New Orleans Leviathan Foxtrot Orchestra play pre-jazz-band music or pianist Tom McDermott conducting one of his revelatory duet performances at Snug Harbor. McDermott, a virtuoso pianist and composer and one of the city's masterful accompanists, always made his duet partner sound magnificent, whether it was vocalist Meschiya Lake, Evan Christopher on clarinet, Connie Jones on trumpet, or Jason Marsalis on vibraphone.

The affable, laid-back McDermott could be a bit character from Mark Twain's *Life on the Mississippi*, a reference that traces McDermott's biography to St. Louis, where he was born in 1957. As a teenager, he was already playing the music of Jelly Roll Morton and Scott Joplin before moving downriver to New Orleans to search for the wellspring of James Booker's inspiration.

McDermott's music is another story, an anthropologist's dig through the fossils of New Orleans musical and cultural history. His playing is encyclopedic inasmuch as it references everything from nineteenth-century composer Louis Moreau Gottschalk through ragtime, early jazz, brass band, boogie-woogie, and the eclectic post–World War II R&B of Professor Longhair and James Booker. He has written songs and arrangements for a variety of settings, including music for the Dirty Dozen Brass Band, and cofounded the genre-defying New Orleans Nightcrawlers Brass Band.

McDermott began playing piano as a child in St. Louis, where he heard his mother playing rags and novelty pieces from the '20s. While his contemporaries were listening to punk rock and jazz fusion, McDermott was exploring traditional jazz forms, studying Gunther Schuller's analysis of ragtime in *The Red Back Book* and comparing it to the complexities of the Beatles' compositions.

"There's a guy in St. Louis named Trebor Tichenor, who probably knows more about ragtime than anyone alive," said McDermott:

> He keeps the largest piano-roll collection in the world. He had a show on the public radio station, so some time around age thirteen, I was hearing Jelly Roll Morton, Fats Waller, Eubie Blake, and Scott Joplin. Then the Joplin revival started around '72, '73, with Joshua Rifkin and Gunther Schuller putting out *The Red Back Book* and stuff like that, then *The Sting* came out in '74, but I was into it a little before that. St. Louis was the first big urban center to embrace ragtime, so they made as much of it as they could. I heard Jelly Roll early on, and I loved it. I was playing Jelly Roll stuff by the time I was sixteen.

McDermott began visiting New Orleans on his own when he was a teenager, and by the time he was in his early twenties, he had moved there for good:

> I had had a music-critic job for the morning paper in St. Louis, and when that gig ended, I also had a girlfriend I broke up with, who wanted me out of the apartment, and I had a gig connected with the World's Fair. And I had gone absolutely crazy over James Booker. It seems like it was destiny that brought me here. I heard Booker for the first time around '82, and I just went apeshit. Unfortunately, I didn't move here until '84, and Booker died in November of '83. I did get to hear him once, although he didn't do much of a performance. He played a little bit, and then some guy got up and started rapping, and that was the end of the show, and Booker just went off somewhere.

McDermott scuffled around. He played the steamboat *Natchez* for about three years with the Dukes of Dixieland. "I liked it better in the winter because I played on an old upright, which I loved," he said. "In the summer we played on the deck, and I had to play a synthesizer. I played in the Dukes from '90 to '98 with a couple of sabbaticals in there." McDermott's ability to draw from a variety of musical vocabularies came together in his 1996 album, *All the Keys & Then Some*, an exercise in composing a piece in all twenty-four keys on the piano, with a second suite of piano pieces that offered tributes to his musical influences. McDermott's eclecticism is in full flower in these exercises, which range from traditional Western classical pieces to swing-time excursions, rags, and New Orleans second-line songs. His sense of humor and love of the Beatles surface simultaneously when he samples the final chord of the Beatles' "A Day in the Life" in the composition "Andrew's Antics."

In recent years, McDermott has been particularly interested in rhythms that some might not consider part of traditional jazz but are part of the African Diaspora, rhythms from the Caribbean and South America. "South America didn't impact New Orleans music," he explains, "but the music of the Caribbean, especially Cuba, did a lot, so I love bringing other rhythmic elements to it."

McDermott's interest in rhythm led him to musician and writer Ned Sublette's book *The World That Made New Orleans*. "Ned pointed out to me that some rhythms that I hadn't thought about in such terms emanated in Africa, then went to Cuba and became disseminated elsewhere," he notes:

> I had never thought about the rhythm called the *cinquillo* [he plays the five-note rhythmic figure on a nearby piano], and it's in ragtime. It's a core rhythm of ragtime, but it comes from Cuba. Ragtime rhythm comes from Cuba; that was quite a revelation to me. People think the tango was an Argentine thing, but the tango comes from the *habanera*, the root rhythm of which comes from the Congo in Africa. It was first used in a compositional sense in Cuba, and then it spilled out. Ned points out in the book that the first use of the word "tango" comes from a document that talks about New Orleans musicians. He makes connections I wasn't aware of, and I'm very intrigued by that aspect, certainly with *choro* and ragtime, in which I'm also interested. I really see the connections between early Brazilian music and early North American music. I can say proudly that the Brazilians really liked my ideas about the relationship between *choros* and Scott Joplin rags. I made that connection, and it turned into a good record, *Choro do Norte*. So in a way I'm very traditional, and in a way I'm not. I'm looking for new ways to combine things.

That search is evident on *Creole Nocturne*, a duet project designed to showcase the improvisational genius of Connie Jones, one of the most respected trumpet players in the city, yet someone who McDermott feels is underappreciated. He met Jones in 1990, when Jones was subbing for the Dukes of Dixieland's piano player. It wasn't until later that he learned that Jones's main instrument was the cornet. "He was a good piano player," McDermott says. "His harmony and melody instincts are just so good."

McDermott had followed Jones's recordings, and he was frustrated by how little space he left for himself. "He has good players, but it was always one solo after another, so he only got about one-sixth of the solo space on his own records. I resolved to correct that by putting out *Creole Nocturne*." McDermott had already featured Jones on his first album as a leader, *Tom McDermott and His Jazz Hellions*, but this time he placed Jones in a variety of unusual settings, including the title track, which is based on a Chopin nocturne.

McDermott and Jones recorded the album at Piety Street Studio, where they covered material that ranged from Gottschalk through Jelly Roll Morton and Louis Armstrong right up to McDermott's originals. "Connie wasn't familiar with Gottschalk," McDermott admitted,

> but nobody here is improvising on Gottschalk. Anybody covering him is doing it straight. We're simplifying it and improvising on it at the same time. I'm pretty conscious of trying to vary timbre as much as possible with a duet album, so I had a couple of piano solos, and I have Connie singing on a couple of things, playing mute on another, just to get different sounds. We actually moved the piano around in the studio, so some of the tracks sound a little different. If you listen to "Sleepy Time Down South," it has a certain ambience that's different from "Satchmo Speaks" because we recorded it in a different part of the room. It sounds dreamier, airier. There are little tricks like that you can do to keep the tracks from sounding alike.

McDermott's work with Jones prefigured 2009's *Duets*, which consists of twenty-one exchanges with New Orleans musicians from Louis Armstrong to John Boutté. Through it all McDermott refused to call attention to himself and instead used his encyclopedic talents in service of the myriad of musical genres he presented, a waiter at his own banquet. While several of McDermott's partners on the project, like Jones and clarinetist Tim Laughlin, were obvious choices, most of them weren't, creating an atmosphere of constant surprise as the record spins along with the pace of a theatrical revue. The thought and meticulous care McDermott exhibited in collecting these trinkets and treasures were the result of six years of patient work and essential curatorial help from Tim Stambaugh at Word of Mouth Studios and Mark Bingham and John Fischbach at Piety Street Studios.

Most of the compositions were McDermott's, ranging from the Brazilian *choro* of "Irresistival," with Christopher, to the stately classical pieces "Opulence," with Aurora Nealand, and "Leyla's Lullaby," with cellist Helen Gillet. McDermott contrasted a cunning piece of social criticism, the antiwar song "Sportsman's Paradise," delivered perfectly by Anders Osborne, with "I Don't Want Nuthin' for Christmas," a simple, unassuming piece with John Fohl singing and playing guitar. McDermott is a great accompanist to vocalists, a talent much in evidence in the beautifully straightforward reading of "These Foolish Things," with Judith Owen; "Our Love Rolls On," with Topsy Chapman; and his own compositions "That's What I Saw at Mardi Gras," with Debbie Davis, and "To Kill Our Brothers Now," with Cindy Scott. The greatest of these moments, though, was the duet with John Boutté on Sam Cooke's "Cupid." I've often felt Cooke's spirit in the room while listening to Boutté, and McDermott captured that genie in a bottle.

McDermott has explored the connections between different branches of the African diaspora, work that is reflected in the amazing reconfiguration of Louis Moreau Gottschalk's "Manchega," with percussionist Michael Skinkus, and another experiment in Brazilian music, "Conversa de Botequim," with drummer/vocalist Eduardo Tozzatto.

Mostly, McDermott's musical imagination seems to have no limits. His duet with sousaphonist Matt Perrine on "The Stars and Stripes Forever" adds qualities of humor and variation to revive a composition that has been wrung dry over the years. Similarly, his complete deconstruction of "Blueberry Hill," with African percussionist Seguenon Kone, transforms a familiar tune into something novel but still essentially New Orleans. Accompanying Jelly Roll Morton's a capella track from the Library of Congress sessions, "Tricks Ain't Walkin' No More," is a clever idea, but the mashup of trumpet and vocal riffs from Louis Armstrong's 1920s' recordings, "Some Satchmo Sampling," is revelatory. After hearing this track, one is tempted to think that Armstrong could well be featured on a future Li'l Wayne release.

CHAPTER 30

Cyril's Nightmare

More than four years after the federal flood, Cyril Neville still couldn't shake the nightmares. The ordinary ones were bad enough—images of his home and neighborhood before Katrina, happy memories lost over and over again in the recurrent dreams. However, it was the other nightmares that really gave him the creeps, images that did not reflect his own experience but were based on stories others told him about being trapped in New Orleans for a week, then herded like animals and sent to faraway destinations.

"I have nightmares about shit that people told me about," he said:

> We had a couple of young brothers that got trapped in New Orleans, and they had to swim, walk, wade through all of this foul water, pushing dead bodies out of the way, all the way to the Superdome. They told me harrowing stories about the three nights that they stayed in the Super-dome and the night they decided to break out because they'd rather take their chances out on the street than stay another night in the dome.
>
> We played in Oklahoma not that long ago. I didn't know they had that many black people in Oklahoma. Everywhere we go we can identify the enclaves of people exiled from New Orleans at our shows, standing on their chairs, waving their handkerchiefs at us. It bring tears to your eyes even though they're out there dancing [because] this is the only taste of New Orleans they can get.

Neville is among the thousands of New Orleans residents who were displaced by the flood and were unable to make it back. He had some harsh words for the way people were treated after Hurricane Katrina, but he was shocked at the reaction to his charges because he'd been saying most of the same things before the flood. The difference was that nobody had paid attention to him back then, but once the city was depopulated, Neville's words became amplified by the national media.

Ironically, Neville's career blossomed after he moved to Austin, Texas, where he became a leader of the exiled New Orleans community as he fought to keep its culture alive. Neville has been a charismatic front man in a variety of New Orleans All-Star projects and supplemented his work with the Neville Brothers with his own band, Tribe 13. He recorded what may well be the best album of his career, *Brand New Blues*, which documents contemporary blues themes from post-Katrina stress to people's losing their retirement savings in the Wall Street meltdown.

Everywhere he went around the country with the Neville Brothers, Cyril ran into pockets of New Orleans natives who had about as much chance of returning to the communities they had once lived in as their ancestors who were brought to America as slaves did. "I didn't just wake up one morning and say I'm moving to Austin," Neville pointed out. "I got there the same way a lot of other people wound up in places that they never thought they would be in. It just so happened I landed somewhere with people like Marcia Ball and Eddie Wilson from Threadgill's and Papa Mali, people who reached out and helped."

Neville has tried to maintain his identity as a New Orleans native in a new environment even though generations of intricate family ties were gone forever. Neville knew he wasn't alone in this new diaspora, a theme that runs through *Brand New Blues*.

"This is an ongoing agony for a lot of us," he said:

> In Austin, me and Big Chief Kevin Goodman have put together something called Project Chumbo. It's what happens after the gumbo spills into the chili. It's what happens when Austin musicians and New Orleans musicians start playing together. Now there's a brass band called Austin Nights that didn't exist before we got there. My band, Tribe 13, is made up of a combination of musicians from New Orleans and cats from Austin, Texas. Project Chumbo is an outgrowth of the culture that we brought to Austin and the thing that continues to develop between people from Austin and people from New Orleans. We even got people trying to figure out how to make chumbo. You gotta be able to taste both things. Some people you could never get to eat that.

Neville envisioned Project Chumbo as a way to transport New Orleans culture to new environments. "We've got a social aid and pleasure club in Austin, and we're gonna have second lines. We've already had a couple of Mardi Gras there," he said. "One in particular I'll never forget. We were sitting outside playing drums, and the cats was dancing, and these Mexican brothers passed, two carloads of them. About twenty minutes later those same two cars came back, and the brothers got out of the car with their instruments, and we jammed. It was a beautiful thing."

Neville kept running into people who had been trapped in the Convention Center or the Superdome after Katrina and then found themselves living in Texas. He organized a concert for them:

> Even though I wasn't trapped in the dome or the Convention Center, I just felt the collective feeling of all of those people who had been in there who realized "We have been misused. We have really been screwed over." That's where I hooked up with Big Chief Kevin from the Flaming Arrows. He wound up coming up onstage, and we played New Orleans music to a New Orleans crowd, and I saw people in there in wheelchairs spinning around on the floor, happy for that moment to be back in New Orleans. Kevin wrote this song "Boy, We Come Out That Water." Like most Mardi Gras Indian songs it's about something that actually happened. He put a Mardi Gras Indian groove to a story about the agony that these people went through.

Neville grew up during the 1960s, when the civil rights and antiwar movements were intertwined and skepticism about the country's political leadership was rampant. Organizations from Students for a Democratic Society to the Black Panthers offered alternatives to the traditional pathways of social organization, and Neville was clearly influenced by some of these ideas. The youngest member of the Neville Brothers wrote a number of politically charged songs for the band that were considered too controversial for inclusion on its albums. Cyril's own work always reflected his political views, and his observations about the way the poorest and most helpless people in New Orleans were treated the worst in the wake of the flood are consistent with the message he's been preaching his whole career. In fact, Neville had been arguing that the tradition-bearing conduits for African American culture were in jeopardy years before the storm.

Neville has become a lightning rod for criticism from some who believe that his time away from the city has exacerbated his apocalyptic visions and from others who don't want any negative information about New Orleans to find its way to potential tourists. Many well-meaning civic boosters argue that the city's cultural traditions are no longer in danger of disappearing, an observation that is underscored by the city's highest-profile cultural organization, the New Orleans Jazz and Heritage Festival. The festival claimed that its 2009 renewal featured more Mardi Gras Indians and brass bands than ever before. However, the musicians' aid organization, Sweet Home New Orleans, noted that many Indians have to commute from other cities to participate in the masking rituals.

Neville's argument had irrefutable anecdotal weight. Despite pockets of development in the upper Ninth Ward (the Musician's Village), the lower Ninth (Brad Pitt's Make It Right Foundation), and Gentilly (Barnes and Noble founder

Lennie Riggio's Project Home Again), many of the city's legendary African American communities are nothing like what they were before the flood. Neville was trying to rebuild his home in Gentilly but had been frustrated by what he calls the "Roadblock to Recovery" program.

"My neighborhood, Gentilly, it looks basically the same. Some people have tried to come back and fix their houses," Neville said:

> but it's not a neighborhood any more, and it probably never will be again. Somebody might live there, but what was there is gone. You can go into several different parts of the city and get that same feeling. In some places where I used to go visit people, now it's just flat ground. Not just the lower Ninth. I had friends in the Lafitte project, in the St. Bernard project, in the Magnolia project. I was born and raised in the Calliope project. A lot of it really could have been fixed.

Neville made frequent returns to New Orleans to visit his friend James Andrews. In the fall of 2009 they visited Kermit Ruffins's bar, Sidney's, in the Seventh Ward and then took a walk through Treme. "It was good to see that Kermit had something going in what was left of that neighborhood," says Neville:

> Then we took a walk to the Candlelight Lounge, and we walked the same route that we used to walk, but it was all dark. All the places that used to be there are gone. It wasn't just an idle stroll. We got to the Candlelight, and the Treme brass band was playing. James told me, "This is what's left of what we used to call Treme." It ain't enough that it's four years after the storm, and a lot of people I knew and places I knew I'll never see again—to know that one of the most beloved areas of the city, where I got a lot of who I am from, once that last place goes, that whole area of the city is lost forever, like Rampart Street, like a whole lot of other things that make up the culture of New Orleans that people come from all over the world to see.

Cyril Neville knew he could never return to the New Orleans he grew up in. Nevertheless, if he could no longer live there, Neville was certain that his New Orleans would always live in him. "It's beautiful to be from New Orleans," he said. "Nothing like it on the planet. And whatever people say I say or don't say, they can't take that from me. I'm part of New Orleans history. I'm part of New Orleans culture. They can't take that from me."

CHAPTER 31

The Wizard of Piety Street

On a hotter than July afternoon in 2009 I took a walk down the block to see what Mark Bingham was up to at Piety Street Studios. The enigmatic, wisecracking Bingham was always good for some hilarious conversation, along with breaking news about what was happening in the New Orleans recording scene. Bingham is good at multitasking, a jack of all trades on his home turf.

"There's a cartoon somewhere," Bingham mused that day, brown eyes winking sardonically, "where the producer's pressing the talkback button and saying, 'That really sucks. Come back in four hours, and it will be great.' " Bingham chuckled at his joke and ambled out to the kitchen, where he was performing another of his favorite duties at the studio, cooking. "I'm improvising today because there's nothing left in the refrigerator," he mused. "I think I'll make pasta with some periwinkle meat in it. Mix that with squid and anchovies."

Bingham also plays a variety of instruments in various sessions, most often guitar or banjo. At the studio he'd just recorded an ambient music concert that consisted of "me on banjo and two laptops. Two of the pieces already have deals." Bingham also had nine albums he'd produced, composed, or played on over the last forty years, all due out later that year, including a brand new record, *Psalms of Vengeance*, recorded at Piety Street. The record is as complex a piece of art as Bingham is a person: dense, beautiful, and foreboding, the nihilistic imagination of a man whose father was tortured for four years in World War II and ended up shooting himself. There's a song about his father on *Vengeance* called "It Never Goes Away."

Delfeayo Marsalis was in Studio A that day with house engineer Wesley Fontenot, recording a quartet with ten children on vocals. Bingham was in Studio B telling stories.

Even though Marsalis, who produces all of his own sessions, wasn't working directly with Bingham, he had high praise for him. "Mark's a good guy," said Delfeayo, "and Piety Street still has the analog equipment which I prefer. Mark grew up in the analog era, and he has a great deal of respect for analog recording. That's very important to me."

Bingham does not look like a man who runs the most in-demand recording studio in New Orleans; he looks more like an affable local shopkeeper, a middle-aged man of average height and build, with thinning hair cropped closely to his scalp, and a mostly expressionless demeanor that sets up his often startling wit. Sociable without being particularly outgoing, Bingham has the kind of evenhanded personality that allows him to deal easily with some of the most eccentric figures on the New Orleans music scene. At the same time, Bingham is notoriously flinty with music business hustlers and has been known to walk out of lucrative deals that rubbed him the wrong way.

Bingham basically lives in a back room at Piety Street Studios around the corner from the Dauphine Street house owned by his business partner, Shawn Hall, and her dog, Oliver. The arrangement is particularly suitable to Oliver in that the studio is across the street from Bywater's Markey Park, the neighborhood's top canine social-networking destination. The studio building is an old white stucco structure with vaulted ceilings and a warren of rooms for recording, rehearsal, production, mastering, and sleeping. The couches may be pooched and torn, but they're certainly comfortable. The recording equipment ranges from primitive to postmodern, two-track analog tape to Pro-Tools, and it all serves a purpose. The walls are covered with Hall's vivid, spiritual paintings—she's a well-regarded local artist whose work is part of the Ogden Museum's permanent collection— along with various photographs and posters. The platinum records that usually adorn the foyers of recording studios are located discreetly in this cabinet of curiosities. The copy of Stevie Wonder's *Songs in the Key of Life* that was awarded to Bingham's production partner and mastering engineer, John Fischbach, is unobtrusively placed on a side wall, the kind of credential that doesn't have to be overplayed to impress. The overall impression inside Piety Street is that you're in the home of an eccentric artist whose collection of artifacts have slightly outgrown the space. It's a little mysterious—and a lot to take in; you're aware of being in a special place.

A number of important New Orleans records were recorded here over the years, but since Katrina, Piety Street has been a production line that turns out memorable sessions, a creative run that hasn't been seen in this city since Allen Toussaint's heyday at Cosimo Matassa's legendary recording space on North Rampart Street. Toussaint himself recorded *The River in Reverse* at Piety with Elvis Costello. Since *River,* Piety Street has turned out a series of definitive New Orleans recordings, as well as some outstanding records by national acts. The list includes James Blood Ulmer's *Bad Blood in the City: The Piety Street Sessions,* Ed Sanders of the Fugs' *Poems for New Orleans,* trumpeter Nicholas Peyton's *Into the Blue,* and the Blind Boys of Alabama's session with the Hot 8 Brass Band. Earlier in 2009 the Dave Matthews Band cut Big *Whiskey and the GrooGrux King* during Mardi Gras at Piety Street, and guitarist John Scofield named the album he recorded there, as well as his touring band, after the studio. The parade of local talent through Piety went on and on—Alex McMurray and Jonathan Freilich (the Tom Paines), Paul Sanchez, John Boutté, Brother Tyrone, the Happy Talk Band, the Zydepunks, Ronnie Golden, and Leroy Jones all recorded there after the flood.

Bingham likes to quote Dorothy Parker and enjoys telling elaborate stories, lending an offhanded genius to his method that has drawn people to work with him. "Over the years I've done a few sessions with him, and I've watched him work with John Boutté," said Paul Sanchez, who recorded *A Stew Called New Orleans* with Boutté at Piety Street:

> John Boutté is a really sensitive fellow, and Mark has a casual, sort of sarcastic way of dealing with him, which seems to work. When it came time to make *Stew*, John just didn't want to spend any time in the studio. He didn't want to do the record. I said, what if we just do it very easy, rehearse the songs, and then just go in and play it live? We don't even have to think about it.
>
> Boutté came in, Mark told him a dirty joke, everybody laughed, we played the material, and John never had to think about the fact that Mark had spent a day and a half miking the room in different corners, with live mikes near John's face but not in his face. We sat down and played the thing like it was live music. That's just not possible without a guy like Mark, who's first of all that good at what he does but also sensitive enough to deal with a guy like John Boutté's aesthetic. Mark's ego was just not part of the session. Mark was invisible other than to make John comfortable and make jokes and disappear. He did all the mixing. I went home, then came back to listen to the mix. I came back, and it was perfect. I didn't have to say anything.

Bingham likes it best when the artist doesn't have to say anything. "I don't understand the idea of the producer micromanaging the mixer," Bingham explained:

> When I'm the producer, I don't interfere. I try to keep the delineation of jobs clear. You have sessions where everyone involved has produced records, but there's only one producer. What I've noticed is that most people in that position don't know how to shut up and do their job, so if I shut up and do my job, at least there's one less producer in the room. I just shut up and try to make it sound good. What I like to do is, for example, have Nicholas Peyton and Bob Belden go out on the porch and talk while I do the mixdown. Then I tell them, "What do you need

now?" And they come in and listen, make comments. They go back to the porch, and I fix it to their liking.

Bingham has been on the fringes of the big time throughout the rock era, but he never found himself comfortable with it until he moved to New Orleans in 1982:

> New Orleans was a place where I could play music and enjoy doing it, and musicians had friends other than musicians and artists, people who actually worked for a living as plumbers or carpenters. It was real. I ended up moving into a house next to Aaron Neville and teaching a bunch of kids in the Thirteenth Ward to play some of the pieces I was writing, stuff with treated guitars and all the guitars tuned to one string, the kind of stuff I had been doing in New York. Nobody in New Orleans was playing anything like that back then.

Bingham's first major New Orleans project was a remote recording of Monk Boudreaux and the Golden Eagles Mardi Gras Indians, which is widely considered one of the most important documents of that culture:

> I went to the H&R bar in 1987, Steve Pierce at WWOZ had some equipment, and I had some equipment, so we pooled it, and I set up in the back of a van with an early digital recording system that was a Sony Betamax rigged with a convertor that would print the audio on a CD level, 44, 16 bit, which is not that good, really. It was pretty much like an Indian practice except they were on stage because this had to be a little more focused. It still sounds cool, but it was made in the most minimal conditions.

In 1993 he opened his first New Orleans studio, the Boiler Room, and began making a series of great recordings, including *Cubanismo!* and records by Astral Project, Mem Shannon, Leroy Jones, and Wessel ("Warmdaddy") Anderson, among others. Bingham moved his operation into Piety Street in 2001 and has become the chief partisan of New Orleans music by turning the place into a kind of shrine. "It's one of the last of the great studios," says Shannon McNally, who has been on numerous sessions at Piety. "It's as much of a church as anyplace I've ever been to. New Orleans took a serious blow, but it's still there, maybe a little shell shocked, but the soul of the place is still there. New Orleans is still there to me because Piety is still there and because Mark and Shawn are still there, people with the intelligence and compassion for enabling other people to express themselves."

Bingham takes an almost bitter pride in surviving as the rest of the music industry around him is going into the tank. "The *New York Times* declared the recording industry was dead ten years ago," he said with a wry smile:

> Who needs studios when you can make a record on your home computer? And it's true—if you know what you're doing, you can make a good recording anywhere. The catch is you have to know what you're doing.
>
> I always say you can fix the recording, but you can't fix the people. That was why, in my limited time of being in the big-time music business, I immediately wanted to get out. The higher up the money food chain you get, the crazier it gets. That's why I'm sort of hiding out in New Orleans and working with people instead of waiting around for three producer gigs a year, where you get fifty grand for each one, which is what some of my friends from the old days are still doing, living in the shitty apartment in New York, waiting for the next call.

"The secret to success is to come in and do the work every day," he said flatly:

> There are a lot of studios that have hot tubs and luxury accommodations. People go in there, and they have a great time, and nothing gets done. When it comes time to record again, they have to ask the question, "Do we want to go into the super-tricked-out studio with the hot tubs and the blow jobs, or do we want to go to the place where we had fun and still got all the work done?"
>
> How do we stay above water in the current economic climate? That's a really good question. This week we had a jazz record on Monday, something else on Tuesday, something completely different on Wednesday, Green Day on Thursday, the ambient concert and recordings on Saturday. I keep getting tapes out of New Orleans from people. I had a homeless rapper in here the other day, cutting to looped samples from a second line. So much of it has to do with pricing. This studio runs like a street market in Sierra Leone—it's all negotiable. There is a book rate, but only Dave Matthews and the Dixie Chicks pay it-because they can. Shawn basically takes care of the day-to-day business, making sure people are happy and have what they need. We do a lot of the work around here ourselves. She taught me how to sew, and I sewed all the curtains. So now I'm simpatico with the Indians. Sewing's a cool thing because it really calms your brain. I've always thought if you do something well, something's going to work out. If you do it all right, and then you fail, that's cool. That hasn't happened here yet.

Bingham was one of the musicians who participated in the annual Bywater music fest, the Mirliton Festival, which takes place across the street from his studio. Ratty Scurvics, the bizarre keyboardist, playwright, and performance artist who lives up the block from me got things going in fine style later in 2009 at what was billed as the Twentieth Mirliton festival. Ratty harangued the crowd as he blurted out catchy keyboard licks accompanied by a young woman who twirled a hula hoop as he played. At the end of Ratty's overamped performance he hurled his keyboard from the stage. Hurray for the Riff Raff, featuring the eccentric vocalist Alyndra Lee Segarra, won over the crowd with strong songwriting. Guitar Lightning Lee tore it up in anticipation of his Saturday-night throwdown at Melvin's, a bar on St. Claude Avenue, then hung out on his motorcycle to catch the R. Scully Rough 7, which did not disappoint a suddenly animated crowd. With Ratty back on keyboards, Scully, formerly with the Morning 40 Federation, took no prisoners as he turned out savage guitar licks alongside fellow stringmasher Rob Cambre. Happy Talk Band then played a great set with Luke Allen singing and playing guitar, Alex McMurray on electric guitar, Helen Gillet on cello, and Bingham on bass. McMurray and Gillet challenged each other with magnificent virtuoso turns, and things got so hot that, toward the end of the set, some loon charged through the crowd yelling "Stop it! Stop it!" When he reached the front of the stage, hands waving in the air, he apparently said something about Alex McMurray's mother because McMurray charged off the stage after him. Bingham, looking extra mad, dived immediately into the fracas. The whole exchange almost seemed like it was the opening act of the Fringe Festival, but the guy did get thrown out, so I guess it was all real. "I think he objected to Alex writhing around on the stage," observed Bingham. Fortunately, DJ Jubilee was up next to chill everybody out with his bounce mix before McMurray reintroduced the mayhem, leading the Valparaiso Men's Chorus with Schatzy on accordion, Matt Perrine on sousaphone, and a "chorus" of twenty, including Jonathan Freilich singing sea shanties tailored to the occasion with titles such as "Give Me Some Time to Back That Ass Up." Mirliton executives rewarded the crowd by offering free beer toward the end of the set.

CHAPTER 32

Blues Come Down like Rain

"The Cuckoo" was the first song the Radiators played at the two nights of blues that a fan commissioned to benefit the Tipitina's Foundation. "I sing that one," Ed Volker noted when I spoke to him on his Bayou St. John porch on a hot, early October night in 2009, when every breeze from Lake Pontchartrain was a breath of blessed relief. As if to comment on our colloquy, a mockingbird hidden in the evergreen tree just off Volker's porch screeched out in response to his observation. The bird would continue to deliver his coded messages from time to time throughout the night.

The program at Tipitina's was divided into two sections, the mostly rural pre–World War II blues and the mostly urban blues coined after 1945. Volker took the assignment less as a challenge than a discipline and an opportunity for musical philosophizing. Many of the country blues songs coined in the fields and played in the small towns of the south during the sharecropping era were found objects when they were first played by the attributed authors. "It's like some of the material in the Harry Smith anthology," said Volker. "How old are these songs? The folk tradition can be older than the written word."

The choice of "The Cuckoo" certainly is beginning at the beginning, recalling the thirteenth-century English round that is the first item usually included in anthologies of the English language:

> *Sumer is icumen in,*
> *Lhude sing cuccu!*

I marveled at how much is known about the post-1945 blues and how little about its rural ancestor, separated by so few years. Why is so little known about Robert Johnson?

"They probably weren't asking the right questions," Volker offered. The mockingbird screeched in agreement. "Who cares what color tie Robert Johnson was wearing? The more interesting question becomes something like, 'How long did he play a song?' The people doing the recording were looking for something very different than the live performances, which is what that music was about. They had to fit it all into a time frame."

The second song the Radiators played on night one was an old jug-band tune, "Stealin'," a great sing-along that many of the people in the audience probably recognized through the version by the Grateful Dead. Ed sang that one, too, with a great vocal harmony part from Dave Malone.

Out came guitarist John Mooney, who played an opening set that created a most appropriate atmosphere for the evening. Malone sang a gravel-throated "Tell Him I'm Sorry," followed by a song that is inexorably linked to "The Cuckoo," "Corrina." The link is partly based on the narrator's bird, a bird that "whistles and sings" but is nothing without Corrina. Taj Mahal forged the link forever by including the two songs on his *Natch'l Blues* album, a record that would most likely show up on just about everybody's top 10 blues albums list.

Later in the set the band would play another song from that album, "She Caught the Katy and Left Me a Mule to Ride." This time Malone sang, noting "A 'katy' is a wagon." When Radiators bassist Reggie Scanlan first met Malone, they bonded over their mutual tastes in music, and that classic Taj Mahal recording was the one album Scanlan made a point of referencing.

The Radiators have an intricate two-guitar interchange between Malone and the eccentric master of fills, rhythmic patterns, and stunt guitar solos, Camile Baudoin. It's not easy to add a third guitar into such a delicate balance, but Mooney fit in like he was born to the role. In fact, Mooney learned directly from one of greatest players of the country-blues era, Son House, who befriended the teenage Mooney and guided him toward his destiny as a master blues guitarist, a living embodiment of the ancient tradition. Mooney sliced his way into the mix of guitars, traded back and forth, supported the other soloists, added clever fills and rhythm patterns of his own design, and thus brought the whole gestalt of the Radiators sound to another level.

Sitting on his porch with a Latin jazz record by vibraphonist Cal Tjader playing softly in the background, Volker made another point. "There's no reason why we can't expand the concept to include some of our own songs that exist in that prewar framework." The mockingbird emphatically agreed.

As the Tipitina's crowd buzzed with excitement at Mooney's perfect integration with the Radiators, Volker took the microphone and began to chant, "Have you ever seen that vigilante man?" before beginning the rolling introduction to one of his own takes on pre-WWII blues, Blind Willie Johnson's "City of Refuge." Dave took the reigns again for Robert Johnson's "Come On in My Kitchen," which featured an amazing slide solo from Camile, followed by an even more amazing turn from Mooney.

Mooney left the stage to great congratulations from Jazz Fest producer Quint Davis and hugs from his wife, while Ed Volker moaned in a slow, spooky voice, "keep your lamps trimmed and burning," evoking the itinerant's lament, "Everybody Ought to Treat a Stranger Right." Dave played a nasty wah-wah guitar intro to "No More Cane on the Brazos," with its timely reference to the year 1910, when "all them women dressed just like men." Ed delivered the eerie, mournful dirge "Delia's Gone," then Dave announced, "We've got one more song about killing your girlfriend," as Ed launched into "No. 2 Pencil," getting the crowd to shout along in response.

Mooney was onstage from the beginning for the second set, which began with a wacky rendition of the Three Stooges' theme. Dave opened it up in jolly fashion, singing "Mississippi River, so big and wide," as he celebrated the departure of a lover with the Mississippi Sheiks classic, "Sitting on Top of the World." Mooney was fully engaged as the three guitars sang in joyous chorus through the tune, then fired away on the Volker-shouted "Broken-down Engine," which went into overdrive with a three-chorus slide solo from Mooney. When the song stopped on a dime, the crowd shouted with exuberant joy. The band began playing a nameless blues, and suddenly Mooney sang the line "I saw the Rads last night" over and over, then improvised another repeated line: "Dave is playing wah wah/you know it's gonna be all right."

Everybody on stage was laughing as Dave led the band into the mirror reflection of the blues, a gospel version of "Jesus Is on the Mainline," with Camile and Mooney trading slide solos. After Ed sang "Last Deal Gone Down" and Dave "Bring Me a Little Water, Sylvie," Ed began a "Jack of Diamonds" that was obviously going to be an epic performance. Midway through the song Johnny Sansone strode on stage, grabbed Mooney's slide, and played a solo on the neck while Mooney fingered the strings right-handed, then whipped out his harmonica, and joined the fray for the finale.

CHAPTER 33

Cyril Comes Full Circle

In late October 2009 Cyril Neville went to Bonfouca, a Native American Choctaw (Chahta) village in Slidell, Louisiana, just northeast of New Orleans across Lake Pontchartrain, on what he called a quest "to complete the circle that has been broken."

Neville had long been aware of his blood relation to the Choctaw nation, ancestry communicated to him by his parents. He had started a cultural exchange with Native American and African American children and opened communication with Elwin Gillum, Chief Warhorse of the Chahta, who joined the Neville Brothers onstage for their thirtieth reunion show at Jazz Fest. Now Gillum was about to return the favor by naming Neville ambassador of the joint tribes of Native Americans from the area.[1]

"To heal my family, I have to help heal your family," Gillum told Neville. The two researched tribal rosters and property maps together, and two lines from Neville's mother's ancestry produced the names Melon and Williams, who were listed in the Native American records.

"This is the culmination of a long journey I've been on a long time," said Neville, "trying to put the two parts of me together to be whole. The truth is, I am what [my] family told me I was. I am a Chahta Indian, and that is what I want to pass down to my children and grandchildren. My daughter, my son, wife, grandkids—everybody is feeling and acting different, and it is very positive because when you know where you come from, you can chart a course where you're going."

CHAPTER 34

Marching In

Something amazing and wonderful started to happen in New Orleans in the last months of 2009. The New Orleans Saints were having an improbably great season, and the city began sensing each victory as a metaphoric step in its recovery. The effect was psychological up to a point, but there was a concurrent boost to tourism that definitely helped the economy. As the Saints kept winning, more people came to town to see them, and the locals started to believe that their team might actually make it to the Super Bowl to play in the NFL championship game for the first time in the team's history. The "Who dat?" chant took on new meaning, not just as a rallying cry for a sports team but also as a statement of pride for the city. The anthem "When the Saints Go Marching In" started to take on an aura of certainty. And musicians of all descriptions began composing music to celebrate the city's football team. "All I want for Christmas is the Saints in the Super Bowl," sang Kermit Ruffins on a new album released late in 2009.

Saints fever took possession of New Orleans as 2010 began. It was a time of giddy optimism and the uncanny sense that the city had finally turned a corner on Katrina. The same problems still existed, but the inexorable, house-by-house recovery was starting to have a visible effect on some of the blasted neighborhoods, and the prospects of a new mayor (Ray Nagin could not run again because of term-limit restrictions) gave people hope that the next political leader would be able to speed up the recovery process.

Most of all, though, the city was excited because the Saints were winning. New Orleans is the smallest market city in the National Football League, and for many years the team was the city's only major-league franchise, so its fortunes were reflected more dramatically in the population than would be the case for a larger city. The team finished the regular season with the best record in the National Football Conference, which guaranteed them home-field advantage through the Super Bowl. The Saints pushed aside all negative thoughts and gave the people in the city the sense that they were special. Dozens of versions of the Saints fight song, "Who Dat?" and "When the Saints Go Marching In" were recorded by local groups.

The Saints faced the Minnesota Vikings and quarterback Brett Favre at home on January 24, 2010. The winner would go to the Super Bowl, and that weekend New Orleans was packed with Vikings fans who'd made the trip to support their team. The good-natured rivalry between the local fans and the visitors from the headwaters of the Mississippi River created a carnival atmosphere that was especially ribald in the French Quarter. On Bourbon Street the night before the game, Big Al Carson entertained a packed house at the Funky Pirate, where he interspersed his usual numbers with songs dedicated to the big game. Carson had recorded one of the Saints' tribute songs with his old friend, guitarist Marc Stone, and he gleefully teased the Vikings fans in the audience. "Any Brett Favre fans out there tonight?" Carson asked. The Vikings fans, dressed in their purple and gold colors and horned hats, responded with cheers and raised fists. "Well, I have a song for you." Carson began to sing "You're going down" as he raised his giant fists in a thumbs down signal.

Figure 50. Big Al gives a big thumbs-down to Vikings fans on the eve of the 2010 NFC championship game. Photo by John Swenson. Used by permission of John Swenson.

The game was a tense battle that went into overtime, and when the Saints finally won on a field goal, the streets of the city erupted in celebration. After a franchise history of frustration, the New Orleans Saints had finally made it to the Super Bowl. Mass hysteria took over New Orleans: Even if the team didn't win, just making it into the Super Bowl was a historic achievement. For the next two weeks very few musical performances in the city failed to include a rousing version of the "Who dat?" chant.

Trombone Shorty was chosen to perform during the week of celebrations leading up to the Super Bowl. The half-time music at the Super Bowl was provided by The Who, and a Who tribute band appeared in New Orleans, calling itself "The Who Dats." Shorty appeared on "Good Morning America" and played "When the Saints Go Marching In" on ESPN. "That was the most exciting time of my life," said Shorty, a huge Saints fan:

> I went to ESPN to represent the city before the Saints won the Super Bowl. I was very moved to be the representative of the city on national TV playing "When the Saints Go Marching In." The Saints going to the Super Bowl really helped the city. I talked to one of my friends, and he asked, "How is New Orleans?" I said, "New Orleans is smiling right now. The heart is beating, and everyone is excited and just enjoying the time." It's been a long time coming, and we're gonna live it up as much as we can.

The Super Bowl took place during the middle of the Carnival season, which leads up to Mardi Gras, which was on February 16 in 2010. On the afternoon of the game several parades rolled through the city, including the French Quarter parade, the Krewe of Barkus, a parade of dogs. The quarter was packed with revelers, who shouted approval as people showed off thousands of companion animals all dressed in some variation of Saints' costumes.

James Andrews watched the Super Bowl in his living room, and when the Saints won, he pulled out his trumpet, walked out the front door of his house, and began playing. An impromptu second line quickly formed.

Davis Rogan watched the game uptown. "After we won I went to Sidney's and gave Kermit Ruffins and Philip Frazier big hugs. For the 25 years we'd know each other we'd had a losing football team, and that had changed. I've always been the white guy in the black clubs, and I've always put up with or ignored a certain amount of vibing from the brothers and that night it just wasn't there. There was a palatable air of unity in the city, that night and for weeks afterward."

A parade to celebrate the Saints was scheduled on the only off night available before Fat Tuesday. The Saints parade became the largest parade in New Orleans history, drawing more people than the entire population of the city. Highways leading into town were completely blocked with cars hours before the event. Some people left their cars on the highway and climbed down to the street.

On Saturday, February 13, James and Troy Andrews joined the Saints' owner, Tom Benson, on the grand marshal's float of the Endymion parade as it rolled through Mid-City, down Canal Street and past their Treme neighborhood. "It was amazing to be in the Endymion parade during that time with so many people," said Troy:

> I actually got to hold the Lombardi trophy before the parade kicked off. It was an unbelievable experience. I've never felt like that a day in my life. The energy of the city was great. I don't think the energy of the city's been that good since pre-Katrina. Everybody had fun, there was no words, no violence. It was all fun and celebration, celebrating something we never celebrated a day in our lives. It was like a moment of recovery. Everybody was so friendly, walking up the street. People that didn't even know each other were hugging. It was a beautiful sight.

Even after Mardi Gras ended, the Saints celebrations continued. On February 20, Glen David Andrews organized a second-line funeral procession to bury "The 'Aints,'" the nickname fans had attached to the Saints during their years of futility. The marchers assembled at the corner of North Robertson and St. Philip streets in the Treme. This was the site of the vacant lot where Andrews was arrested in 2007 for participation in a funeral celebration for his friend Kerwin James. The lot had been turned into Tuba Fats Park, the place where second lines like the one Glen David organized for that day kick off. Glen David high-fived and fist-bumped friends as the crowd assembled. He talked with the group that would play the event, the Baby Boyz Brass Band, a group of teenage players who are his nephews and cousins. Andrews gave the leader of the Baby Boyz band, trumpeter Glen Hall III, his first instrument.

The Boyz assembled along with a mule-drawn hearse and a casket bearing a sign that read "Aint's [*sic*] No More," symbolizing the end of an era when depressed Saints fans expressed their mood by wearing paper bags over their heads at home games. This jazz funeral was burying a tradition of negativity for the new Super Bowl champions and at the same time creating another tradition by demonstrating that a new generation of musicians was more than capable of performing the crucial New Orleans function of a jazz funeral.

The crowd was several hundred strong as the parade moved through Treme, and the Baby Boyz kept everyone's feet moving with jumping second-line brass rhythms. Dressed in their navy blue T-shirts with the Baby Boyz Brass Band logo across the front, the band was dwarfed by the crowd but loud enough to be heard

Figure 51. Hearse carrying the symbolic corpse of the "Aint's." Photo by John Swenson. Used by permission of John Swenson.

by the growing second line of thousands, who danced along North Rampart Street, down Esplanade, and along Frenchmen street. Hall, the fifteen-year-old leader of the Baby Boyz, blew long and hard, the eye of the storm throughout, just as generations of his ancestors had for the Treme Social Aid and Pleasure Clubs they had belonged to. In keeping with the old ways, Hall was sponsored in the second-line culture by his father, Glen Hall Jr., who organized the Baby Boyz after bringing the family home after the flood.

Glen Hall III had been playing trumpet well before the Baby Boyz. He began playing at age six, staking out his place in a long line of New Orleans trumpet kings. The previous summer Hall joined Kermit Ruffins, James Andrews, and Shamarr Allen in the trumpet jam session that caps off each year's Satchmo Summerfest and more than held his own. "He's really good," said James Andrews, whose son Jenard plays trombone with the Baby Boyz. "He knew what to do up there. That whole band is comin' along real good."

When the "Aints' " funeral second line hit Frenchmen Street, the crowd in the street was as thick as on Mardi Gras day. Glen David Andrews and the Baby Boyz marched right into d.b.a. and onto the stage for a riotous spontaneous concert. The club was packed with members of the Andrews family. Glen David saluted them all and drew particular attention to the "elders" in the crowd before introducing a dozen of his musical nephews. "We are the Andrews Family," he proclaimed. "I am part of the fabric that makes New Orleans." He raised his trombone aloft to cheers from the audience. "This song," he shouted, "is at the roots of New Orleans jazz!" He began playing "Saints." Everyone in the club was singing and bouncing up and down with excitement. As the song progressed, people in front of the stage lifted Glen David off the stage and passed him above their heads all the way through the club and back to the stage.

Glen David Andrews had turned his life around. The complex artist who had bottomed out two years before had completed his transition from despair to redemption. Surrounded by a family that supported him, he was aware that his career was once again bright with promise. "I had to overcome my problems and fix my life," he later told me. "I did it. It's like the whole world is against you. And then you win them over, one by one."

Saints' fever simply did not abate as the year went on. Suddenly it seemed like everyone in the country wanted to be part of the ongoing celebration. The French Quarter Festival smashed all records as hundreds of thousands of music lovers packed the quarter and the stages along the river to listen to local music. There was a triumphant air to the forty-first renewal of the New Orleans Jazz and Heritage Festival. The afterglow of the Saints' winning the Super Bowl and the decisive endorsement the city gave new mayor Mitch Landrieu, with his land-slide victory, made many New Orleanians feel that the trials of Orleans were overbooked; hotel rooms were impossible to come by.

From the gentrified Bayou St. John side of the neighborhood surrounding the Fair Grounds to the French Quarter and its environs, the city swelled in size by roughly a third for Jazz Fest as visitors from around the world made their annual pilgrimage to the event. Many of these visitors to the Holy City of Music have attended the festival numerous times and consider themselves New Orleanians for the eleven days they attend the event. "Be a New Orleanian even when you're not in New Orleans," read the advertisements for the T-shirt company Dirty Coast. The HBO series *Treme* gave the city's music culture a unique showcase. The debut episode, aired on April 11, was almost shockingly realistic in its por-trayal of a city returning to life after a near-death experience. Those of us who lived through those days saw the events of late 2005 replayed as if in a home movie. There were all the familiar places, and familiar people, in a televised "real-ity" that lived up to the name. Driving around the city in the days after *Treme* appeared afforded surreal flashbacks to scenes from the show. The day after the debut show we passed Kermit Ruffins outside Sidney's cooking on his barbecue. The effect on tourists was also profound. Local musicians were suddenly minor TV stars, and Jazz Fest became a kind of Hollywood tour of the stars' homes. There was Kermit Ruffins, looking like he just stepped off your TV screen. There was Trombone Shorty, playing with Amanda Shaw. There was Trombone Shorty again, leading his own band, with New Orleans rap star Mystikal, back on the scene after serving a 6-year prison term, joining him onstage. There was Glen

David Andrews. There was John Boutté, singing the *Treme* theme song, and Tom McDermott and Elvis Costello with Allen Toussaint, and Rebirth, and Dr. John. Overheard conversations during Jazz Fest frequently included knowing references to *Treme*. The series showed how much musicians played their parts in the city's recovery. The show's story line incorporated some of the biggest problems New Orleanians faced in the aftermath of the flood—lack of medical care, a broken school system, a shoddy and corrupt criminal-justice system.

At Jazz Fest, Better than Ezra got a big cheer for the line "Everybody wrote us off, and now we're Super Bowl champions." The band played with a version of Tom Petty's "Mary Jane's Last Dance," changing the lyric from "Indiana" to "Louisiana" and featuring a Mark Mullins trombone solo. Most of the crowd was on hand for My Morning Jacket, which delivered a great set—Jim James and Carl Broemel have one of the most creative two-guitar approaches in contemporary rock—complete with a Preservation Hall collaboration.

On the recent benefit record I felt that Preservation Hall's music was somehow denatured by the non–New Orleans musicians who joined the traditional New Orleans jazz band, but the exchange with My Morning Jacket was warmer and much more convincing in person on "Mother-in-Law" and "Carnival Time," which featured a cameo by Al Johnson. Just as the New Orleans culture was becoming more a part of mainstream America due to the post-Katrina attention paid to the city and the influence of *Treme*, its music was being assimilated into mainstream pop similar to the way that world music is becoming part of that language.

James Andrews played ringmaster to a veritable sideshow of New Orleans musicians assembled for a Jazz Fest version of the Crescent City All-Stars, including three guitars and a five-piece horn section that featured baritone giant Roger Lewis of the Dirty Dozen Brass Band. Andrews, with help from Alfred Doucette and his wife, Karen, on guest vocals, had the crowd partying to a hit-heavy program: "You Talk Too Much," "See You Later, Alligator," "Caledonia," "Flip, Flop, and Fly," and, of course, Grandpa Jessie Hill's "Ooh Poo Pah Doo." Andrews kept urging the blues tent crowd to "get out front and second line!" even as the security people kept making them sit down.

Along with Wyclef Gordon and Victor Goines, Andrews surfaced again at the "Wonderful World of Louis Armstrong" tribute, which closed out the Economy Hall tent's first weekend. Of the three, Andrews came the closest to touching Armstrong's infectious personality. "My bucket's got a hole in it," he announced, introducing the classic Satchmo vehicle, "and guess what? We can't buy no beer!"

Whether he was singing "My Bucket's Got a Hole in It" or "Hello, Dolly," Andrews avoided being overly reverent, offering asides and getting the audience to sing along. However, he really showed his stuff on the inevitable version of "What a Wonderful World" by toying with the melody and phrasing, stepping aside to ask the audience, "Hey, somebody say…" before going to the tag line. He handled the dynamics of the vocal beautifully and got the crowd to sing "I love you," then personalized the last line before Gordon played a stirring trombone break. At the end of the solo Andrews jumped in with the set-up line "Like Satchmo says," then went to a pure Armstrong chorus, gravel voice and all, before reverting to his own voice, pulling the phrasing apart and offering a shout-out to Satchmo in the last line.

Troy Andrews had an even more dramatic Jazz Fest as an enormous buzz began to build behind his just-released album, *Backatown*. The title, a reference to the Treme neighborhood, which he had grown up in, also recalled the nickname for the Place des Nègres, the marketplace where African Americans kept alive the tradition that Troy was now one of the primary caretakers of.

"It's really amazing to think about my grandfather Jessie Hill and listen to some of what he did," said Troy. "It's just amazing to think about having a family that's so musically inclined and that played and performed, and we continue to do it today. It's just a beautiful thing to keep that legacy going."

Backatown was an impressive series of well-crafted songs that reflected the influence of contemporary hip-hop and heavy-rock production textures while remaining deeply rooted in the funk and second-line traditions Shorty grew up listening to. Though he's a virtuoso on trombone, trumpet, and drums and played all three instruments on the album, what really stood out on *Backatown* was the cohesion among all of the elements that make up his band, Orleans Avenue. Shorty himself was steeped in funk and jazz, but drummer Joey Peebles and guitarist Pete Murano added a solid rock foundation to the band's sound, which Shorty described as "supafunkrock."

"I'm really proud of the band on this record," said Shorty. "We wanted to make sure we captured Pete's sound. We'll have Joey come in one day and just do his sound. Then we'll spend a couple of days just on guitar, working out different tones, different rhythms, different textures."

Most New Orleans records are made quickly on low budgets, but producer Ben Ellman and the band spent entire days during the *Backatown* sessions getting the right drum or guitar sound. "We took a lot of time on this record and worked out its best presentation," said Shorty:

> It's been five years. I think we took the right amount of time to develop the sound on this record. Other records I've been involved with were cut in four days, but on this record we would take four days just to get the groove right on one song. It's been a real learning experience for the next record. It's about patience and making sure you get it the way it's comfortable for you to listen to as an artist.

The songs were terse and densely arranged, so the record spins out like a series of discreet musical statements rather than the intense jam marathon most New Orleans bands try to reproduce in the studio. "We had some things that we went in with that evolved as we recorded," Shorty explained. "The rest of it was just us in the studio coming up with a bunch of different ideas and developing songs. In some cases we recorded by pulling quotes from different songs we were writing and putting them into one thing, making it into full songs. I brought in some ideas on my computer which we recorded as a live band. Then we kept changing it up until it was right for us."

Making terse statements was probably the most important lesson Shorty learned from his time spent in Lenny Kravitz's band. "Something Beautiful" had the contours of a Kravitz hit, and Lenny added a backing vocal and guitar solo to the catchy track. Shorty also included another well sung ballad, "Fallin'."

"I was talking to Lenny Kravitz, and he said, 'You've got to make a *record* when you make a record. It's not a live show,'" said Shorty:

> When you make an album, it has to be its own experience. Then you can play it live, and then you can do long solos or anything you want, but you have to make it a record first. So with this record we wanted to be able to catch people's ears that might not be as interested, that might not have seen us live and understand what we're about. We don't want them to be bored, so we give them a taste of what we do, and when they see us live, we can stretch out and play as much as we want. On this record I thought it was important to stick to the songs and not include a lot of long solos.

Backatown offered a kind of aural picture of New Orleans, particularly Shorty's home neighborhood, Treme. Songs titled "In the Sixth" and "Where Y'at" reinforced that theme. The circular pattern of "Hurricane Season" actually sounded like gusts of wind, and the repeated shouts that punctuated the tune seemed like the chants of a Sixth Ward second-line parade.

"That's what I was thinking, making it sound like a circle," said Shorty:

> And then there's a little second line in there with the crowd chants and everything. I think that just happened naturally. New Orleans is part of us, and no matter where we go, that just happens. The record really is about that. It's about what Treme has done for me. It gave me a foundation to build from, and it's just my interpretation of everything I've been given musically from the neighborhood and just put my own spin on it.

The song that most dramatically represents Shorty's development as an artist is "Right to Complain," a sophisticated piece of writing (with lyricist P. J. Morton) that addressed issues directly related to the post-Katrina recovery, which also could be applied to life in general.

"It's just about people needing to stop complaining and get up and make a difference in their life if they want it to happen," Shorty reasoned,

> because nobody's gonna wait on you. You have to make it happen. That's what all my mentors told me throughout my whole life. If you want anything accomplished, you have to do it yourself and not wait for anybody. We have to do it ourselves. When I come back home and I see people working on their houses, that's what it takes. You can't wait for the government to do it for you if you want it to be done.

Shorty was happy to see people in New Orleans taking responsibility for their future, but he remained dismayed about the way his childhood neighborhood was faring. "Thank god Treme was close to the French Quarter, so it didn't get that much damage. We didn't have to rebuild that much," he said,

> but the most important thing is we have to get the musicians back in Treme. I was on tour a couple of years ago, and it really disturbed me that some of our friends and family were celebrating doing what we do, second-lining for Kerwin James, just to hear that some of my cousins got arrested for playing in Treme. Treme was built around second lines and that whole culture. I was very disturbed when I heard that. We just gotta get the musicians back and get 'em in there so we can do what we do best, which is be around each other and create music and just have that vibe back. It might take a little time, but that's what we really have to do in order to get Treme back. Right now the only thing we're holding on to is the Candlelight bar, with the Treme brass band playing every Wednesday. It's a good hangout, a jam session. I go in there whenever I'm in town and just play whenever I can. We just gotta keep the music going. If we lose that, Treme will never be the same.

The 101 Runners were one of the highlights of the second weekend of the 2010 Jazz Fest. The band reproduced the fire of its just-released live record at the Jazz and Heritage stage. Chris Jones, who led the group on congas, grew up listening to the Mardi Gras Indians at Second and Dryades. Jones remembered "beating on a 40-ounce beer bottle for hours with Geechee Johnson" and became close friends with Johnson's Big Chief, Bo Dollis of the Wild Magnolias.

Jones came back to New Orleans in 2005 after the federal flood and got a unique chance to return the favor to his feathered friends when Maple Leaf's owner, Hank Staples, asked him to put together a Mardi Gras Indian tribute band at a time when few of the Indians had been able to return to the city. With help from Geechee Johnson and a couple of other friends Jones held one of the first Indian performances in the city post-Katrina even though he's not an Indian himself. Jones called his group the 101 Runners after the ad hoc group of unaf-filiated Indians who would meet up on Mardi Gras day even though they didn't belong to a specific gang.

One gig led to another, the Indian vocalists dug what was happening and joined in, and the 101 Runners continued to roll, playing several notable gigs, including the 2006 Jazz Fest and the 2008 Voodoo Fest. At the 2010 Jazz Fest, 101 Runners guitarist June Yamagishi took three solos that fairly levitated the band—a flying series of choruses pitted against a maelstrom of drums in "Shot-gun Joe," a centerpiece showcase in "Sew, Sew, Sew" and the furious coda that brought the set to its apogee on "Shallow Water."

The drummers—Jones on congas, Ajay Mallery on the trap set, Lionel Batiste Jr. on bass drum, Boubacaar Cissikko on African drum, Ike ("the Run-ning Drummer") Kinchen on percussion—delivered a lively, surging pulse throughout and provided the setting for inspired declamations by the vocal-ists. Big Chief Monk Boudreaux of the Golden Eagles and War Chief Juan Pardo of the Golden Comanches sounded completely at home as they threw down, offering a workshop on how to enliven these folk tales with personal observations. On "Old Black Johnny" Monk told the story of his mentor, who didn't mask as a Mardi Gras Indian and didn't even live in New Orleans but came every year to encourage the boy Monk, telling him he'd eventually be a big chief. "You just keep singing," Monk remembers Johnny telling him. "They gonna hear you one day."

The next day the cultural connection between brass bands and Mardi Gras Indians was underscored by the Forgotten Souls Brass Band, which paid tribute to the late Ernest T. Skipper, who recorded the original "Shotgun Joe" in 1983 with Rebirth Brass Band, an obscure single that is thought to be the first com-bination of brass band and Mardi Gras Indians on record. "Shotgun Joe" was played over and over at the festival by both Mardi Gras Indian gangs and brass bands.

The Westbank Steppers, Valley of the Silent Men, and the Pigeon Town Step-pers Social Aid and Pleasure Clubs held one of the best Jazz Fest second lines, with the Baby Boyz Brass Band providing the music. The second line of friends and fest goers grew behind the infectious marching rhythms and inspired blow-ing by the Boyz, with leader Glen Hall III directing the band in the midst of the chaos with hand gestures and musical cues. The band moved with military precision in contrast to the offhandedness of the merry crowd milling around them. One guy in the crowd had taken the Dr. Bob illustration on the cover of *OffBeat* and attached it to the front of his hat. "This is called a second line," the guy told the friend he was with. "It's how *Treme* starts." People danced, took pictures, or just walked along with the parade. A couple of people were doing a good job of skip stepping along in time to the 2/4 beat.

Pearl Jam, perhaps the last of the great stadium-size rock bands, was a perfect fit for Jazz Fest, in large part because New Orleans had the right bands to warm up the crowd. When Anders Osborne played "On the Road to Charlie Parker," you could feel the buzz in the audience. By the time Pepper Keenan joined him toward the end of the set, Osborne had a whole new demographic of followers. When he and Keenan burned through the string-splitting "Darkness at the Bottom," they threw the two-guitar gauntlet down, and the Pearl Jam fans let them know they appreciated it.

Then came Galactic, which had the cramped infield fans at Acura bouncing off of each other with the force of its supercharged hard-rock/bounce take on funk, epitomized by the band's latest album, *Ya-ka-may*. Galactic had undergone a complete transformation since its early days, and Cyril Neville, who alternately sang and played percussion throughout the first half of the set, was the perfect front man. "Funkdefunkdefunkdefunkdefunk," Cyril tongue-tripped, and the band just rolled with him as he finished his part of the set with the Meters' "No More Okey-Doke." Irma Thomas did a great job of translating the tricky "Heart of Steel" to live performance. Corey Henry played trombone and sang throughout the set, and toward the end Trombone Shorty came out, first playing trumpet, then joining Henry for a two-trombone rave-up that pitched it all up to yet another level. At that point Shorty just took over, and Henry had the crowd loudly chanting "hoo-na-nay!" over and over again like a giant Mardi Gras Indian practice. No doubt many in the crowd had heard this chant at the Indian practices depicted in *Treme,* another demonstration of the way the HBO series had brought the language of New Orleans into the mainstream of American vernacular.

I chilled out on the final day of Jazz Fest 2010 as the rain came down intermittently while I strolled in my rain slicker from one stage to another and sipped beers with friends. We camped out in front of the Gentilly stage for a while, where I got to animate "Mr. Jazz," the vintage stuffed toy monkey who has become one of the more popular photo subjects at the fest. At the end of the fest we strolled across the street to a friend's porch on D'Abidie Street just before the deluge began. We began watching the depressing television reports about the BP oil disaster.

That night after I went to bed, I listened to the rain pound against the roof of my house and took comfort in the fact that the roof no longer leaked. It was a cozy night in New Orleans, and my thoughts wandered across the previous five years. I had moved into my house here only weeks after my father had died in 1999, a distance in time that seemed fitting to think of as the last millennium. I thought of the many quietly heroic people who died in this city during and since the flood. I thought of the animals lost in the flood, a lesser tragedy to be sure but definitely another kind of loss for those who loved them. It took two years before local cats resurfaced in our neighborhood. As I drifted off to sleep, thinking of those now gone but still in our memories, I wondered...how many more Jazz Fests will take place? I thought about the oil spill, awed by its enormity, and wondered whether New Orleans would survive another summer...

The Deepwater Horizon tragedy began on April 20, 2010, just before Jazz Fest began. The initial explosion killed eleven workers, but as the weeks went by and the well gushed untold amounts of crude oil into the Gulf of Mexico, it became increasingly apparent that the catastrophe was going to have a generational impact on the ecosystem and the livelihoods of everyone in the Louisiana fishing industry. Just as the recovery from the devastation following Katrina appeared to have turned a corner, a new tragedy threatened New Orleans and south Louisiana. Politicians and business people bickered and tried to shift the blame as the uncontrolled spill just kept gushing. When President Obama announced a moratorium on deepwater drilling, Republican governor Bobby Jindal howled in protest. A Republican judge overturned the moratorium, arguing that it was just one well that blew. The politicians argued, and the oil kept spilling...one day into the next.

The bright Louisiana smiles brought on by the Saints' Super Bowl victory turned into stony frowns as news of the gathering oil disaster in the Gulf grew worse with each successive news cycle. Then P&J Oysters, the distributor that had provided New Orleans restaurants with the city's trademark bivalves for 134 years, closed up shop.

The oysters were gone—who knows for how long. "There are a million small ways in which this is the end of the world for people in the region," said Davis Rogan.

The anguish began taking on artistic shapes. One night I went up Canal Street to see Jolly House at Chickie Wah-Wah. Ed Volker sang mournfully as he turned the ancient lament "House of the Rising Sun" into a funeral dirge about the loss of the Gulf Coast. He began the final chorus, then ad-libbed:

> There is a house in New Orleans
> They call the Rising Sun
> And it's been the ruin of many a poor boy
> all my shrimp are gone
> all my shrimp are gone
> all my shrimp are gone

all my shrimp are gone
all my shrimp are dead and gone
all my shrimp are dead and gone.

With each line Volker's singing grew more intense, the rhythm more insistent. By the end he was screaming, his voice cracking with emotion. He has used the line "all my shrimp are gone" before in his song "Low-Down Alligator," but it took on a chilling new meaning in this context.

Once again it was the musicians who best articulated the sense of loss people were experiencing and spoke out on behalf of the victims of this tragedy. Musicians also organized benefits for the stricken fishing communities in Louisiana. On Sunday, May 16, 2010, New Orleans musicians and some friends from out of town held a benefit concert for the victims of the oil disaster. The concert, called "Gulf Aid," featured the eloquent spokesman for the wetlands, Tab Benoit, along with Cyril Neville, Dr. John, Kermit Ruffins, Jeremy Davenport, Lenny Kravitz, John Legend, Ani DiFranco, Allen Toussaint, the Preservation Hall Jazz Band, and Mos Def. Fans flocked to the concert at Mardi Gras World despite a torrential rainstorm that caused flash flooding throughout the city.

Cyril Neville spoke out for the people of the region, including those he represented in his new position as ambassador for the local Native American tribes, whose fishing grounds were ruined by the catastrophe as crude oil polluted the wetlands.

"Most of what will be affected along the Gulf Coast from Florida around to Texas is owned by people who are more well off than those who live where the land is already disappearing hourly," Neville wrote on his blog:

> Oil companies, rig owners, and builders and refineries will be directly affected, but they all have huge insurance contracts to fall back on. It is not so for the shrimpers and fishermen of South Louisiana. What I would like to see come out of this concert is funding for the people of Bob's Town, Island Jean Charles, Bayou Blue, Bayou Black, and Shrimpers Row to help rebuild and sustain their communities. If hearts and minds are in the right place, this will be the outcome. If not, it will be business as usual, and that's something none of us should stand for.
>
> I found out much of what I know about this subject from someone who has been directly involved with the People of each of these areas' recovery efforts and serves as a true Voice of the Peoples of the Wetlands: Queen/Chief Elwin Warhorse Gillum.

Benoit, the tireless advocate for his native land, was resolute even as he betrayed a sense of futility. Though just as defiant, every bit as determined to tell his story to all he met, Benoit no longer looked like the young idealist ready to tilt at windmills. He railed at BP for not letting the press have access to the contaminated areas. "They won't let us do flyovers down there," said the pilot who once serviced the Gulf rigs himself. "It's restricted air space. If you try to go in there, they'll force you down."

Like the skipper of a foundering vessel caught at the lip of the perfect storm, Benoit grimly continued to articulate his mission in the face of disaster. "If we lose the coast of Louisiana, we lose everything," said Benoit. "We will lose our way of life in the United States."

For years Dr. John had been fighting the oil companies, but this time his position took on the aspect of a last stand. "President Obama might give us a choice for some square goods," he speculated:

> I don't think anybody else was gonna deal us square goods. Hey, all we wanna hear is a yea or a nay. If it's ixnay, people gotta make the choice to go find somewhere else to live or tough it out.
>
> I have been a little political over the years, but I only do something when I think it's really important to do. I ain't going out of my way to be political for no reason. This is my home. This is my roots. This is our home. This is sacred land, and when y'all start playing around with some sacred land, somethin' bad gonna happen. It's been misused just about in all of the indigenous lands. One of the problems that cause all of this which is namely oil. That's one of the major contributors to the whole mess. The oil spill is there, but just the pipelines, the saltwater canals dug into the wetlands is makin' them disappear faster.

In the end Mac would not predict what the future held for Louisiana.

"There's a two-way possibility here," he reasoned. "Either something's gonna happen, or it ain't. If it don't happen, the future is weak. If something happens, it could be wonderful, a renaissance of spirituality coming true that this planet has always needed. I don't have no expectation. I have only belief in what is a possibility."

NOTES

Chapter 2

1. Jazz historians note that Back o' Town, or "the Battlefield," was a specific area uptown from Canal Street, where many saloons and dance halls featured early jazz from the beginning of the twentieth century to the 1920s. Louis Armstrong grew up in that section of the city and later referenced it by singing "Back o' Town Blues." Though Back o' Town was on the other side of Canal Street from Treme, the whole area to the lake side of Rampart Street has been colloquially called Back of Town, or, as in Trombone Shorty's 2010 release, "Backatown." One of the blogs covering the HBO series *Treme* is even called Back of Town.

Chapter 3

1. New Orleans residents commonly refer to the inundation of the city as a "federal flood." They argue that the flooding was caused by the failure of poorly constructed levees, not Hurricane Katrina, and thus was an artificial disaster, not a natural one. The point is well dramatized by John Goodman's rants as Creighton Bernette in the HBO series *Treme*.

Chapter 9

1. "Five Teenagers Shot Dead in New Orleans." http://www.reuters.com, June 17, 2006.
2. "Man Stabbed to Death on Bourbon St.," *New Orleans Times-Picayune,* from staff reports (Nov. 27, 2006, B1–3).
3. "Two Die in New Orleans Shootings," by Gwen Filosa, *New Orleans Times-Picayune* (Dec. 29, 2006, B1–3).

Chapter 10

1. "Killings Bring the City to Its Knees." http://blog.nola.com/tpcrimearchive/2007/01/killings_bring_the_city_to_its.html, Jan. 26, 2007 (accessed Oct. 30, 2010).
2. The circular breathing technique, favored by jazz musicians who want to play lengthy tones without interruption, involves breathing in through the nose while forcing air out through the instrument simultaneously.

Chapter 13

1. Tad Jones was a jazz historian who discovered Armstrong's true birthdate of August 4, 1901, not July 4, 1900, as Armstrong himself believed.

2. Colley Charpentier, "Fatal Stabbing Shocks City Numb to Violence," *New Orleans Times-Picayune* (Aug. 16, 2007, B1–3).

Chapter 18

1. In 2010 the Ponderosa Stomp ended its association with Jazz Fest season and moved to a weekend in September.

Chapter 22

1. Patches are the pictures or illustrated themes some of the Mardi Gras Indians sew into their suits.

Chapter 33

1. Sharon Sharpe, "Cyril Neville Named Ambassador of Chahta Indian tribe," *New Orleans Times-Picayune* (Oct. 30, 2009).

Index

Page numbers and figure numbers written in italics refer to photographs.

Nelson, Prince La La, 86
Nelson, Tracy, 147
Nelson, Walter, 86
Nelson, Willie, 161–62
Neville, Aaron, 25, 64, 98, 145, 166
Neville, Art, 144–45, 217
Neville Brothers, 25, 98, 138, 144, 148–49, 251
    See also individual family members
Neville, Carlos, 88
Neville, Charles, 26, 186
Neville, Cyril:
    despair over loss of old New Orleans, 26, 238,
        239, 240–41
    exile in Austin, 24, 25, 166, 239–40
    friendship with James Andrews, 87, 88, 241
    Gulf Aid concert, 265
    importance to New Orleans culture, 98, 239
    Jazz Fest appearances, 263
    Native American heritage, 148–49, 185–86,
        251, 265
    protesting treatment of African American
        community, 14, 25, 26–27, 41, 120, 238,
        240–41
    and *Sing Me Back Home* project, 25–26
    Voice of the Wetlands recording, 3, 5, 6–7, 8,
        9, 11
Neville, Ian, 64, 148
Neville, Ivan, 26, 64–65, 148, 150
Neville, Jason, 88
Neville, Omari, 87–88
New Birth Brass Band, 60, 86, 90, 98, 112,
    117–18, 119
Newcomb College, 177
New Kids Brass Band, 120
Newman, Randy, 61
New Orleans:
    flora and fauna, 12–13
    future of, v, 266
    neighborhoods and wards, 17
    segregation and racism, 14, 43, 181, 185,
        187, 188
    settlers and early history, 13–14
    See also city government; crime; festivals
        of New Orleans; Hurricane Katrina;
        music of New Orleans; New Orleans after
        Katrina; New Orleans culture; *specific
        neighborhoods*
New Orleans after Katrina:
    crime and lawlessness, 17, 41, 63, 72, 77–78,
        166, 201
    curfews, 16, 19, 77, 78
    depopulation and displacement, 14, 63, 127,
        138–39, 238, 239
    electricity, 17, 19, 44, 52, 55, 59, 62, 166
    emotional state of residents, 45, 62, 67, 72
    fires, 165, 178
    garbage, 17, 39, 165

illnesses, 39
importance of music to, 19, 21, 29–30, 34, 44,
    62, 134, 164, 167, 191
levee repairs, 166
loss of housing, 16, 25, 39, 165, 241
as lure for artists and adventurers, 18, 166
medical services, 134, 166, 258
refrigerators, 17, 39, 52, fig. 7
relief agencies, 30–31, 44, 62, 78, 165
schools, 52, 54, 57, 66, 115, 134, 166, 224, 258
services, 44, 52, 134, 165
stores, 17, 165
threats of further hurricanes, 62, 166, 178
tourism, 52–53, 134, 165, 166–67, 252
toxic sludge, 74, 123
water supply, 62, 166
widespread destruction, 16–17, 22, 23–24, 29,
    39, 165–66, 252
See also city government; crime; federal
    government; FEMA (Federal Emergency
    Management Agency); Hurricane Katrina;
    specific neighborhoods
The New Orleans Bingo! Show (band), 97,
    125, 177
New Orleans Center for the Creative Arts
    (NOCCA), 90, 94
New Orleans Cultural Conservatory, 88
New Orleans culture:
    cuisine, 192–93
    eccentricity, 18
    joie de vivre, 44
    mainstreaming of, 258, 263
    music/musicians key to, 15, 44, 52, 164,
        193, 196
    street performers, 18, 116–17
    threats to, 25, 139–40, 240–41
    See also brass bands; festivals of New Orleans;
        jazz funerals; Mardi Gras Indians; music of
        New Orleans; second-line parades
New Orleans east, 127, 138
New Orleans Jazz and Heritage Festival:
    children's artwork, 141–42
    corporate sponsorships, 139, 151, 152, 218
    demographic shifts in, 138–39
    indie alternatives to, 150–56
    non-local musicians at, 154–55, 220–21, 227
    tourist attendance, 43, 139, 154–55, 257
    in 2003, 96
    in 2005, 21, 91
    in 2006 (post-Katrina), 57–61, 91, 262
    in 2007, 93–94, 128
    in 2008, 138–49
    in 2009, 219–26, 240
    in 2010, 257, 258–59, 261, 262–63
New Orleans Jazz Babies, 88
New Orleans Jazz Orchestra (NOJO), 58, 192,
    194, 195